Teacher's Resource Manual

for

USING STATISTICS

Kenneth J. Travers

William F. Stout

James H. Swift

Joan Sextro

Addison-Wesley Publishing Company

Menlo Park, Califoria • Reading, Massachusetts
Don Mills, Ontario • Wokingham, England • Amsterdam
Sydney • Singapore • Tokyo • Madrid • Bogotá
Santiago • San Juan

About the authors:

Kenneth J. Travers has taught elementary, secondary, and college level mathematics as well as workshops in statistics for teachers at both high school and college level. He has been professor of Mathematics Education at the University of Illinois since 1971 and is currently Chairman of the International Mathematics Committee for the Second IEA International Mathematics Study.

William F. Stout, Professor of Mathematics and Statistics at the University of Illinois and Fellow of the Institute of Mathematical Statistics, has written numerous research articles on probability and statistics and recently developed a course at the University of Illinois in applied statistics for non-mathematics majors.

Jim Swift has taught mathematics and statistics in the schools of England, Kenya, and Canada. He was a member of the American Statistical Association/National Council of Teachers of Mathematics Joint Committee on the Curriculum in Statistics and Probability for several years and more recently served as chairman. At present, he is a member of the Task Force of the International Statistical Institute on Teaching Statistics at the School Level.

Joan Sextro holds a BA degree in mathematics and an MA degree in mathematics education. She has taught junior and senior high school mathematics including statistics, to students with a wide range of ability levels. She is currently head of the Mathematics Department of New Trier High School, Winnetka, Illinois.

This book is published by the Addison-Wesley Innovative Division.

The blackline masters in this publication are designed to be used with appropriate duplicating equipment to reproduce copies for classroom use. Addison-Wesley Publishing Company grants permission to classroom teachers to reproduce these masters.

ISBN 0-201-20118-6

ABCDEFGHIJKL-AL-89876

Table of Contents

PART I   Introduction

This Manual contains a variety of resources to help enrich your teaching of <u>Using Statistics</u>. If you are pressed for time, the introduction and in particular the <u>Recipes for Success</u> are especially useful.

The Art of Teaching Statistics

There is an art to teaching any subject and statistics is no exception. The art of teaching is acquired with experience and with the determination to continue to look for improved methods of presentation. Such is also the case with teaching statistics. But "USING STATISTICS" was not written with the assumption that you, the teacher, already have experience in teaching the subject. The primary purpose of this teachers' resource manual is to provide some guidance, particularly for those teachers who have not had extensive experience teaching statistics. We hope that the book will encourage those who have never taught this subject to venture into this interesting, stimulating, and important area. Even for the experienced teacher of statistics there is much useful material here to assist in the use of this particular textbook.

Statistics are encountered every day, in all areas of life. Sports, for instance, abound in examples of the use of data. Every professional team pays great attention to (and money for) the collection of data on opposing teams. No matter where a person's interest lies, examples of the use of data can always be found, and used as a means of exciting interest in the topic.

In government and business, modern technology combined with statistical methods has lead to improved decision-making procedures, including efficient data collection and rapid ways of calculating gains or losses associated with decisions that could be made.

Probability and statistics are now part of the language of the daily newspaper. Considering that most newspapers attempt to write at a rather low reading level, it is interesting to speculate how many people are assumed to have a working knowledge of the language of probability and statistics. Statistics, along with the skills of collecting and interpreting data, should be considered among the essentials of a basic curriculum.

Recipes for Success

There is no single recipe for success in teaching statistics, but rather a collection of approaches that can valuably be incorporated into your own particular style.

A.   Take account of the interests of the students in the class.

Everyone is all too familiar with the effects of teaching statistics as merely a collection of techniques, and the boredom that accompanies calculations of means and variances, when there appears to be no reason for doing such a thing. The techniques that one learns in statistics are but stepping stones, which lead to the goal of better understanding a set of data. If a person has no interest in, say, automobiles, it is difficult for that individual to get excited about performance ratios or data on cornering ability. But, on the other hand, someone with such an interest will be far more inclined to examine data on various models of cars to discover new ways of becoming better informed. The teacher who spots and feeds these interests will develop a more interesting course for the students.

B.   Recognize the numerous examples of statistics all around you.

During the second world war, the British mathematician J. G. Bennett was involved with research on fuel and power. During his travels he realized that he could look at a coal truck and observe the type of coal it carried, where it came from, and its possible destination and use. He called this "professional noticing". Any person with training will notice things that will pass by other people completely. Once you, as a teacher of statistics, start noticing applications of your subject, you may be surprised how easy it is to use these illustrations to enhance your lessons. Even .nore important, students will learn to develop similar habits in their area of interest. One student, with an interest in hockey, developed an article in Sports Illustrated on the use of data collection by one of the National Hockey League teams into a project using data collected during matches of the minor hockey team that he coached in his spare time. Effective statistics courses inevitably will produce similar success stories.

C.   Take the course outside the classroom.

Statistics is a practical subject. Most teachers of statistics at this level have come from a background of teaching mathematics. The tendency is for such teachers to teach the course just as they would a mathematics course, spending a lot of time on examples and exercises from the text book. This approach does not draw out the more interesting aspects of the subject. So, in every chapter of this text, there are opportunities for project work. It is the experience of most successful teachers of statistics that this kind of approach adds greatly to the students' level of interest, and results in a stimulating course. It is interesting to note that in Britain, where external examinations have dominated the secondary school statistics courses for a long time, several examinations now include the requirement that a project must be undertaken. Possible topics for projects often can arise out of visits to the classroom of practicing statisticians from the community. Such visits, perhaps accompanied by field trips to a quality control lab, or other examples of applied statistics, do provide relevance to the course, which could otherwise degenerate into the kind of cookbook approach to the subject that all too often is found in statistics classes.

D.   Integrate the computer into the course as much as possible.

The motivation that results from the

use of the computer, together with its ability to reduce the labor required by involved calculations and simulation runs, combine to bring life and vitality to statistics. And, of course, there is the fact that every practicing statistician now regards the computer as an essential tool of the trade.

E. Encourage collection of newspaper or magazine clippings.

One of the most important objectives of a statistics course at this level is to show the widespread use of statistics in all walks of life. There are many ways to accomplish this objective, but one that has always been successful is the compilation of a collection of clippings from newspapers or magazines. The student finds such a collection or "scrapbook" useful in many ways:

(a) the collection illuminates the content of the course as examples of the contents of each chapter are found in the collection;

(b) the student can observe the fact that statistics is a discipline vitally important to the running of an information society;

(c) the student learns to recognise fallacious arguments and the misuse of statistics;

(d) ideas for further development into major projects often arise from a seemingly inconsequential clipping;

(e) the clipping shows something of the work of statisticians, and perhaps reveals career openings that might otherwise not be considered;

(f) a student's interest in a hobby, sport, or topic, can be incorporated into the course, adding a strong element of motivation;

(g) the teacher's use of clippings that a student has found can bring a sense of

achievement to a student who may be having difficulties with the subject;

(h) the use of students' clippings in unit tests can further motivate students to observe their world with a statistical eye.

Teachers who have used this technique consistently throughout the course find that the scrapbook, at the end of the course, makes a useful record of the student's progress through the course, especially if the student is encouraged to write comments that tie each of the clippings to the content of each chapter. Clippings related to some topics in statistics are not commonly seen and it may be a few weeks before, for example, an application of the use of chi square is found. Such clippings, however, are often seen in articles on a medical subject. Reports of the data from control groups and other groups, often yield appropriate clippings. Over the years it is useful to keep file copies of the better clippings. Once such a file is started, you will soon realise the need to keep only the better clippings, since the collection soon reaches the hundreds.

The key word in this aspect of the course is relevance. Once statistics is seen to be relevant, many of the obstacles to developing an interesting course are brushed aside.

F. Keep in touch with other teachers and statisticians.

Every successful statistics course contains ideas, examples and information drawn from other teachers and professionals in the field. Such persons have many useful examples, case studies and illustrations to contribute to a statistics class. Some colleges and high schools, for instance, have organized Statistics Days for students and teachers. Such programs illustrate the value of fruitful cooperation between university statisticians and school teachers. The ASA/NCTM Joint Committee on the Curriculum in Statistics and Probability have organised a STATISTICS TEACHER NETWORK. Statistics teachers use this network to keep in touch with each other and to share ideas, problems and experiences. Further information about this network can be obtained from NCTM headquarters, 1906 Association Drive, Reston, VA 22091 (telephone 703-620-9840).

The above items certainly do not encompass all the recipes for a successful statistics course. The remainder of this resource manual has been prepared with the hope that it will help you bring excitement and the joy of learning to your statistics classes. GOOD LUCK.

Interdisciplinary References

More than perhaps most subjects, statistics offers the opportunity to relate topics in the same course to other subjects in the curriculum. This may be particularly true of social studies and biology. Drawing on the examples and experiences of teachers in those courses, and your sharing with them, can be fruitful. Sometimes it might be possible to encourage the dissolution of subject matter boundaries by offering credit in statistics for work done in other courses. Usually, it is the students themselves who, when suitably encouraged, will bring examples from other courses to statistics class. When students begin to do this without the encouragement of you, the teacher, then the course will have achieved an important objective -- that of providing students the opportunity to see statistical methods at work in the world around them.

Projects

An important component of a statistics class is project work. Suggestions for projects are given in Appendix C.

CHAPTER

1

Descriptive Statistics
TELLING IT
LIKE IT IS

1. PREAMBLE.

The most important commodity in the world of the 1980's is INFORMATION. The ability of computers to store, manipulate, and retrieve information incredibly quickly has changed the pattern of society. The dominant force in our economy is no longer industry--it is information. Over half the working population of North America have jobs that relate to the collection, compilation, storage, or transmission of information. Much of that information is numerical. There is not one of us who will be able to go through life without having to look at some numerical data and then draw some conclusion from the data. These days there are many, many professionals whose job it is to seek out and find data, draw conclusions, and summarize those conclusions with appropriate reasons. The skills of data analysis that we begin to teach at this level will probably be needed and used by students for the rest of their lives. At the present time, one needs only to examine the statistical arguments so widely used by politicians to see how they make full use of the ignorance of the population concerning statistical arguments. Hopefully, by giving more attention to data analysis in our schools, the situation will improve.

Our task begins with getting students to ask the question, "What does it tell me?" when confronted with a collection of data. The first chapter in this book has this as one of its aims. The techniques described in the chapter are merely tools to be used to illuminate data. The student must "want to discover", if the tools are to become ways to reach an end and not ends in themselves.

2.   LEARNING OUTCOMES.

Students will be able to:

(a)   describe some of the uses of statistics and data analysis;

(b)   construct a stem-and-leaf plot of a collection of data;

(c)   answer questions relating to data presented in stemplot, tabular, graphical or report form;

(d)   make appropriate use of the terms proportion, experimental probability, cumulative frequency, theoretical probability, and the notation p(heads) and P(heads);

(e)   give interpretations of stem-and-leaf plots using the language of probability;

(f)   describe any misrepresentations in statistical plots, arguments, and reports;

(g)   ask appropriate questions when presented with a collection of data.

3.   TEACHING COMMENTARY.

Since descriptive statistics has often been associated with boredom, it is worth going to some lengths to avoid this stigma. Too often, the main point of descriptive statistics is lost in the process of teaching techniques. The main point is of course to prompt the reader (viewer) to ask questions of the data. Having the appropriate subject matter makes it easier for students to be willing to ask such questions. It is worth making an effort to provide as interesting a collection of data as possible--the course will be much more successful if students are continually motivated to ask the kind of questions that will illuminate the data. The infor-

mation that comes out of such an exercise is sometimes quite surprising--information that at first glance was not at all obvious.

The use of computer data banks is also a good way of generating interest.

Section 1.1 Working with data

Here is the whole point of the course and the book - working with and drawing conclusions from data. To work with data, there must be an underlying motivation, which for most students would be an interest in the subject matter, rather than in the mere collection of numbers. If the student has an interest in the subject matter it makes the task of question generation a lot more relevant. Data exploration must be seen as a task that is worth doing.

There are a number of question-raising examples in this section. These are useful as a start to the process of working with data. Perhaps the most interesting examples will be those that rely on the efforts of the students to collect data in which they are interested. The success of questions such as 1.4 to 1.6 depends to a great extent on the way that the assignment is presented. It can become a most fruitful exercise or a tedious chore. This is one of those situations where the first year is the most difficult. In subsequent years, you will have a collection of interesting work from the students of previous years. If you succeed in getting the students to find data that interest them, your efforts will be well worthwhile.

Section 1.2 Stems and leaves

The stem and leaf plot may be a new idea for you. The main point of this plot is that the grouping of the data is revealed while PRE-

SERVING THE ORIGINAL DATA IN THE PLOT. Thus individual bits of data can be seen relative to the overall picture of the distribution. Also the exercise of constructing the plot requires you to look at each item to determine its place in the plot. If you do this as simply a mechanical process, then you will lose the opportunity of using the process to examine the figures more carefully. As you enter the figures in the plot, it is much more useful to let a stream of questions and observations run through your mind: that observation is unusually large, why are there two distinct groupings, why are all the numbers even, why are there so few numbers in that group.... It is, of course, important that you acquire the habit of questioning data, whatever the process used. But many users of stem-and-leaf plots have been surprised how easily they find themselves asking questions about the data.

Making such plots without asking questions will become tedious. Hence one must give the students lots of reminders so that they will develop the habit of questioning data.

Remember that such devices as the stem and leaf plot were intended to be used to get a quick look at a set of data. The key word here is QUICK. Making a stem plot is not intended to be an exercise in draftmanship but a method of illuminating the data. Some students will, all too easily, spend 15 minutes making a plot of exemplary neatness and elegance, and fail to realize that THE QUESTIONS CAN BE ANSWERED JUST AS EASILY with the help of a more quickly drawn, less elegant plot. Untidiness in a plot does not have to be associated with speed. The point of all this is that it is answering the questions that is the main idea, not the ability to make neat plots. Of course too much sloppiness can be a problem as well.

Section 1.3 Graphs: pictures of data

The same points apply as in Section 1.2. The section illustrates the relationship of the stemplot with the common bar graph or histogram. (The importance of the histogram is seen in later work when the property of histogram, that the AREA represents frequency or relative frequency, becomes important.) Since the only new idea in this section will probably be the emphasis on quesioning data, it should not be necessary to spend a great deal of time on this section.

Section 1.4 Proportions and probabilities

The language of probability is used here as an alternative way of asking and answering questions about data. The ideas are the intuitive ideas of probability, most of which will not be new to the students. The terms experimental and theoretical probability are introduced together with examples of their use. This section should be considered as an exercise in questioning data using the language of probability.

Section 1.5 It all adds up (cumulative frequencies and proportions)

Cumulative proportions, frequencies and probabilities are necessary to answer such questions as, "What proportion of the observations were greater than 5?" Answering such questions requires the use of the techniques of this section. Notice once more the emphasis on questioning data. It is necessary to know the techniques required, if an answer to the question is to be given. Conversely, you would, perhaps, find it difficult to think of such questions as the one above, if you had not encountered the techniques of cumulative frequencies.

Many users of stem-and-leaf plots write the cumulative frequencies resulting from counting towards the middle from either end. An example is given of this technique below using the stem-and-leaf plot from page 19.

8	899	3
9	2289	7
10	0001335678	17
11	024445789	(9)
12	01255789	24
13	122223447789	16
14	68	4
15	23	2

There are 50 observations, so the middle observations (25th, 26th in rank) will have a stem of 11. The number of leaves for this stem is indicated with a (9) in parentheses to indicate that this is the stemline that includes the middle observation(s). The total number of observations is then calculated by adding to the middle stem (9) the cumulative frequencies above and below (9), i.e., 24+17+9=50.

Section 1.6   Telling it like it isn't

The abuse of statistical argument is made possible by the relative ignorance of the population. Hence the great distrust of such arguments by the majority of the population! The only way to counter such misuse is by a greater willingness to examine such arguments for accuracy and hidden assumptions. There is evidence that such a change is happening. As recently as 5 years ago, it was very rare to find an opinion poll reported in a newspaper with the qualifying statement such as, "For this size of sample the figures are accurate to within 4 percentage points 19 times out of 20". Now such a statement is quite common, at least without the "19 times out of 20". It is still necessary to learn what the statement means, something that will be considered in chapter 5, but it does represent a greater awareness of the problem by the 'media'.

However, it is still very easy to find examples of the misuse of statistical diagrams, drawn in such a way to encourage A PARTICULAR INTERPRETATION OF THE DATA. Getting the students to add examples of misuses to their collections of clippings is the best way of handling this particular section. It is, of course, necessary to present suitable examples first. Your own collection of clippings will, once again, be of great help.

THE KEY PROBLEM - background, use and development

The authorship of disputed papers has been 'decided' with the help of statistical methods. There are many interesting developments along these lines that require very little background knowledge of statistics. Some of these are described in the article by Mosteller and Wallace in Statistics: A Guide to the Unknown (Holden-Day, 1972). The authors of this article give a more extensive treatment of the statistical analysis of the 12 Federalist papers whose authorship was unknown.

4.   STATISTICAL COMMENTARY.

p. 1   It should be noted that the actual statistical analysis of authorship is far more complex than that discussed here, although the basic approach is contained in this presentation.

Section 1.1

p. 2   The "medium and the message" excerpt should not be misinterpreted as establishing that more television viewing causes a high level of fear. This may or may not be the case. See the discussion of this issue in Section 8.7.

p. 3   The extrapolation the students are encouraged to do in Exercise 2 is of course of no practical use. It is dangerous to extrapolate much beyond the range of the data. Mark Twain, commenting on data showing that the Mississippi river was over the years gradually shortening in length, predicted tongue in cheek that in some future year the river would be one mile long.

Section 1.2

p. 4   Despite the rather quaint title, "stem-and-leaf" diagrams are very useful and really are better than bar graphs in that no information about the original data set is lost.

p. 6   The technique of Table 1.5, if covered, needs to be illustrated by several examples for clarity.

Section 1.4

p. 15   The idea that the empirical P(heads) is a good approximation or estimate of the theoretical p(heads) when the number of tosses is large is a very important statistical idea. It will reappear in various guises throughout the book. Be sure that the students understand that P(heads) and p(heads) are conceptually very different. This is the difference (as will be discussed in Chapter Five and later) between a statistic and a parameter. This important distinction is made clear as one progresses through the book.

It may be useful to refer to the theoretical probability as the true probability. Thus, you can use the fact that students know that the (true or theoretical) probability of getting heads on the toss of a fair coin is 0.5.

The statement, "Therefore, in 10,000 tosses....tails" is not technically correct. It is used here for pedagogical reasons. What is true is that the proportion of heads obtained should be approximately equal to the proportion of tails obtained, if the number of trials is very large. In fact, the larger the number of trials, the greater the difference between the number of heads and the number of tails will tend to be! This is rather subtle and paradoxical, and better left alone, the authors believe.

Section 1.5

p. 18   It can be proved, using elementary geometry, that the area under a relative frequency polygon (such as Figure 1.11) is 1.0.

p. 20   In Exercise 2c, iv, although the term "average" has not yet been defined (it comes in Chapter Two), it is assumed that most students are, in fact, familiar with arithmetic average. It is the common-sense understanding of average that is looked for here.

CHAPTER 2

Centers and Spreads

1.   PREAMBLE.

The calculation of means, medians, measures of spread and the like has long been a part of the mathematics curriculum. Usually, teachers left these topics until the end of the course, perhaps hoping that there would not be enough time to cover them. Certainly, not all teachers find it easy to teach this topic with enthusiasm. As a result, what often happens is that students are shown how to do the calculations and given very little explanation of their purpose, of the reason why one would want to calculate these things anyway. This approach misses the fundamental purpose of these activities, which is to ILLUMINATE THE DATA, by whatever means are at hand. It is the data that are important; the calculations are merely means towards the end of data illumination.

For this to make any sense to the students, however, the data must capture their interest, so they come to realize that these measures have meaning. For example, students are increasingly using computer data banks to explore possible career choices, which include comparing the salaries of the different occupations. When a student discovers for himself or herself that the average starting salary for a particular position is $23,000, then that student may be prompted to ask what kind of average has been used, and to discover that the average on its own does not give the full picture; it is also important to look at the range of starting salaries and the variation across different parts of the country, for example.

A new feature of this chapter, which has not previously been a part of statistics at this level, is the BOX-AND-WHISKER plot. The importance of this plot lies in the fact that it provides a quick summary of the entire set of data, including the median, and measures of spread or variation. Devised by Professor John Tukey of Princeton University about ten years ago, it is now widely used, especially when different sets of data are being compared.

The "bottom line" of this chapter, once again, is that these techniques are not ends in themselves, but tools to be used to explore data.

2. LEARNING OUTCOMES.

Students will be able to:

(a) find and interpret measures of central tendency (mean, median and mode) for a small set of data (up to about 100 data points);

(b) compare the properties of the mean and median (such as robustness);

(c) find and interpret a quick measure of variation (the range) of a set of data;

(d) use box-and-whisker plots to give information about the center (median) and spread (range and quartiles) of a set of data;

(e) find and interpret deviation scores for a set of data, another measure of spread;

(f) find and interpret the variance and standard deviation of a set of data, still further measures of spread.

3. TEACHING COMMENTARY.

Section 2.1 Centers (Measures of Central Tendency)

It is important that students acquire the techniques of calculating the various methods of determining the "center" of a set of data. But this is certainly not an end in itself. Skill in calculating the mean, median, and mode is no more important than an understanding of the measures involved and how they are used and misused in everyday life. Yes, students must know calculation methods, but do not leave it there.

A second point to remember is that, in this introductory section, since the students are learning, or re-learning, the methods, the data sets are small and not always of great interest. When the data become interesting, the data sets are often quite large; even the most motivated of students will prefer that the data are available in a form that makes it easy to perform calculations. This may mean giving the data on floppy disks with appropriate software to assist in the exploration.

Section 2.2 Properties of centers

The exercises in this section reinforce calculation skills, but also go further in developing an understanding of the differences between the measures. Perhaps the most important idea to get across is the difference between the mean and the median in the way that they treat extreme values. Statisticians use the word "robust" to describe a measure that is not much affected by large outliers. The median is a "robust" central measure. To illustrate this idea, the following may be used.

Calculate the mean and median of the following sets of data.

1. 1 3 5 7 9
2. 1 3 5 7 19
3. 1 3 5 7 90
4. 1 3 5 7 900

It will also be instructive to collect newspaper cuttings that illustrate the many uses (and misuses) of central measures.

Section 2.3 Spread (measures of variation)

The same broad comments apply to this section as to the previous two sections. This section does not cover all the methods of measuring spread, but concentrates on the intuitive approach that comes from looking at the range of a set of data. Clearly, the range is greatly affected by the extreme values of a set of data; the range is not a robust measure of spread, which is a major disadvantage of this measure.

Section 2.4 Boxes and whiskers

This is the second idea in the book that will be new for most teachers. (The first was the stem-and-leaf plot). The box-and-whisker plot (sometimes shortened to boxplot) is a very useful way of summarizing a set of data, since it gives a visual image of measures of both the center and the spread of a set of data. This plot is widely used by industrial statisticians in their initial exploration of sets of data. Few students have difficulty with this plot, and it becomes especially useful when comparing several sets of data.

A more advanced use of the box-and-whisker plot is in the detection of <u>outliers</u>. An outlier of a set of a data is a value that does not seem to fit in with the rest of the data.

> NOTE: That word <u>seem</u> is an important word in exploring data. One of the important goals in teaching data explora-tion is to get the students to make statements that begin with "It seems that...". I put a lot of emphasis on this goal. Tukey uses the word SEM-BLANCE to describe the statement after the words "it seems that..."

The length of the whiskers of a boxplot is used to detect outliers. Statisticians often use the following rule:

a. Calculate the length of the box.

b. Multiply this by 1.5. This is the maximum length (W) of a whisker.

c. Extend the whiskers from the box to the extremes, or for a length of W, WHICHEVER IS THE LESSER.

d. Denote any values outside the whiskers with an *. These values are called outliers.

The reason that a multiplier of 1.5 is used is that less than 1% (actually about .07%) of the values in a normal distribution will lie outside these whiskers.

At a more elementary level, an easier rule is to make the maximum length of the whiskers EQUAL to the length of the box. This will, of course, produce more outliers. For whiskers of this length you would expect about 4.6% of the values to lie outside the whiskers. This figure is in line with the 95% confidence intervals that are com-monly used in statistics.

The length of the box in a boxplot is a good measure of the spread of data. It is sometimes called the midspread, or the inter-quartile range. It is a robust measure of spread.

Section 2.5 Deviation scores

Section 2.6 Mean deviation

Section 2.7 Variance and standard deviation

These three sections lead the way through to the calculation of the standard deviation, perhaps the most widely used measure of spread, and the one to be found on all statistical calculators.

If a student does not have a cal-culator that performs calculations for standard deviation, then the following formula for the variance is the easiest to use with a 4-function calculator.

Variance = (mean of the squares) - (square of the mean)

The following exercises are used to demonstrate the validity of this formula for those students whose algebraic skills are insufficient to follow the algebraic proof.

i.   Calculate   the   variance   of
1   2   3   4   5

X	dev from 3	square of dev from 3
1	-2	4
2	-1	1
3	0	0
4	1	1
5	2	4
	total	10

Variance = 10/5 = 2

ii.   Now   let   us   assume   that   we have made a mistake in measuring the mean and we proceed with the calculations using a mean of 2. This will obviously make a difference in the variance.   We see how great an error has been made:

X	dev from 2	square of dev from 2
1	-1	1
2	0	0
3	1	1
4	2	4
5	3	9
	total	15

Variance = 15/5 = 3

We made an error of 1 in the mean; the corresponding error in the variance is 1 (that is, 3 - 2 = 1).

iii.   Repeat   question   2   for   a   mean of 1

X	dev from 1	square of dev from 1
1	0	0
2	1	1
3	2	4
4	3	9
5	4	16
	total	30

Variance = 30/5 = 6

We made an error of 2 in the mean; the error in the variance is 4 (that is, 6 - 2   =4).

iv.   Finally,   assuming   the   mean   to be 0, the error in the mean is 3, equal to the actual mean.

X	dev from 0	square of dev from 0
1	1	1
2	2	4
3	3	9
4	4	16
5	5	25
	totals	55

The correct value for the variance is $11 - 3^2$
But 3 is the mean of the values; hence
Variance = (mean of X^2) - (mean of X)^2

4.   STATISTICAL   COMMENTARY.

Section 2.1

pp. 26-28   Students   should   be cautioned that the mean and the median (when the number of scores is even) are not necessarily numbers that were in the original data.   Note that in Example 4, the median value of $800 is not one of the original car prices.

Neither is the mean of these six values.   By contrast, a

modal score must be one of the original scores.

p. 28   The concept of mode is dealt with here for reasons of tradition. However, only the mean and the median are usually used as measures of centering.

Section 2.2

p. 31   The modern theory and practice of statistics puts some emphasis on robust measures. Since measurement errors do occur, it is comforting to have measures that are not unduly influenced by isolated observations out of character with the rest of the data set. These unusual observations are often called "outliers". If outliers are not taken into account, serious misinterpretations of the data can occur. By using robust measures, this pitfall may be avoided.

Section 2.3

p. 34   It is interesting to note that the range is certainly not robust. Indeed, a bad piece of data, resulting, say, from human error, is likely to be a largest or smallest number and hence produce a much larger range than if the bad data had not been included. Range is not seriously used as a measure of the spread of data, except as a "quick and dirty" preliminary indicator.

Section 2.7

p. 47   Although the mean deviation is perhaps easier to interpret than the variance (and standard deviation) it is not used a great deal in advanced statistical work. The latter measures have much more powerful mathematical properties, as shown in advanced courses.

CHAPTER 3

Expected Value

1. PREAMBLE.

Simulation is a technique that is used increasingly often because of the ever growing availability of computers. It also attracts the interest of students, illuminates many important ideas in probability and statistics, and is a very good way of helping students understand the capabilities of the computer. For these reasons, this text makes extensive use of simulation. The basic ideas of exploring data have been introduced. Now we can use, and illuminate, those ideas by means of simulation. This chapter on expected value introduces a method that will be used often in the book. This 5-step method has been found useful in structuring the process of simulation, and allows students to design their own simulation as a method of solving problems.

Problem solving is enjoying a great deal of publicity at the present time, and rightly so, since the essence of the practical application of what we teach in mathematics is to solve problems. Many problems contain the word EXPECT in the statement of the problem. Some of those problems have a solution that can be determined: "What can I expect to have to pay for my car if I take out this loan?" Such problems are well suited to the tools of conventional mathematics and algebra. Other problems, less comfortable perhaps, do not have deterministic solutions. Such problems involve the use of variability, probability, and chance. These are not as amenable to the use of traditional areas of mathematics, yet they are the most important kinds of problems in many areas of industry, business, government, and yes, even in sports. The manager of a baseball team is constantly thinking about probabilities and expectations in every decision he or she has to make - what lineup of players will have the largest expected number of runs in today's game? Note that the solution is probabilistic, not deterministic in that the number of runs produced, like the number of cities receiving rain, is controlled by chance. It is decisions such as these that the technique of simulation can help us to answer problems involving EXPECTED VALUE.

2. LEARNING OUTCOMES.

Students will be able to:

  (a) identify an appropriate model for a situation using random digits or dice or other devices;
  (b) define the trial that simulates a given phenomenon of interest;
  (c) state the statistic of interest in the trial;
  (d) record the statistic of interest from repeated trials using a stem-and-leaf plot;
  (e) calculate approximately the expected value of the statistic using an average from the stem-and-leaf plot;
  (f) design simulation models for investigating the independence of events;
  (g) design simulation models using the 5 step process.

3. TEACHING COMMENTARY.

The primary tasks in teaching this chapter are to introduce the Monte Carlo method and to provide the opportunity for students to design and conduct their own simulations.

Section 3.1 Rain, rain go away

The example given is simple enough to be able to give an intuitive answer. But the question of variability in the answer is not so obvious. The simulation serves to illustrate the intention behind giving probabilities of rainfall in a given area. The key idea in this section, namely the representation of rainfall by the tossing of a coin, is a straightforward idea. The remainder of the section serves to review the notion of an average.

Section 3.2 Models of chance

Some time must be spent on developing the idea of representation mentioned above. The most useful approach, (to be introduced in Section 4.3), seems to be lists of random digits. Students need to learn which set of random digits to use for a given problem.

Explanation of the model is naturally an important topic in this section. Interesting examples, preferably of local interest, or drawing on the interests of the class are most desirable in the presentation. Try to find examples where discovery of the expected value is of interest.

Section 3.3 Independence

The concept of independent events is open to several levels of presentation. The definition of independent events; namely, that events A and B are independent if and only if $p(A \text{ and } B) = p(A) \times p(B)$, often seems to teachers to be a backwards way of looking at the product law for probabilities since the formula is so devoid of motivation. But it is possible to illuminate this concept with the use of suitable simulations. See section 4.9 in this resource manual. In this section of the book, however, the aim is not so much to undertake a technical discussion of independence but to illustrate the concept with some straightforward simulations that appeal to an intuitive idea of independence.

Section 3.4 About how many...

The section develops greater variety in the kinds of problems that can be investigated by the simulation technique.

Section 3.5 Pass it on!

Two interesting applications of simulation are described in this section. The investigation of epidemics has often made use of simulation techniques and this example of hermits on an island has become a quite well known simple example of the method. This simulation has also been described in several forms for use on a microcomputer; for an example see the article, "Epidemic", by Andy Gamble in the May 1981 issue of Compute magazine.

Section 3.6   Take a walk, by chance!

This section makes an interesting project for a computer science student. Many physical problems are insoluble by the analytical methods of pure mathematics. A great deal of information can be gained about such problems by the application of Monte Carlo techniques, one of which is the random walk. The heat flow problem involving a rectangular plate is used in this section to illustrate how the random walk method is used. This problem can be solved analytically using partial differential equations.

Further teaching notes

THE KEY PROBLEM - background, use and development

The collector's problem is becoming an increasingly well known instructional problem. It has been described in several places including the 1981 NCTM yearbook and in the materials of Mathematics Resource Project published by Creative Publications. It may not be so widely known that the expected number of sticks of gum is given by

$$\frac{n}{1} + \frac{n}{2} + \frac{n}{3} + \frac{n}{4} + \frac{n}{5} + \ldots + \frac{n}{n} ,$$

where n is the number of cards in the set to be collected.

The problem is typical of those mentioned in the preamble that are not easily amenable to solution by traditional methods of mathematics. Setting up a probability model for such a problem is not within the capabilities of most students at this level. Yet the problem can be investigated very easily if a simulation is set up using a fair die. An added attraction to this problem is that the solution is not intuitively obvious. This makes the investigation more interesting.

4.   STATISTICAL COMMENTARY.

Section 3.1

p. 54   When students are asked for "other objections", the hope is that some will suggest that one trial of telephoning the 12 cities could not possibly answer the question, "on the average." Note that this idea is somehow easier to explain, and understand, using (as does the text) the idea of the experiment of tossing 12 coins; i.e. the model helps the students' understanding.

p. 56   In simulation experiments, there are often two quantities involved. In addition to the number of simulation trials, usually chosen to be 50 or 100 in examples of Chapter 3, there are often several stages of each trial, for example 12 tosses of a coin per trial. Since students often find these distinctions difficult, the teacher should do everything possible to prevent confusion on this.

Section 3.2

p. 57   In advanced courses, the three-child family problem would be approached using a mathematical model instead of the physical model of tossing a coin three times. Indeed, the number of girls in a three-child family would be modeled by a binomial distribution with n=3 and p=½.

The probability of k girls in a family of n children is then given by

$$\binom{n}{k}(p^k)(1-p)^{n-k}$$

For example, for k=2 we have

$$\binom{3}{2}(\tfrac{1}{2})^2(\tfrac{1}{2})^1 = 3/8$$

Using the Monte Carlo approach, the value of 3/8 is estimated by either an actual physical model (such as a coin) or a simulated model (such as a random number generator).

p. 58   Another way of physically modeling the situation, which is equivalent, is to toss three coins each once. Here, each coin represents a child.

p. 58   It may be interesting to have some idea of the accuracy obtained with the Monte Carlo approach of this section, as a function of the number trials n. Consider a simulation where each trial consists of N coin tosses. In the example of this section, n=100 and N=3. The statistical concept of a confidence interval and the Central Limit Theorem of probability, both covered in Chapter 11 of this book, provide an approximate answer. Using these, it can be shown that approximately 95% of the time that one conducts a simulation, (n tosses of N coins) the difference between the average computed in Step 5 and the theoretical expected value will be less than $\sqrt{N}/n$, which for the example is about .17. That is, most of the time (95% of the time), the simulated expected value will be within $\sqrt{N}/n$ of the theoretical expected value.

Section 3.3

p. 60   Note that the concept of independence is not introduced by giving the usual formula for independence [that is, p(A and B) = p(A) times p(B)]. Rather, the intuitive idea of independence is stated in the second paragraph of Section 3.3. Then, simulations of situations where independence is appropriate to assume (such as raining in Chicago and raining in San Juan) are achieved by using physical models that clearly behave independently of one another (e.g. a penny and a nickel).

Section 3.4

p. 63   Eysenck's statement of equal thirds of course depends upon his definition of what constitutes an introvert, extrovert, and ambivert.

p. 64   Note that for the example of section 3.4 it is not quite as easy to guess the theoretical expected value. Hence students can have the experience of discovering (approximating) a theoretical expected value they could not otherwise obtain (e.g. by simple intuition).

Section 3.6

p. 69   The mathematical definition of a random walk is that it is the sum of independent identically distributed random variables.

CHAPTER 4

Probability

1. PREAMBLE.

The second major application of simulation is to illuminate the concept of probability. Just about every problem that involves the calculation of a probability can be simulated and with the use of the computer to generate a large number of trials, these simulations can be very reliable. Indeed, there are many problems for which a simulation approach is the only method of solution for students at this level. Simulation of probabilities can also give insight into some of the puzzling paradoxes in probability. For example, consider the following problem.

I know that my new neighbor has just 2 children, but I do not know their sex. When a visitor calls on them, I see that one of the children, a boy, answers the door. What is the probability that the children are both boys?

The two arguments often used are these:

1. The probability that they are both boys is the probability that the child who didn't answer the door is a boy, which is 0.5.

2. I can eliminate the possibility of 2 girls, so there are three possibilities for the children BG GB BB, so the probability that both are boys is .3333..

A simulation helps to clarify the solution. A trial is throwing two coins that contain at least one head (B). A successful trial is HH.

As with the previous chapter, the use of a computer helps to add much-needed motivation, especially with more mature students. Some care should be taken with very long runs on the computer - students frequently like to keep the computer running all night to see if (say) an accurate value of pi can be found. Some random number generators have relatively short cycling times. See Section 13.5 for a further discussion of randomness.

2. LEARNING OUTCOMES.

Students will be able to:

  (a) identify an appropriate model for a situation using random digits or dice or other devices;
  (b) define the trial that simulates a given occurrence;
  (c) classify the trial as being successful or not;
  (d) record the results from repeated trials;
  (e) estimate the probability of the outcome;
  (f) design simulation models, using the 5-step process, for estimating the probability of an event;
  (g) construct tree diagrams to determine the probability of a set of independent events;
  (h) find the probability of an event given the probability of its complement;
  (i) find the probability of failure of a system, given the probabilities of failure for each of the component parts.

3. TEACHING COMMENTARY.

Section 4.1 Relative frequency

This chapter develops an intuitive approach to probability, namely the long-run relative frequency model. This is the approach with which most people are familiar. Experimental models for determining probabilities using relative frequency are introduced in this section. The main objective of the section is to develop an intuitive understanding of the method, and to introduce the terminology. Over the next three sections a more formal method of performing the experiments is developed using the 5-step method used in chapter 3.

Section 4.2 What are the chances?

The 5-step model used to determine expected values in chapter 3 is modified a little to allow it to be used to find probabilities. Once again, the most difficult part of the model are steps 2 and 3, describing a trial and a successful trial. Much practice is needed before most students become comfortable with these 2 steps.

Section 4.3 Random digits

Some students may soon tire of throwing coins and rolling dice. A more appealing approach for them may be to use random digit tables. Once again, use of these tables does not come easily to some students, and careful explanations are needed. The tables are used to reinforce steps 2 and 3 of the model.

Also, there will likely be some students who want to go directly to the computer to generate and count the appropriate digits. This provides an opportunity for some instruction in the use of RND in BASIC, for those students who have not had the experience. (For further details on this, see Section 14.1.)

Section 4.4 Independent events

The question of independence can lead to some difficult ideas. At this level, the idea of independence that is used is the intuitive one that event A has no effect upon event B. This idea is formalized somewhat with the "Law of Experimental Independence." The use of computer-based activities to demonstrate this law is encouraged. This law leads up to the "Law of Theoretical Independence," discussed in Section 4.5.

Section 4.5   Theoretically speaking

This section presents the view of probability based on the idea of equally likely simple events.   The idea of a tree diagram plays a central role in this development. These diagrams have been found to be very useful in describing quite complex situations.

Section 4.6   Thanks for the complement

The idea of complementary events is a simple one, and one which is very useful in the solution of a number of probability problems that can be long and involved without the use of complementary events.   It may be easier to first find the probability that an event will NOT happen.   An example of such a problem is the question of finding, among 10 people, the probability that at least 2 of them have birthdays on the same day.   In this case, it is easier to find the probability that they all have different birthdays.

4.   STATISTICAL   COMMENTARY.

p. 75   The   question   of   the independence   of   the   four wheels   of   an   automobile   is actually very subtle.   It turns out   that   the   assumption   of probabilistic independence is a good   one   here   if   the   car traveled   fairly   far   before returning to the same parking spot.

Section 4.1

p. 76   It is interesting to look at   the   pattern   of   Kerrich's relative frequencies (or experimental   probabilities).   As probability   theory   says   (the "weak"   and   "strong"   laws   of large   numbers)   the   relative frequencies after a large number of tosses stay close to the theoretical   value. But   the approach of the relative frequencies   to   the   theoretical value   is   not   monotone.   For example,   as   the   number   of tosses   increased   from   9000   to 10,000, the relative frequency actually moved away from 0.5.

p. 76   Kerrich's experiment contains   the   very   essence of how one should   interpret   what   it means to say that p(heads)=½. When one says, for example, that p(A)=1/3, for some event A,   what   is   meant   is   that   if there   were   many   experiments conducted,   then   the   event   A would   have   occurred   about   1/3 of the time.   The viewpoint is called   the   relative   frequency interpretation   of   probability.

p. 77   One   major   thrust of this book   is   to   use   as   much   as possible   experimental   probabilities   instead   of   theoretical probabilities.   This   is   sound for three reasons:

(a)   It   allows   a   satisfactorily fast pace to be maintained with   major   emphasis   on statistical   concepts   rather than   on   mathematical techniques.   Since   the purpose of the book is to teach   students   how   to reason   statistically,   this is a justifiable approach.

(b)   Many,   perhaps   most, students   of   elementary statistics   find   the   mathematics   of   statistics extremely   difficult   to understand.

(c)   The experimental approach is   very   helpful   in   leading students   to   mastery   of basic   statistical   concepts. From   the   statistical   viewpoint, a student is better off really understanding, for example, that a theoretical probability is merely the limit of experimental probabilities as the number of trials increases (of course, the formal concept of limit is not used in this book) rather than being able to recite the axioms of theoretical probability.

To be sure, mathematically strong students can often handle and benefit from the study of properties of theoretical probability as well. Teachers should provide for such students supplementary references such as Mosteller, Rourke and Thomas or others referred to in the bibliography of this manual (Appendix F). The use of set theory concepts, combinatorics and even, perhaps, integration, can be introduced, depending upon the sophistication of the student.

Section 4.2

p. 80   One may wish to know or even present to the class some idea of the accuracy obtained with the 5-step Monte Carlo approach to estimating theoretical probabilities. The "page 58" remark essentially carries over with N=1. That is, it can be shown that approximately 95% of the time that simulation is done, the difference between the experimental and the theoretical probability will be less than 1/ n, n being the number of trials of a simulation. Thus when n=50, we expect to be within 0.14 of the theoretical probability, most (95%) of the time. Since the theoretical probability of three girls is .125, the error using Table 4.4 is 0.035, well

within the expected accuracy. It may be emphasized that if high accuracy is desired, n merely need be large and, if time is a factor, a computer should be used to do the simulating. For example, n = 10,000 (recall Kerrich's data) yields a maximum error of 0.01. Recall that his actual error for 10,000 was 0.007.

Section 4.3

p. 83   We are now developing sophistication and speed in carrying out simulations. Clearly, the use of random digits, rapidly generated by a microcomputer, or hand-held calculator, is an enormous advance over tossing coins or throwing dice. And, of course, computers can be programmed to carry out simulations. It is an easy computer-programming exercise to develop a program to simulate Kerrich's experiment for example. Monte Carlo simulation is an invaluable tool for scientists and statisticians to estimate probabilities, where it is too difficult or impossible to solve for the theoretical probabilities. Students might find it interesting to know that the basic method of the book is more than merely a teaching device. For example, the famous mathematician S. Ulam used the Monte Carlo method in his research, and gives an interesting account of it in the book Mathematical Thinking in the Behavioral Sciences.

Section 4.4

p. 88   It is a property of random digits that they appear to be independent of each other. Thus the trial described in Step 2 of the example of Section 4.4 assumes that rainfall in San Juan is independent of that in Chicago since different (and hence independent) random digits are used for each.

p.89   Note that the law of (theoretical) independence is,

$$p(A \text{ and } B) = p(A) \, p(B).$$

Section 4.5

p. 93   It is important to realize that not all experiments involve equally likely outcomes. Thus it really needs to be emphasized that the formula p(success) = S/N should only be used when the outcomes of the experiment are assumed to be equally likely. For example, it might be calculated that p (life on at least one of three planets) = 7/8, based on the assumption that life is just as likely as no life for each of these three planets. This model would be scientifically silly and hence the 7/8 is silly too.

pp. 93-94   In more advanced courses one typically does a fair amount of theoretical analysis of equally likely outcome models. A reference that really brings out the power of this approach is Feller's Volume I of Probability Theory and Its Applications. This work is also a wonderful source of examples.

p. 95   Many would say that the concept of independence is one of the most important concepts of probability and statistics.

p. 97   Notice that it has been pointed out in Exercise 6, Section 1.1 (page 16) that the world's population is made up of slightly more women than men. Thus, taking p(boy) = 0.5 as a model is only an approximation (though for most purposes a good one.)

Section 4.6

p. 98   Students sometimes have linguistic difficulties with finding the complement of a verbally described event. For example, the complement of the event of at least one girl in a three-child family is often given as "at most one girl in a three-child family," where it should be "no girls in a three-child family". The complement of three heads, in the example of Section 4.6 is sometimes incorrectly given as "no heads" (instead of "at most two heads").

CHAPTER 5

Making Statistical Decisions

1. PREAMBLE.

Over the years, many recommendations have been made for a greater emphasis on statistical concepts in the school curriculum. Some authorities have gone further and suggested specific topics for inclusion. The concept of sampling has been on most such lists. The fact that a sample from a population can provide reliable information about the entire population is the foundation for entire industries - those of survey sampling and market research. The Gallup Poll, the Harris poll, and the Neilsen ratings, are as familiar to many of us as our daily newspaper. There are two important aspects to be considered:

1. The scientific basis of sampling and why it works.
2. Questions of the rights of individual privacy compared with the pollster's "need to know."

The second question only becomes meaningful when students have had the experience either of being interviewed by a canvasser for one of the polling organisations or having participated in a door-to-door survey or telephone survey. Nowadays, it has become almost commonplace for organizations, such as School Board, Parent-Teacher groups or local newspapers, to ask statistics teachers to help conduct surveys. This activity provides a useful service to the community as well as making the whole process more meaningful for the students.

There is a broad consensus among those who have taught this topic that the concept of obtaining information from samples has opened up a completely new attitude to the subject. Where teachers had previously thought of statistics as being confined to calculations about means, etc., they now discovered a new, interesting, motivating and relevant approach to statistics. Teachers see that statistics need not be a dull subject, postponed until the end of the school year; it can become an interesting, useful and motivating discipline. The same can also be said about students' approaches to the subject.

The material contains no difficult mathematics and has been successfully taught to students with a wide range of mathematical backgrounds. Needless to say, the more practical you can make this chapter, the more rewarding it will turn out to be.

2.   LEARNING OUTCOMES.

Students will be able to:

(a)   determine, from statistical information in a newspaper or TV report, the population and the sample being referred to (or implied);

(b)   use the five-step method to use information from a sample to make statements about the population from which the sample was taken;

(c)   use the sample box procedure to make statements about a population based on information from a sample taken from that population (optional);

(d)   decide the appropriateness of a probability model used to carry out an experiment to solve a statistical problem;

(e)   choose an appropriate statistical model for solving a given problem;

(f)   use the Median Test to help in deciding whether two populations differ in their mean values (optional);

3.   TEACHING COMMENTARY.

The fact that a sample taken from a population can provide reasonably accurate information about the population itself is one of the central ideas in statistics. It is also one of the least understood ideas, despite the widespread use of sampling today. There are numerous ways of approaching this topic. This chapter looks at sampling to obtain information about the mean of a population and about the proportion in a population who might answer 'yes' to a particular question.

Section 5.1 Samples and populations

The basic ideas and vocabulary are first introduced. The example used concerns means and variances of populations and samples. It is not necessary, or desirable to go into lots of detail about biased estimators. It is sufficient to convey the idea that the mean of a sample is close to the mean of the population if the sample is large enough. The other important objective of the section is that the students should be able to identify the difference between a sample and a population.

It is very useful to begin this chapter with a project to compile a collection of clippings each of which uses the language introduced in this section. Such a collection reinforces the use of the terminology and adds relevance to the subject. Students should, at all times, question the information given by opinion polls. Of particular importance is the question of representative samples. For example, a widely-quoted survey suggested that teenagers today are sexually much more active than teenagers were 10 years ago. It wasn't until a person read the description more carefully that it was learned that the data had been collected from teenagers attending birth control clinics. It is very doubtful if the sample was representative of the population of teenagers - it certainly was not a random sample of teenagers.

Methods of sampling should be given very careful attention. If possible, arrange for a visit from a representative of a market research firm, or the Harris or Gallup polling organizations. These groups provide some interesting and informative pamphlets on sampling. The American Statistical Association also publishes a useful inexpensive booklet entitled "What is a Sample".

Section 5.2 Using information from samples

The subtitle of this section might be "WHAT IF...". The approach used links the simulation framework with an investigation of the information gained from a population that is evenly split (50-50) on an issue (for example, raising the minimum age for a driving license). This may seem a backwards way of doing things - aren't we trying to get information about the actual population rather than from a 50-50 population? The point here is that you need knowledge of what might be called a reference distribution. If we know the kind of samples we are likely to get from a 50-50 split population, then we can look at the sample obtained from the actual population and assess whether such a sample is very likely if the actual population were a 50-50 population. If the sample is sufficiently unlikely to have come from a 50-50 population, we are then willing to conclude that the actual population is <u>not</u> a 50-50 population. This approach is intellectually subtle and needs to be very carefully explained and illustrated by examples.

The essence of the technique known as sampling is to obtain information about a population. It will be explored more fully in Section 5.4. At this stage in the student's learning, the experience that gives information on the range of likely samples has not yet been aquired. We do not want merely to give formulae or tables that provide this information - that stage will come later. So in this, and subsequent sections, the objective is to build experience about different populations and samples that are likely to occur, using the simulation framework of previous chapters.

Section 5.3 Yes-no populations

The YES-NO population has been found to be a very useful vehicle for teaching about sampling. There is only one variable being studied - the proportion in a population who would answer YES to a particular question. The aim here is to give experience with populations other than 50-50 populations. One of the authors has used a set of sampling boxes for several years and has found their value worth the initial effort in making the set of 5 boxes. Later he added 4 more boxes to the collection to provide populations containing 5%, 10%, 15%, ... 50% colored BB shot. But the section does not depend entirely on the manufacture of a set of these boxes. The exercises in this section, however, do not use the complete set of boxes but concentrate on the 50-50 YES-NO population, providing experience with the distribution of samples that occur from such a population.

The simulation framework has been adapted for use with teaching the concept of checking models. The two stages of the process are covered in sections 5.4 and 5.5. In Section 5.4, the student is presented with information (called the STATISTIC OF INTEREST) from some sample. The aim is to obtain an estimate of the probability that this STATISTIC OF INTEREST came from a 50-50 population. This theme is developed in the exercises that follow. It is important to present the ingredients of the situation in such a way that the reasoning behind the activities become clear. These exercises are laying the foundation for the reasoning behind accepting a model in the next section. Essentially the basis of the work in Section 5.4 is, given a statistic of interest from a sample, what is the probability that it came from a 50-50 YES-NO population?

Section 5.4 Accepting a model

The crux of the argument referred to above in Section 5.2 is developed. The critical point is that this is a lesson in reasoning. Many examples may be necessary before all students understand the chain of reasoning involved. But this is the central idea of this chapter and it is important that some understanding be gained of the principle of rejecting or failing to reject a model. The simulation framework is once again used to clarify the ideas involved.

The final step of the argument follows the estimate based on the assumption that the statistic of interest comes from a 50-50 population. If this estimated probability is low (0.1 in our book) then the argument is made that that sample is not likely to have come from such a population. We will either fail to reject a 50-50 population as a possible model, or such a model will be rejected. Clarification of principles in your own mind is again important.

Section 5.5 Different models for different problems

Clearly, not all models will be 50-50 population models. The same procedures as were described in Section 5.4 can be used with other population models if you have a means of generating the required samples from such populations. The set of sampling boxes (provided the total number of shot or beads used is quite large) can be used, but computer-generated samples may be more convenient. The procedure is identical to that of Section 5.4.

Section 5.6 The median test

The students now have the background to be able to compare two samples using an interesting technique known as the median test. This simple test can be used in a number of interesting projects involving 2 groups of students. The project approach is one of the most effective ways of concluding

this chapter. Most of the important ideas in this chapter can be tested in this way.

The investigative technique described in this section is very similar to one of the new computer-based techniques that has recently been introduced into statistics. The technique is known as the bootstrap method. It was developed by Bradley Efron and is clearly discussed by him in the May 1983 issue of Scientific American.

With this method it is possible to take a set of data that has been collected and see if the results of that set of data have unusual characteristics. In the case of the example in the book, 7 of the method A results were above the median of the combined samples. Is this an unusually high number or an unusually low number? If we now use the 21 numbers and take repeated samples of size 12 (the number of students taught by "Method A"), it is possible to observe how often we got 7 or more numbers greater than 16; one can also see if 7 values above the median is unusual. One of the really important features of this method is that no assumptions are made about the underlying distribution. Almost all tests of significance require one to make certain assumptions about the distribution of the parent population; often it must be assumed that this distribution is normal. Many statisticians have welcomed the "nonparametric" methods, such as the median test, with their freedom from questionable assumptions.

4.   STATISTICAL   COMMENTARY.

Section 5.1

p. 102   It is essential that a sample be representative of the population about which it is providing information. The fact that, say, 42% of the

Drama 427 class at Central College are regular users of marijuana should certainly not be used to infer that approximately 42% of all of the students at Central College are regular users of marijuana. One time-honored way of achieving representative sampling is <u>random sampling</u>, guaranteeing that each population member has an <u>equal chance</u> of appearing in the sample.

p. 102   An idea is touched on here that will come up frequently in the book. Sample values (mean and variance, for example) are often used to estimate corresponding population values (called parameters) of interest.

p. 104   Exercise 1(e). It might be of interest to ask the class whether this method of sampling will be representative, given that concrete is being produced and used all day.

Section 5.2

p. 106   What is really being introduced in Section 5.2 is hypothesis testing. It is perhaps worth noting that if 18 people had favored raising the driving age, then we would likely have been willing to conclude that the community favors raising the driving age, since P(18 or more in favor) = 0.02 is really quite small. Such a large number favoring raising the driving age is unlikely to have occurred if the community were in fact split 50-50 on the issue.

p. 106   In Step 5, the estimated probability 0.23 is called the descriptive level of significance in more advanced courses. Philosophically, it is a measure of how strong the evidence is

(from the data) for rejection. Very small values constitute strong evidence, while larger values constitute weak evidence. Conventionally 0.05 is usually taken as small enough to suggest rejection. As stated elsewhere, we use 0.10 in the book.

Section 5.3

p. 109   The bead box is actually a physical model for the hypergeometric probability law. That is, if a bead box contains W white and B black beads, then in a sample of size n, the probability of w white (and hence n-w black beads) is theoretically given by

$$\frac{\binom{W}{w}\binom{B}{n-w}}{\binom{W+B}{n}}$$

If the population size W+B is large and the sample size is modest compared with W+B, then the above hypergeometric probability is well approximated by the binomial probability

$$\binom{n}{w}\left(\frac{W}{W+B}\right)^{w}\left(\frac{B}{W+B}\right)^{n-w}$$

In more advanced courses, the hypergeometric and binomial formulas are important.

It might occur to the teacher to use the bead box for independent outcome processes such as the ESP problem (Section 5.4). The probability theory allows this as an approximation to independent sampling provided that the population size (total number of beads) is taken to be quite large.

Section 5.4

p.113   If Rob is just guessing, then p(7 or more correct) =

$$\sum_{j=7}^{10} \binom{10}{j} \left(\tfrac{1}{2}\right)^{10}$$

In Table 5.8, this theoretical probability is estimated by the Monte Carlo Method to be 0.21.

p. 114   Note that the conclusion resulting from 0.21 is that "Rob's score is not convincing evidence of anything other than chance behavior." This wording was very carefully chosen by the authors because of an issue that professional statisticians consider very important. In our context, 7 out of 10 correct does not tell us we should accept the conclusion that Rob does not have ESP. It merely tells us we should not conclude that Rob does have ESP. A full discussion of this matter would take us too far afield. It involves a thorough understanding of the issue of the statistical power of hypothesis testing. Most elementary, and quite a few advanced textbooks, leave students with the impression that one either "accepts" or "rejects" based on the data. The truth in most cases is rather that one either rejects (i.e., concludes ESP present) or fails to reject (i.e., concludes we don't know whether ESP is present or not). Only for large data sets is it sometimes appropriate to "accept" (i.e., conclude Rob does not have ESP).

p. 115   Note that if Rob were an anti-social type and told us that he was going to use ESP to produce incorrect answers, we would then decide Rob has ESP or not based on how few answers Rob gets correct. That is, sometimes we want to obtain P(obtained statistics or less). See, for instance, Example 2, page 117.

p. 115   Using 0.10 as conventional in this book (instead of 0.05 or an even smaller value such as 0.01), was a deliberate attempt to increase interest, since rejection of a hypothesis is usually the more exciting conclusion. Occasionally, 0.10 is used in actual practice but the standard value is 0.05.

CHAPTER 6

Chi-Square

1. PREAMBLE.

In chapter 3, students learned that when a certain outcome of an experiment is expected, the results (OBSERVED VALUES) usually differ from the EXPECTED VALUES. This chapter explores the differences between the expected values under a certain model, such as assuming a fair die, and the observed values that have been obtained from experiments. We look at two different ways of measuring these differences. At this point, if we say that the measure of observed difference is 5.6, there is no way of knowing whether this is a large amount or a small one. So we examine the DISTRIBUTION of the measurements. Such a distribution may be called a REFERENCE distribution, although this terminology is not used in the book. In the case we are considering, the difference between expected and observed outcomes, the reference distribution is tied to the assumptions that are made in calculating the expected values. Hence, a reference distribution can be used to find out if a set of assumptions seems valid or not. The chi-square method of measuring the differences is very widely used in statistics and yet the concept is simple enough that most students have little difficulty understanding basic applications of the method. It is one of the more attractive features of this topic, that it can be used to introduce students to many of the central ideas in statistics and, at the same time, give them the opportunity of practical work.

The chi-square test is a very important concept, not only in statistics, but in science in general. Indeed, in Science '84 (November 1984), it has been listed as one of the most important scientific advances of this century (along with the inventions of plastics and transistors, for example).

2. LEARNING OUTCOMES.

Students will be able to:

(a) calculate the expected outcomes of an experiment;

(b) calculate the D statistic measuring the difference between observed and expected outcomes;

(c) calculate the chi-square statistic measuring the difference between observed and expected outcomes;

(d) find the number of degrees of freedom of a table of outcomes;

(e) read information from a stem-and-leaf plot or a table of chi-square values, concerning the probability of getting given chi-square values;

(f) use the chi-square method to test the uniformity of an experimental distribution;

(g) test a model to see if it fits a given set of observed outcomes.

3. TEACHING COMMENTARY.

It is easy to let the approach used in this chapter fall to the level of what has become known as the "cook-book" approach to statistics. This approach, found all too often in many courses, consists mainly of putting numbers into formulae and then putting the resulting value into a table. This approach is far from the intentions of the authors. Rather, a set of experiences should be provided that will lead students through the following stages.

(a) Look at the expected outcomes of an experiment and observe the differences between what was expected and what has been observed. The

vehicle we have used for the activity in this chapter is rolling a fair die.

(b) Establish a method of measuring the difference between the expected and observed outcomes. The first method simply uses the absolute value of the difference between the observed and expected frequencies. This is a convenient way of developing the idea of a statistic that MEASURES some characteristic of a sample and can be used to reinforce the idea of a REFERENCE distribution first introduced in chapter 5 (see e.g. Table 5.3, p. 106). Class results for the experiments provide a distribution of 20-30 values of the D statistic and show the values that can be considered likely and those that can be considered unlikely.

(c) Develop the chi-square statistic as another way of measuring the difference between the observed and expected frequencies. For a number of reasons, explained in later sections of this manual, the chi-square statistic is preferable to the D statistic for serious use.

(d) Produce reference distribution for chi-square statistics. Several distributions are needed since the number of degrees of freedom usually differs from experiment to experiment. The distributions simply tell us which measures are likely and which are not likely.

(e) Observe that for larger samples, the distribution becomes smoother. The shape is an approximation to the theoretical distribution known as the chi-square (χ^2) distribution. Tables of this distribution can be used wherever the size of the sample is large enough (all expected frequencies greater than 5).

In general, the more practical you make the treatment of this chapter, the less likely it is that a cookbook approach will occur. There is considerable scope in this chapter for computer enhancement. The development and use of the concept of a reference distribution, begun in chapter 5, is a crucial element in this treatment. Some teachers have even emphasized this aspect of the chapter to the exclusion of the use of tables. Stem-and-leaf plots were used to summarize the reference distributions for coins, for dice and for random digits. Such reference plots cover most of the applications of the chapter, and build on the knowledge that was acquired in chapter 5.

Section 6.1   Is the die fair?

Since the important idea in this chapter is the difference between the expected and observed outcomes, it is necessary to build up a base of experiences from which conclusions can be drawn. Hence this first section deals with the concept of fairness, in particular the idea of a fair die. Fairness, in this case, is connected with the idea of each of the faces being equally likely to occur, in other words, the idea of a UNIFORM distribution. We expect each of the faces to occur equally often. But this expectation is not always realized, so we begin this chapter by looking at the results of throwing fair dice and observing the differences between what we would expect and what we actually observe.

Section 6.2   What you expect and what you get

A simple way of looking at the difference between the observed (0) and expected (E) frequencies is to look at the absolute value of 0 - E. This exercise sets the stage for the introduction of the D statistic in the next section. All the time, the emphasis is on observing the kinds of variations that are produced by a fair die.

Section 6.3   The D Statistic

The D statistic is merely used to lead up to the more commonly used statistic known as chi-squared. It is an intuitively straightforward concept, and one that is used to reinforce the use of a REFERENCE DISTRIBUTION introduced in the previous chapter. By means of such a distribution, students learn what values of D are likely and what values are unlikely. Some classes may be able to pass by the D statistic and proceed directly to the chi-square statistic.

Section   6.4   Here's   chi-square

The only difference in the methods for D and for chi-square calculation is that we square (0-E) rather than finding the absolute value of (0-E). Once again, it is necessary to build up a REFERENCE DISTRIBUTION to illustrate the likely and unlikely values of chi-square.

Section 6.5   Six steps to chi-square

To this point in the chapter, the probabilities of getting values of χ^2 have been obtained using data obtained from class experiments. Now we take this to a logical conclusion by considering the distribution of chi-square for an "infinite" number of observations, namely the theoretical distribution of chi-square. The theoretical distribution is tabulated and such a table is used in this section. The use of the theoretical probabilities for chi-square requires a knowledge of degrees of freedom from the previous section.

An appropriate statement would be: "Since the probability of a chi-square value as large or larger than the observed 5.84 is large (0.6), under the assumption (model) of a fair die, there is no evidence that one should reject the fair die model and assume the die is biased."

Note: The earlier examples of the calculation of the chi-square statistic are all restricted to situations of equally likely outcomes. Students will probably have developed a habit of adding $(O-E)^2$ for all the categories and then dividing the result by E. This presents no problems if E is the same for all categories, but will lead to errors otherwise.

Section 6.6 Smooth chi-square curves

Smoothing a curve is an important idea and activity. It represents moving from an experimental to a theoretical basis. Here, for example, the move is from graphs based on many experimental trials to the graph of a well-defined theoretical (mathematical) function.

Section 6.7 The chi square table

The students have already used a table as a source of random digits. Hopefully, that experience was a successful one for them--a natural extension of ongoing class activity.

In this section, the use of a table should be introduced just as naturally.

FURTHER PRACTICE WITH CALCULATIONS.

Some of the following six-sided dice are biased. That is, they do not produce uniform distributions. There are 3 kinds of dice. Fair dice, biased dice, and heavily biased dice. Calculate chi-square for each set of 120 rolls and see if you can say which dice are biased and which are not.

Trial Number	Die Face 1	2	3	4	5	6
1	24	21	23	18	16	18
2	13	16	3	36	28	24
3	16	18	29	15	19	23
4	7	12	17	23	26	25
5	23	13	22	18	30	14
6	18	19	25	19	19	20
7	14	17	14	28	22	25
8	16	26	18	23	19	18
9	20	14	14	14	27	31
10	5	9	16	26	32	32
11	9	3	14	23	32	39
12	18	32	15	13	22	20
13	22	14	30	7	18	29
14	22	10	14	25	29	20
15	24	18	17	16	22	23
16	17	17	5	26	25	30
17	14	14	12	19	22	39
18	14	8	10	38	20	30
19	13	10	5	34	20	38
20	18	16	14	31	26	15
21	11	18	16	37	26	12
22	16	12	12	30	27	23
23	11	23	13	20	27	21
24	25	23	15	17	19	21
25	20	17	18	29	21	15
26	16	16	26	23	19	20
27	24	17	19	13	32	15
28	20	23	17	19	23	18
29	25	8	3	37	28	19
30	16	22	14	28	10	30
31	31	37	26	7	8	11
32	24	17	30	13	11	25
33	31	13	19	20	28	9
34	19	21	21	25	17	17
35	16	19	10	28	22	25
36	17	23	19	17	27	17
37	26	15	27	20	23	9

	1	2	3	4	5	6
38	26	16	19	14	16	29
39	22	26	17	14	19	22
40	11	19	25	22	15	28
41	24	18	22	16	18	22
42	20	25	10	24	28	13
43	17	17	20	26	18	22
44	14	18	9	30	18	31
45	32	21	26	11	21	9
46	21	14	19	22	21	23
47	15	8	15	21	31	30
48	27	18	13	21	18	23
49	24	16	15	25	23	17
50	20	13	8	33	19	27
51	23	15	8	30	35	9
52	23	15	17	16	24	25
53	16	12	17	27	23	25
54	8	27	16	13	26	30
55	20	6	12	31	33	18
56	21	20	18	21	23	17
57	14	22	16	23	22	23
58	7	11	13	30	29	30
59	18	15	10	31	27	19
60	7	16	10	31	26	30

Note: Each of the 60 dice has been tossed 120 times.

Values of chi-square for the above dice are given below, together with the bias of the dice. 0 = fair 1 = biased 2 = heavily biased

1	2	3	4
2.5	34.5	6.8	25.6
0	2	0	2

5	6	7	8
10.1	1.6	8.7	3.5
0	0	2	1

9	10	11	12
13.9	34.3	48	11.3
0	2	2	1

13	14	15	16
19.7	12.3	2.9	20.2
1	1	0	2

17	18	19	20
25.1	35.2	44.7	11.9
1	2	2	1

21	22	23	24
24.5	15.1	7.2	3.5
2	1	0	0

25	26	27	28
6	3.9	12.2	1.6
0	0	0	0

29	30	31	32
40.6	16	42	14
2	1	2	1

33	34	35	36
17.8	2.3	10.5	4.3
1	0	1	0

37	38	39	40
12	9.3	4.5	10
1	0	0	1

41	42	43	44
2.4	12.7	3.1	19.3
0	1	0	2

45	46	47	48
19.2	2.6	20.8	5.8
0	0	2	0

49	50	51	52
5	20.6	31.2	5
1	2	2	1

53	54	55	56
8.6	19.7	27.7	1.2
1	2	2	0

57	58	59	60
3.9	29	15	27.1
0	2	1	2

Some of these results will be very surprising. The method used to arrive at these data was to create a non-uniform string of 30 numbers using 1-6 in a microcomputer. 120 numbers were selected at random from this string. A fair die would have 5 of each number in its string. To get a biased string, 3 of the numbers, 1, 2, and 3 in the string, were replaced with 6, 5, and 4. And for a heavily-biased string, 6 of the 15 numbers 1, 2, 3, were replaced with 6, 5, 4. Finally, after all the 120 numbers were tabulated, the frequencies were rearranged randomly among the numbers 1, 2, 3, 4, 5, 6.

4.   STATISTICAL   COMMENTARY.

Section 6.1

p. 124   As remarked in the comments for Chapter 2, Section 2.1, the approach of P(1) to 0.15 is not monotonic. That is, P(1) will fluctuate up and down on both sides of 0.15 as it approaches 0.15.

Section 6.6

p. 145   One needs to be sure that students do not confuse the number of (Monte Carlo) trials (30, 60, 100) and the number of rolls of the die (90) on each trial. Otherwise, the materials becomes hopelessly confusing for the student.

p. 147   The idea that relative frequency polygons can be approximated by smooth curves, (called density functions) is a powerful one. A mathematical treatment of this topic would need graduate level mathematics. But, used informally, as in Figure 6.8, it is very useful in this book. The study of such limiting distributions of statistics is called large-sample theory. The best known and most important example is the Central Limit Theorem, dealt with in Chapter 11.

p. 148   One might wonder why D is not widely used, while chi-square is. The major reason is demonstrated in Figure 6.9. The point is that we can use the same theoretical distribution for reference, with good approximation, regardless of how many observations have been taken, as long as the number is large. This is very useful, and simply not true for the D statistic. Thus, we do not know many properties of the distribution of the D statistic whereas those of the chi-square statistic are very well known. Hence, practitioners routinely use the chi-square statistic.

p. 153   What we really have here is a departure from the Monte Carlo approach to using a approach based upon probability theory, namely the theory of the χ^2 distribution. Since all that is required intellectually to do this is to teach how to use a set of tables, this departure is clearly appropriate. We avoid mathematical theory only when it would be too time-consuming, or too difficult, or when it would distract from a clear focus on central statistical concepts.

Special note: Throughout Chapter 6, all the chi-square problems have involved equal expected cell frequencies (e.g., assuming a fair die). In Chapter 13, unequal expected cell frequencies will be dealt with. (Here, the model to be used is a loaded rather than a fair die.)

p. 153   A chi-square random variable is an example of a random variable that is continuous. This simply means that probabilities are obtained by finding the appropriate area under the appropriate curve, (called a density). Symbolically, $p(2 \leq x \leq 3)$ = area under f(x) from x=2 to x=3. Thus, integral calculus is required to yield a rigorous treatment of random variables of continuous type. One useful fact is that

$$p(x \leq 3) = p(x < 3)$$

as discussed in the note in Appendix B of the Student Text. This is true since the area is the same whether the boundary line x=3 is included in the area or not. Alternatively, $p(x=3)=0$ for any random variable x of continuous type. Many of the random variables dealt with in a basic statistics course (chi-square, t, normal) are of continuous type.

CHAPTER 7

Statistics In Two Variables

1.   PREAMBLE.

The New York Times makes extensive use of statistical graphics. They were once asked why they had never shown a scatterplot involving two variables. Their reason was that they thought that very few people would understand such a graph. It is regrettably true that very few instructional programs include the use of scatter plots in their curriculum. Yet, at the same time, people have a tendency to compare things, and investigating the relation between variables is one of the most important applications in statistics. Perhaps one of the difficulties is that there seems to be such a big difference between the precision of finding the equation of a line that passes through a set of (X,Y) coordinates that lie exactly in a line, and the uncertaintly in that same problem when the points are scattered around the plane so that they only "tend" to lie in a line. Learning how to cope with this kind of uncertainty is becoming an important part of the curriculum, one that should not be neglected to the extent that occurs at present.

The work on statistics in two variables is covered in chapters 7 and 8. The work of chapter 7 deals with the necessary background in linear relations. All investigations into relationships in two variables eventually make use of the linear function. The linear relation, like earlier calculations of the mean, should be seen as a tool to be used in the illumination of data rather than an end in itself. You may have noticed that students learn a technique much more effectively if it is not the main point of the lesson, but a part of something that is perceived to be more interesting. Such is the background for this chapter.

2.   LEARNING OUTCOMES.

Students will be able to:

(a) identify the two variables being referred to in a report or article describing relationships;

(b) given a table of values exhibiting a simple linear relationship, identify the rule which produces those values;

(c) determine the slope and Y-intercept of a line, given its equation;

(d) given a table of values in two variables, plot the data in a "scatterplot";

(e) given a set of data in two variables, find the mean error deviation for an equation of a line which is fitted to the data;

(f) given a table of values for two variables, find the median fit line for these data.

3.   TEACHING COMMENTARY.

The content of this chapter may be familiar to students who have taken science courses that involve graphing experimental data. The purpose of such experiments was to determine the laws that relate two variables. Such techniques are also an important part of statistics. In this chapter, students will have the opportunity to reinforce their knowledge of linear relations and gain insight into the reasons why linear relationships are so important.

Section 7.1   Relating two measures

This section concentrates on the idea of the variables involved in a relationship. Many such relationships are reported in newspapers, often in the field of public health; the relationship between the number of cigarettes smoked per day and the risk of contracting lung cancer is one example. Once more, the newspapers are a useful source of ideas and examples about the relationship between two variables. The first stage in the investigation of relationships is to identify the variables involved. This is best accomplished by the presentation and discussion of a number of examples. Your own file of newspaper reports will supplement those in the text and also add the local element that is so useful in teaching statistics.

Section 7.2   What's my rule?

This material, which may be too elementary for some students, is essential for understanding the remainder of Chapter Seven.

Section 7.3   Graphs of relationships

How to plot data in two variables is, like the content of Section 7.2, essential material.

You may wish to use one or two of the exercises on page 171 to determine whether your class has a grasp of this section.

Section 7.4   The equation of a line

The comment for Section 7.3 applies here, as well.

Section 7.5   Fitting rules to data

The data obtained from experiments, even when the variables fit a linear relation, will rarely fit on a straight line when plotted. The examples in this section provide points that are close to a straight line. The aim then is to fit the "best" line to the points. This is one reason for the importance of the linear relation. It is much, much easier to fit a straight line to a set of points than it is to fit a curve to a set of points. Later in the book, students will meet sets of points that do not lie even approximately near a straight line. But at this stage, the aim is to fit relations to data that are close to being linearly related. Thus, no new mathematical skills are needed at the stage where the concept of a linear relation between two variables is being explored.

Section 7.6   How good is the rule?

Having acquired, or resurrected the skills of handling linear relations, it is possible to break new ground and ask how good is the relationship, if it is not exact. Here, the ground is being laid for the introduction of the idea of residuals, a most important concept in data analysis. Once a line has been drawn which fits the data as closely as possible, it is then possible to measure the distance from the line of each one of the points, i.e. the deviation from the line. This measurement naturally leads to the idea of the mean deviation. Students with programming skills can present different lines to a set of points on the screen of a micro and calculate the mean deviation for each line. It soon becomes evident which line gives the least mean deviation.

Section 7.7   The median fit

The median fit is a very quick, occasionally used method of fitting a straight line to a set of data. It is particularly useful if it is not immediately obvious that we should try to fit a straight line to the data. The median fit provides three guide points. If these three points do not lie on a straight line, then it may be inappropriate even to try to fit a line. More capable students may, in such a case, try to transform the data $X \to X^2$ or $Y \to \sqrt{Y}$ and replot the data. Of course, this is where the plotting power of a good microcomputer package is invaluable.

4.   STATISTICAL COMMENTARY.

Section 7.5

p. 180   Barb's approach is of course vague and subjective. We do not propose it as a serious approach to regression.

Section 7.7

p. 187   The advantage of the median fit approach is that it is quick. It is not an often-used approach in current statistical practice.

Special note: The inquisitive reader will be pleased to know that there is a large theory of curve fitting in the presence of random error that allows for nonlinear equations to be used as well. Further, a dependent variable can be fitted to several independent variables, yielding the widely-used technique of multiple regression. All of this lies beyond the scope of this course. The modest, yet important purpose of chapters 7 and 8 is to present one important and frequently used special case-- that of a linear relationship between a dependent variable and one independent variable in the presence of random error.

<u>Errata Correction</u> for page 218 <u>Using Statistics</u> student text

The sequence for calculating covariance requires five steps; Step 1 on page 218 should be followed by Steps 2 through 5. All five steps are given below.

<u>Step 1</u>:   Find the mean of the X (spelling) scores and the Y (reading) scores. As is seen from Table 8.44:

$$\bar{X} = \text{mean of } X = \frac{70}{10} = 7.0$$

$$\bar{Y} = \text{mean of } Y = \frac{103}{10} = 10.3$$

<u>Step 2</u>:   Find the deviation score for each X and Y score. That is, find X - $\bar{X}$ and Y - $\bar{Y}$. You may want to review Chapter 3 for this.

<u>Step 3</u>:   Find the product of each pair of corresponding X deviation score and Y deviation score. That is, find $(X - \bar{X})(Y - \bar{Y})$.

<u>Step 4</u>:   Find the sum of these products from Step 3. From Table 8.44, this sum is 152.0.

<u>Step 5</u>:   Find the average of these products from Step 3. This average is $\frac{152.0}{10}$ = 15.2.

The covariance of X and Y (that is, the average of the sum of the products of the deviation scores) is

$$\frac{152.0}{10} = 15.2$$

CHAPTER 8

Regression and Correlation

1.   PREAMBLE.

The story of correlation and regression is one of relationships. To understand these relationships it is necessary to be able to interpret scatter plots. There is, however, an important CAVEAT that will be mentioned several times in these notes. That is the ever-present temptation to think of cause-and-effect relationships when correlation is discussed. It will be necessary to face this problem right from the start, because the key problem concerns cancer mortality rates and exposure to radiation. The causation-correlation arguments are examined in section 8.7 of this chapter.

Another difficulty with this subject is the fact that many of the arguments over controversial issues (e.g., smoking and lung cancer, radiation and cancer) are based on a background of knowledge about correlation. They are also emotionally-charged arguments. It requires a certain maturity of outlook to be able to consider the statistical arguments correctly in the face of (sometimes emotional) attachments to the various positions. This represents another argument in favor of a greater emphasis on statistical reasoning in schools.

2.   LEARNING OUTCOMES.

Students will be able to:

   (a)   given a set of bivariate data (table of values in two variables), draw a line with a given slope through the mean data point and calculate the mean error for this line;

   (b)   using mean error as criterion, do a search to find the slope of the best-fitting line and then find its equation;

   (c)   given a table of values that shows the deviation and squared deviation for each data point (for a given equation), find the mean square error for that equation;

   (d)   using mean squared error as criterion do a search to find the slope of the best fitting line and find its equation;

   (e)   calculate and interpret the covariance of a set of bivariate data;

   (f)   estimate from a scatter-plot the correlation of the data represented.

3.   TEACHING COMMENTARY.

By far the most important teaching point in this chapter is really a CAVEAT. The existence of a (perhaps almost linear) relation between two variables DOES NOT MEAN that there is a cause and effect connection between the variables. Two examples that illustrate this point: Sighting of storks in a German village compared with the number of babies born, and convictions for drunkenness in the southern states compared with the number of ordinations of Baptist ministers. In these two cases, both quantities increased over a number of years, hence the variables were positively correlated.

Give examples, during this chapter, of variables that clearly do not have a cause and effect relationship, but do appear to be related when graphed on a scatterplot.

Section 8.1   Linear regression

The terminology of regression is introduced. The method of calculating a line of 'best-fit' is developed over the first three sections of the chapter. At this point the student is given the method of calculating the 'mean point' of a set of data, and then asked to calculate the 'mean error' for line fits that pass through the mean point. Some teachers have found it effective to draw parallels between finding the mean point and the physics problem of find the center of gravity of a set of equal masses.

One of the advantages of this part of the course is the strong reinforcement given to knowledge previously acquired about linear relations.

The technique can be reinforced by programming assignments for those students with programming skills.

It is easy to fall into the trap of using computers to assist with the calculation too early in the work. There does not seem to be a great problem with those students who, finding many calculations tedious, move to the computer and write the program that does the calculation for them. This exercise is sufficiently demanding of knowledge of the technique. But other students, who have not yet understood the process, and who have not the progamming skills necessary to write their own program, often use the programs written by other students to obtain numerically correct answers, without having understood the means by which the answers are obtained. Sometimes, in such cases, the student can be asked to describe, verbally, the program he or she is using. Such a request can help with the development of programming skills as well as statistical skills.

Section 8.2   Least mean error

Mean error is, rather naturally, the mean (or average) distance of points from the regression line. Students should be encouraged to see the analogy of mean error to mean deviation (the mean distance of points from their mean) as presented in Section 2.6.

Section 8.3   Least mean square error

Mean square error, the mean (or average) squared distance of points from the regression line, is the analogy in two dimensions to variance (discussed in Section 2.7).

The many calculations required in the investigations of these sections suggest the use of groups. Each person in the group finds the mean error of a different line through the median point. Once again, the computer can take most of the tedium out of the calculations and demonstrate the principle of least mean error or least mean square error. (See section 8.7 of this chapter for further suggestions.)

The difference between the two methods is connected with the way that each method is affected by extreme values. Extreme values (those that lie a long way from the line) have a greater influence on the least squares method than on the least mean error. The word used in this context by statisticians is ROBUST. They would say that the least mean error method is MORE ROBUST than the least squares method. The idea is that the estimated regression line should not be overly influenced by any single point, which may, in fact, be in error.

Section 8.4   Negative slope

An example of a best-fit line that has a negative slope is used to compare the methods developed in this chapter with the method of the median fit. The discussion of the

meaning of best fit continues with this section.

Section 8.5   Covariance

In presenting the concept of covariance, it may be helpful to break up the term into its parts:

"co" means "together"; and "variance" means "how much data varies".

So, covariance is a measure of the extent to which data in two variables <u>vary</u> <u>together</u>.

Section 8.6   Correlation

Having developed the techniques using lengthy calculations, it is now necessary to provide some short cuts to the calculations. The concept of covariance, the 2-variable analogy to variance, is required. The method of calculating the covariance and then the Pearson Correlation Coefficient are the principal topics of Sections 8.5 and 8.6. It is important to convey some intuitive understanding of these measures, as well as the technique for their calculation.

Section 8.7   Relation and causation

The last section of this chapter should be closely connected with the task of exploring newspapers, magazines, etc. for misuses of the argument of correlation. Many teachers consider this the most important objective of this chapter. Students should acquire enough of the principles of correlation to detect the frequent misuses of the argument. Go back to the Key Problem at the beginning of this chapter and examine your own reactions to the story. Notice the ease with which one is tempted to blame the exposure to radioactivity for the cancer deaths. But such conclusions cannot be drawn FROM THE DATA that are presented here!!! This is not an easy point to make in a situation such as this, but replace the variables with "less connected" variables and the lack of a cause-and-effect relationship can more easily be demonstrated (for example the shoe size as being "caused" by the level of mathematical knowledge--see the student text).

4. STATISTICAL COMMENTARY.

Section 8.1

p. 195   The terms "prediction" and "estimation" have different technical meanings. Parameters are estimated and values of unknown random variables are predicted. Thus, Andolsek's weight loss (a random variable) is predicted.

P. 200   In Table 8.11, the line with mean error 4.99 is not the best line among all possible lines, but merely the best line in Table 8.11. A similar comment applies to Table 8.12 and many other places.

Section 8.3

p. 205   Even though the mean error criterion is more robust than the mean square error criterion, the mean square criterion is far more widely used. Indeed, "least squares" solutions permeate statistics. The reason is that least squares approaches invariably produce beautiful mathematical theories, whereas least mean error approaches do not. Thus, what is probably the more sensible approach much of the time simply has little mathematical theory to back it up. (Note the corresponding comments in Chapter Two for the use of variance and standard deviation rather than mean deviation.)

p. 207   The "best" fitting line using mean square error as the criterion will in general be different from the "best" fitting line using mean error.

Section 8.6   Correlation

p. 221   Two technical points need to be made. First, r actually measures the strength of the <u>linear</u> relationship between two variables. For example, the points

$$(-2,4) \ (-1,1) \ (0,0) \ (1,1) \ (2,4)$$

have the correlation $r = 0$ even though the points fall exactly on the (non-linear) curve $Y=X^2$. This property of r may be too subtle for many students in an introductory course in statistics.

Second, the description of the type of relationship and the value of r ignores the fact that r can, just by chance, be large, when the underlying relationship is not strong or positive. The point to be made is that r is just an estimate of the population correlation coefficient, and hence can be off, especially if the number of data points is not large.

p. 225 S_e^2 is also often called the error sum of squares or residual sum of squares. It is the amount of variation in the data "unexplained" by the regression line.

The formula $r^2 = \dfrac{S_Y^2 - S_e^2}{S_Y^2}$

is rather well known. It says that the square of the correlation is given by

$$\frac{\text{total variation in Y} - \text{unexplained variation in Y}}{\text{total variation in Y}} .$$

CHAPTER 9

Working with Data

1.   PREAMBLE.

The technique of transforming a set of data is one of the most common techniques in statistics. It is used in this chapter as a preparation for the study of the normal distribution. Given any collection of data, its mean and standard deviation can be computed. The transformations discussed in this chapter enable one to change data to sets of data having other desired means and standard deviations. The main element in the technique of transformation is how to choose the transformation so that the mean and standard deviation can be changed to any desired value, often a mean of 0 and a standard deviation of 1.

Once again, as in chapter 7, much use is made of the knowledge of linear relations.

2.   LEARNING OUTCOMES

Students will be able to:

(a) perform "slides" or "stretches" of given sizes on a set of data and determine their effects on the mean of the data;

(b) perform sequential slides and stretches on a set of data, and determine the resulting effects on the mean and variance (and standard deviation) of the set of data;

(c) given a set of data, change them to corresponding z scores;

(d) change a set of data so that they have a given mean and standard deviation;

(e) for a given set of data, draw a relative frequency polygon of the data and then draw the smooth curve to fit these data;

(f) read a table of normal curve areas and
     i. find a probability (area) given a z-score; and
     ii. find a z-score given a probability (area);

(g) solve probability problems using the table of normal curve areas;

(h) recognize distributions of data that are non-normally distributed (and are not uniformly distributed).

3.   TEACHING COMMENTARY.

Section 9.1   Sliding, stretching and shrinking

Section 9.2   Tailor-made scores

Section 9.3   Standard scores

These three sections draw on useful mathematical techniques that reinforce the intuitive understanding of variables, number, linear relations, and sequences. Students who have used sliding, stretching transformations in learning to sketch curves will find this chapter straightforward. Students who do not have this background will acquire a useful background in the ideas.

The important idea in these sections is to demonstrate the effect of sliding and stretching a set of numbers on the mean, variance, and other statistics. When these effects have been observed, they can be applied to the process of transforming a set of data to produce a new mean and standard deviation. Such standardization is often necessary for the use of normal curve tables.

Section 9.4   The uniform (flat) curve

Another aspect of working with data is the ability to "smooth out" the chance variations that occur in random processes. This section deals with the context of equally likely outcomes. In such cases, the underlying distribution is the uniform distribution. The section paves the way for an examination of one of the important distributions in statistics, the normal distribution.

9.5 The normal (bell-shaped) curve

The normal curve is introduced as the limiting case of the distribution of a set of heights. It should be pointed out, however, that the normal distribution curve is a precise, mathematical distribution. Many distributions found in real life seem to fit this distribution so very closely that the mathematical properties of the normal distribution can be applied to such "real life distributions". One of the more commonly applied results is the fact that 2/3 of the data in a normal distribution lie within one standard deviation of the mean (that is, one standard deviation either side of the mean).

9.6   Normal curve tables

The goal of this section is that students should be able to read the normal curve tables and be able to calculate such probabilities as

$$p(z<1.2), \qquad p(z>1.2),$$
$$p(-1<z<2).$$

In all cases, it is important to insist, in the initial stages, that students draw appropriate diagrams using shading to indicate the required area.

Students should also be able to read the tables in reverse and to determine the appropriate value for a in statements as

$$p(z < a) = .95$$
$$p((z < -a) \text{ or } (z > a)) = .05$$

A certain amount of drill will be required for students to acquire these skills.

9.7 Applications of the normal curve

These applications include those mentioned in 9.5 above. The examples in this section include the more common applications of the properties of the normal curve. Often they center around questions concerning the number of members of a population that can be expected to lie within a given range. The ability to make predictions is, of course, one of the more important aspects of statistics.

9.8 Non-normal data

Students should not be given the idea that all distributions are normal. This is far from being the case; data from some non-normal distributions should be collected to reinforce this point. Traffic counts along a freeway (number of cars per time interval) is a good example of a nonnormal distribution.

4. STATISTICAL COMMENTARY.

Section 9.2

p. 240   Note in "5 x old score + 3" that multiplication is done _before_ addition.

p. 245   One might wonder why it is appropriate, even desirable, to convert to a new scale of measurement where the mean is 0 and the standard deviation is 1. The fact is that many measurements in the social sciences do not have a preferred scale. Indeed, the purpose of the scale is often simply to compare scores or to rank scores. Thus, that John got the best score in the class may be of more interest than his actual score on the original scale. When the actual scale is not important, it has become conventional to report scores in units such that the mean is 0 and the standard deviation 1. So, a score of 1.5 is immediately seen to be 1.5 deviations above the mean. Thus, we have z-scores or standard scores. See p. 247 of the textbook for further useful discussion.

Section 9.4

p. 250   In one sense, we do subjectively and visually, using the relative frequency polygon, what is done by chi-square testing in Chapter 6. That is, taking the fair die question as illustrative, we should reject or not reject the hypothesis of the uniform distribution, not because of the observed value of a chi-square statistic, but rather on the basis of the visual appearance (the "lack of bumpiness") of Figure 9.9 (page 252). More abstractly, if a relative frequency polygon is sufficiently close to a theoretical distribution, we use the theoretical distribution as a model for the data. Such a decision should be made only if we have used lots of data to obtain the relative frequency polygon. Underlying this informal approach is the mathematical fact that the observed frequency polygon approaches the theoretical distribution as the amount of data gets greater and greater. Thus, if we have lots of data, when we look at the relative frequency polygon, we are seeing the theoretical distribution (almost).

There are two kinds of theoretical distributions, discrete, where one adds to compute probabilities, and continuous, where one integrates to compute probabilities. Any standard calculus-based probability or statistics textbook can be consulted for information on this. These "smooth" distributions are not necessarily horizontal as in Figure 9.10. Distributions (densities) come in all shapes, including the famous bell-shaped normal distribution dealt with later in this chapter. The uniform distribution is only one of many.

Section 9.5

p. 261   It is not meant here that one can on the basis of Figure 9.13b automatically come up with the bell shaped curve of Figure 9.14. Rather, if one smooths Figure 9.13, one will get something like the normal density of Figure 9.14. Thus we decide indeed to smooth Figure 9.13b to the normal density in Figure 9.14. The point is that the subjective process of smoothing Figure 9.13b can result in many similar densities, that of Figure 9.14 being one good choice.

p. 263   All that has been defined up to this point in the book is the (sample) median. That is, given a set of numbers, we can compute its median. Distributions have (theoretical) medians too. But, for pedagogical reasons, we do not confront this. Actually, for a distribution like the normal, where finding a probability is done by finding an area (i.e., integration), the median is simply the number for which 1/2 of the area under the distribution lies to each side. This is more or less implicit in the discussion on page 263.

p. 264   In a random variable of continous type like the normal, with a density denoted by f(x), the theoretical mean and standard deviation are defined by

$$\mu = \int_{-\infty}^{\infty} x f(x)\, dx$$

$$\sigma = \sqrt{\int_{-\infty}^{\infty} (x-\mu)^2 f(x)\, dx}$$

The formula for the bell-shaped density of a normal variable is given by

$$f(x) = \frac{1}{\sqrt{2\pi}\sigma}\, e^{-(x-\mu)^2/(2\sigma^2)}$$

The information about μ and σ given in Figures 9.18, 9.19, 9.20, and 9.21 are really based on this integral calculus material.

p. 264   This is perhaps a good place to emphasize that in statistics, the standard measures (mean, variance, standard deviation, and median), are defined both for samples and for populations. The means and standard deviations talked about on pages 262-264 are theoretical (population) parameters rather than quantities computed from samples (i.e. data). Thus, for example, one has both a sample variance and a population variance.

pp. 264-265   The argument begun in the last paragraph of page 264 and continued on page 265 is rather subtle and, because of pedagogical considerations, not really made clear. The sequence of steps is the following: (1) In the theoretical normal distribution, 2/3 of the area lies within one standard deviation of the mean. (2) From the data, the theoretical mean is estimated to be 118.67 and the theoretical standard deviation is estimated to be 16.91. (3) The relative frequency polygon, which describes the spread of the actual 100 girls, is approximately the same as its theoretical distribution, with mean estimated to be 118.67, and standard deviation estimated to be 16.91. (4) Thus, if the theoretical distribution is normal, then about 68% of the girls should be within 118.67 ± 16.91. It turns out that actually 63% lie in this interval. This is some evidence in support of using a normal distribution for modeling the heights.

p. 265   It might be interesting to note that, in a more advanced course, students would be taught to use a chi-square test to determine whether the weights of the 100 girls can be well modeled by a normal distribution. The informal argument in the last paragraph on p. 265 actually merely says that 63% is not too far off from the theoretically predicted 68%, thus 68% was computed under the assumption of normality. This is not be be considered a serious statistically reasoned argument, but merely to be suggestive.

Section 9.7

p. 275   Notice that Figure 9.28, as well as others to follow, contains two horizontal scales. The upper scale is in standard deviation units and the lower scale is in the actual units of the problem. The two scales are aligned. Thus, we can see that 1.33 standard deviations above the mean correspond in our problem to 220 hours. This correspondence of scales is useful and should be made clear to the students.

Section 9.8

p. 279   There is a very rich theory for non-normal distributions. For example, if we, as a simplifying approximation, assume that light bulbs do not wear out over time (a better assumption for solid state electronic components, well maintained aircraft or young adults, than light bulbs) then the probability that a light bulb lasts at most x hours is computed by

$$\frac{1}{\mu}\int_0^x e^{-y/\mu}\,dy$$

where μ is a parameter that is the population mean (theoretical) lifetime of lightbulbs. In a more advanced course, example 1 would be dealt with in this manner.

p. 281   Example 3 is actually that of a (continuous) uniform density. That is, probabilities are found by computing the appropriate area under a density that looks like:

In our example a = 1200 and b = 1205

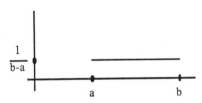

p. 282   U-shaped (and hence bimodal) distributions are used rather infrequently, but they do occur.

CHAPTER

10

Measure-ment

1.   PREAMBLE.

The Normal distribution had its beginnings in a study of the theory of measurement and, in particular, in the errors that are associated with any form of measurement. With the widespread use of hand calculators, a study of errors in measurement is becoming more important. If a student is able to calculate to 8 or more "significant" digits, then he or she should also know when quoting such a result is appropriate. The ability to "read" numerical data correctly, with the underlying information about the goodness of the data is another neglected part of the curriculum.

This chapter gives an excellent opportunity to relate the material to the students' study of science; perhaps members of the science faculty at your school should be consulted. Errors of measurement and how to deal with them are of great importance in laboratory work. This topic is not typically dealt with in other mathematics courses and so warrants careful attention.

2. LEARNING OUTCOMES.

The student will be able to:

    (a) recognize that errors are a part of all measurements;

    (b) know ways of reducing errors of measurement;

    (c) compute the standard error of the mean for sets of measurements;

    (d) identify sources of bias in measurement;

    (e) find way of determining the accuracy of measurement;

    (f) apply concepts of measurement in a laboratory setting.

3. TEACHING COMMENTARY.

Having acquired knowledge of the normal curve, we are now in a position to examine one of its important applications. While DeMoivre (1667-1754) is credited with the first work on the normal curve, it is with Gauss (1777-1855) that the normal curve is most often associated. It was through his work on errors in measurement that Gauss was led to the normal curve. He asked the question,

"What distribution law should be obeyed by errors of measurement, in order to make the arithmetic mean of a set of measurements the most likely value of the true magnitude?"

The normal distribution thus became Gauss' model for the distribution of measurement errors.

This chapter is of particular importance to those proceeding into the sciences. Knowledge of the mathematics of measurement and its associated errors is a sadly neglected part of the mathematics curriculum. It is also a vital prerequisite for the following chapter.

Section 10.1   Measurements vary

The notion of error is introduced. Students should be encouraged to collect some measurements, perhaps from experiments in a science class.

Section 10.2   Measuring carefully

Careful measurement is linked to variance. Investigation, including field trips, of a quality control laboratory will provide an interesting and illuminating background to the entire subject of measurement errors. Manufacturing processes are designed to reduce the variability inherent in any manufacturing process. Quality control engineers help to maintain low variability.

Section 10.3   Standard error

Finding the mean of a set of measurements is one way of obtaining a better estimate of the true measurement. But the means of such a set will also vary. The variability of the mean of a set of measurements will, however, have less variability than the individual measurements themselves. How much variability there is in the mean of a set of measurements is the subject of this section.

Much work of an intuitive nature is necessary to lay the background for a more formal treatment of standard error later in the book. The treatment should not belabor the relation between individual measurement and means of sets of measurements, but students should certainly acquire an intuitive appreciation of the relation. Good visual displays are helpful, including comparative stem-and-leaf plots of measurements and of means of sets of measurements.

Section 10.4   Systematic error (bias)

The example of "sliding" data, adding a constant to a set of measurements might be thought of as a strange thing to do. It may seem a good example to be used in demonstrating the difference between precision and accuracy, but is it a realistic thing to do--does it ever happen? The answer is that it certainly does happen. A cutting tool on a lathe can slip out of adjustment. All items might then be a few "mils" larger than they are supposed to be. It is necessary, in quality control situations to 'calibrate' measuring instruments to help prevent bias from entering the measuring process. Once again, the language of quality control helps to give a visual and concrete image of the abstract ideas being considered here. It is valuable to make use of this idea wherever possible in this chapter.

Section 10.5   Accuracy

Accuracy and precision can be linked to the work of sliding data in an earlier chapter. If we slide data, the variance is not changed, hence the precision is not changed, but we certainly change the accuracy if we add 10 millimetres onto each one of a set of measured lengths.

This idea is developed in the exercises. Some discussion of the difference between precision and accuracy will be necessary to clarify the point.

Section 10.6   Applications of measurement

These two examples given in the text may be of special interest to students in science classes. Consult teachers of other courses for suggestions for other applications.

4. STATISTICAL COMMENTARY.

Section 10.4

p. 294   In this chapter the word "precise" is synonomous with "varies little". "Precise" does not mean "accurate" because, as explained in Section 10.4 one can, because of bias, have low accuracy in the presence of high precision. But low precision does imply low accuracy, whether there is a bias present or not. High accuracy is guaranteed by both high precision (i.e. low standard error of measurement) and little (or no) bias. Because of its great importance in science, we have included the consideration of experimental bias. Most elementary textbooks in statistics do not deal with this topic, leading people to conclude falsely that high precision implies high accuracy. It is true, however, that any improvement in precision will produce a corresponding improvement in accuracy.

CHAPTER

11

Estimation

1.   PREAMBLE.

With the topic of estimation, we return once again, to one of THE most important applications of statistics. The ability to estimate values of the parameters of a population using statistics measured from a sample is a basic part of the subject of Statistics. In an earlier chapter, the application of this principle was studied in the context of YES/NO populations. It is now studied in the context of measurement populations, for which the data have been obtained by measurement rather than by counting.

The subject of statistical bias is an important component of the subject of estimation techniques. Statistical bias is defined as a systematic error in an estimator. Given such a "bald" definition, many students may not really understand the definition. In such cases, experimentation with computer simulations, especially if graphic capabilities are exploited in the software, is a useful way of overcoming this problem.

2. LEARNING OUTCOMES.

Students will be able to:

(a) distinguish between populations and samples;

(b) define "parameter" and "statistic" and give examples of each;

(c) give examples of biased and unbiased statistics;

(d) indicate the basic ideas given by the Central Limit Theorem;

(e) set up a confidence interval for estimating a population mean, using sample information.

3. TEACHING COMMENTARY.

Section 11.1 Samples and populations revisited

This introductory section formalizes some of the language relating to samples and the populations from which they come - PARAMETERS, to denote values computed from a POPULATION, and STATISTICS to denote values computed from a SAMPLE. The essence of this chapter is that SAMPLE STATISTICS inform about POPULATION PARAMETERS. The usual convention of using Greek letters for parameters and Roman letters for statistics is introduced. A discussion format works well with this introduction. Extra motivation is added if the class has previously collected some data of interest that involve measurement. One such activity that has been found successful is that of measuring reaction times of the left and right hands, for male and female subjects, for left- and right-handed people, and for parents and teenagers. See the projects section for further details.

The exercise 11.1 is brief and well handled as an oral exercise. See Newspaper Enhancement for comments about question 11.1.4.

Section 11.2 Estimating population means

This is one of the most widely used techniques of elementary statistics. It is a good idea to build on the intuitive feel that the mean of sample should be close to the mean of the population, a fact that causes no surprise. The important question is, "how close?". It will be necessary to develop experimentally the fact that the "closeness" is related to sample size. Computer simulations will help. The concept of standard error becomes difficult if visual examples are not used. (Some teachers believe that a verbal approach is sufficient - "the standard error is just the standard deviation of the distribution of sample means".) If this approach is successful then the class has a much better verbal ability than most classes. It seems that a graphic approach brings better results.

11.3 Estimating population variances

The principal point of the section is the fact that for small samples the sample variance is in one sense not a good estimate of the population variance; a better estimate is $n/(n-1)$ x sample variance. This introduces the idea of a biased estimator, that is an estimator that is <u>consistently</u> above or below the true value. Once again a computer approach, particularly one incorporating good graphics, is advisable.

Section 11.4 The Central Limit Theorem

The main point to keep in mind in this section is that the section is a DEMONSTRATION of the Theorem, not a proof. The result that the standard deviation of the distribution of sample means is $\sigma/\sqrt{N}$ is shown to be reasonable, rather than proved. It is easy to fall into the trap of merely teaching the correct use of certain formulae to get an answer in this section. One way of avoiding this is to consider a specific problem of interest to the students. The reaction times mentioned earlier is one example. In addition, constant use of the notion of probability will develop this concept, and provide the background necessary to answer such questions as:

If the mean of the population is 83 what is the probability that the mean of a sample (size 16) lies in the interval [81,85]?

Section 11.5   Confidence intervals for mu (large samples)

Both point and interval estimates are developed. The mean of the sample is an unbiased estimator of the mean of the population. This concept is intuitively acceptable, and does not appear to cause any difficulties. More care is necessary with the interval estimate. The use of visual aids has been found to be very helpful. The entire section is built around an understanding of the standard error of the mean, and the use of transparencies helps in establishing a clear idea of this key concept. The success of this section will, to some extent, depend on the students' understanding of the idea of a distribution, and familiarity with such ideas as "95% of the population will be within 2 standard deviations of the mean." This idea is well illustrated by graphic means including the use of box-and-whisker plots. Also the box-and-whisker plots tie in well with the earlier unit on sampling from YES/NO populations.

Key points in the development can be summarized, using the following example as an illustration.
A sample of 9 teenagers had a mean reaction time of 175 m/secs and variance 105 m/sec^2

(a) The sample provides an estimate of the population standard deviation by using

$$\sqrt{105} = 10.25$$

(b) Using this estimated value of the population standard deviation, find the standard error of the mean.

standard error = 10.25/3 = 3.42

(c) Make a 95% box and whisker plot of the distribution of sample means. This is where the visual aid is helpful, because the mean of the population is unknown.

4.   STATISTICAL COMMENTARY.

Section 11.2

pp. 310-313   Be sure the students realize that in "real life", statisticians take only one sample and compute $\bar{X}$ to estimate μ. The repeated sampling to produce many $\bar{X}$s is done to teach students that inherent variation in $\bar{X}$ is a function of the sample size. The means (50.5, 50.2, 49.9) reported at the bottom of Tables 11.1, 11.2, 11.3 are grand means, i.e. means of means. As one would expect, these grand means are all close to the theoretical mean of 50.

p. 313   Our definition of an unbiased statistic is logically equivalent to, but is not the same as, the usual textbook definition of unbiasedness. For those who understand expected value from a college probability or statistics course, $\bar{X}$ would be said to be unbiased if $E(\bar{X}) = \mu$. Our definition avoids the formalism of introducing theoretical expected value and yet captures the real meaning of an unbiased statistic rather well; i.e., if one were to have many samples, the average of the statistic over all these samples should be close to the true parameter value being estimated. One might try telling perceptive students that an unbiased statistic may not be very good because (e.g. in the N = 4 case) it may not be very precise. The ideas of Chapter 10 (accuracy, precision) are relevant here. In actual statistical practice, it occasionally happens that a slightly biased statistic will be preferable, because of its higher precision (i.e. standard error small) over an unbiased statistic with slightly lower precision.

Section 11.4

p. 324   In the sampling procedure of Section 11.4 as well as that elsewhere in the Chapter, the sampling is from a normal population. This choice was one of convenience. Actually, one could start with a population shaped very differently from that of a normal population and still obtain the appropriate bell-shaped distribution for the $\bar{X}$'s.

p. 327   The Central Limit Theorem is the most important and useful theoretical result in all of statistics. It tells us that regardless of the shape of the original population distribution that the shape of the relative frequency polygon resulting from sampling a large number of $\bar{X}$s will be approximately normal provided the sample size is also large. This is a very complex statement. If N is fixed and we choose more and more samples, then a smooth relative frequency polygon (i.e., distribution) will result, which will <u>not</u> in general be normal. But, as N gets large, this smooth relative frequency polygon becomes more and more like a normal density. Thus, if <u>both</u> the number of samples n and the sample size N are large, then the relative frequency polygon will be close to a normal distribution. This is the case in Table 11.13 (c) where both the number of samples (100) and the sample size (36) are fairly large. A good rule of thumb is that N > 20 and n > 100 are required in order that the approximation be a good one.

Section 11.5

p. 333   Earlier in the chapter, to estimate the standard error of a sample mean of size N, many samples of size N were chosen and the standard deviation of their resulting sample means was computed. For example, the standard error of 1.7 in Table 11.3 was found in this way. But here a much simpler procedure is used. Since we <u>know</u> that the standard error is $\sigma/\sqrt{N}$ we can estimate it with just <u>one</u> sample by computing the sample standard deviation S and then estimating the standard error by $S/\sqrt{N}$.

STOP

p. 336   The rather intuitive way of finding confidence intervals can be carefully theoretically justified as producing an approximately 95% confidence interval provided N, the sample size, is large (i.e., N > 20). This is a very useful application of the Central Limit Theorem.

CHAPTER

12

Hypothesis Testing

1.   PREAMBLE.

Hypothesis testing is a subject full of pitfalls for the unwary teacher. It is very easy to pass on incorrect impressions, and be unaware that misconceptions have taken place. Most of the work of the earlier chapters in this book have been laying the foundation for understanding of the principles explored in these later chapters. Technical language has been avoided in favor of developing an intuitive understanding of the processes involved. Such also is the case in this chapter. The model developed in earlier work on probablity, expected values, and decision making is used once again in this chapter. The aim is to provide students with an intuitive understanding of hypothesis testing, not the mechanical, cookbook knowledge so common in introductory college courses.

Hypothesis testing is also the cornerstone of the scientific method. Once again, tying the topic into work in the sciences will be advantageous for those students with an interest in this direction.

2.   LEARNING OUTCOMES.

Students will be able to:

(a)   use information from large samples to test hypotheses about population means;

(b)   recognize decision errors of Type I and Type II;

(c)   use Student's t (for small samples) in testing hypotheses about population means;

(d)   use Student's t to estimate population means, using information from small samples.

3.   TEACHING COMMENTARY.

Section 12.1   Making statistical claims--revisited

The ideas of chapter 11 are used in the context of a problem involving the manufacture of light bulbs. A framework for the discussion of the problem is developed. This framework is similar to those used in earlier chapters on Probability and Simulation. The overriding emphasis is to demonstrate the NATURE OF STATISTICAL REASONING, not to give a cookbook approach that could be applied in an unthinking way.

The argument is similar to that used in any scientific investigation. Make some assumption, examine the consequences of that assumption, compare those consequences with the experimental evidence and see if the evidence contradicts the assumption. The assumptions we make in this kind of argument are assumptions about the population from which the samples have been taken. The technique of computer simulation is then used to produce a distribution of sample means against which the original sample is compared.

The six steps of the framework present the major steps of the argument. The students should become very familiar with the steps of the argument as they follow the examples given in the text and also work through the exercises using the same framework. They should also, once again, be encouraged to devise their own hypotheses, and look for examples of this type of argument in the newspapers.

Some students may have difficulty with the fact that we find the probability of obtaining the test statistic, OR LESS. If the test statistic casts doubt on the claimed value of the population mean, then certainly lower values of the test statistic would also cast doubt. What we are really finding is the probability of obtaining those values (relative to the test statistic) that would cast doubt on the value of the claimed population mean.

Section 12.2   Testing hypotheses about mu (large samples)

The method of reasoning that was developed in the first section used simulation in Steps 2, 3 and 4. The knowledge obtained in chapter 11 can be applied to this simulation enabling us to calculate the probability of obtaining the test statistic, or less, without doing any simulation. This would give a theoretical probability (which is of course better) rather than estimated probability. But the nature of the argument remains the same.

Section 12.3   Wrong decisions

Any decision-making process is accompanied by the possibility of a wrong decision. Statistical decision making arguments share this hazard. But it is possible, using the arguments that have been developed, to estimate the probability of making a wrong decision. Some students have found the following table useful in discussing the kinds of mistakes that can be made.

Two observations are made:
(a) the assumption is either TRUE or FALSE.
(b) the assumption is either ACCEPTED or REJECTED.

There are, therefore, four combinations of these alternatives. They are arranged in the shape of a 2x2 table.

	TRUE	FALSE
ACCEPT	OK	MISTAKE 2
REJECT	MISTAKE 1	OK

Thus the statistician either accepts or rejects a hypothesis which is either true or false.

Many students find the concept of TYPE I and TYPE II errors difficult. Most can handle the idea of TYPE I error but fewer students are comfortable with calculating the probability of a TYPE II error. The principal objective at this level is to acquire an intuitive understanding that 2 types of error are possible. We make no effort at estimating or computing the probability of Type II errors.

Section 12.4   Student's t

One of the important steps in the previous sections was the use of the sample variance to obtain an unbiased estimate of the population variance. For small samples, the error inherent in using the sample variance in place of an unknown population variance may be large enough to make all the difference between accepting and rejecting the hypothesis. "Small," in this context, usually means less than 30. The problem of small samples is investigated in this section and in section 12.5. First, the method of sections 12.1 - 12.3 is used in several examples that involve small samples. Then in this section,

students are introduced to a method that avoids the error of estimating the population variance.

The essence of the calculation in Section 12.2 was to find the value of the z statistic

$$\frac{(\bar{X} - \mu)}{\sigma/\sqrt{N}} \simeq \frac{\bar{X} - \mu}{S/\sqrt{N}}$$

where N is large and hence the observed standard error S/N is very close to the theoretical value σ/N.

The use of the observed standard error involves ESTIMATION when N is small, hence error. Then the t statistic

$$t = \frac{(\bar{X} - \mu)}{S / \sqrt{N}}$$

(where N is the sample size) will not behave in the same way as does the z statistic.

$$z = \frac{\bar{X} - \mu}{\sigma / \sqrt{N}}$$

A different set of tables, including BOTH t and the sample size N, is required. These tables were devised by Gosset.

Students should be encouraged to examine the tables and note how they compare closely with the Normal Distribution tables (for z) when the size of the sample is large.

Section 12.5   Confidence intervals for mu (Small Samples)

Section 12.6   Testing hypotheses without mu (Small Samples)

One of the most common activities of human beings is to compare things. The average salaries of different occupations, of men and women, and so on. The techniques developed in this chapter can be applied to such comparisons to examine whether the difference between the means of two samples is significant; that is, to examine whether the two samples were, in fact, taken from the same population, or whether the samples came from quite different populations having different means.

Project work on the content of this chapter is most likely to be centered around the techniques of this section.

The development uses the computer simulation method used in section 1. More advanced students could benefit from being assigned the task of investigating the method of calculating the theoretical probabilities rather than using estimation through simulation. The simulation method, however, has many advantages over the theoretical approach, since it involves obtaining a reference distribution based on the assumption that the two samples came from the same population. This approach is a much more effective way of acquiring an understanding of the principles behind the method.

4. STATISTICAL COMMENTARY.

Section 12.1

p. 343   In Chapter 5 we needed an exact model (e.g. 3 fair coins) to simulate a situation. Here the model used by SAMPLE may be quite different from the actual probability distribution of the population of batteries at XYZ, but the Central Limit Theorem makes this difference irrelevant, since the statistical decision depends on getting the distribution of $\bar{X}$ right, independent of the original population distribution.

p. 344   In Example 2, it would be more accurate to say that "We want to estimate... if the actual amount of iron in the mine is only 12% or less." But for pedagogical reasons we say "is only 12%." Even at the college level, hypothesis testing, and in particular, this point, is hard to teach effectively. By developing a statistical procedure that is, as desired, very unlikely to lead us to conclude that iron exceeds 12% when it is only 12% we have also developed a statistical procedure that is even more unlikely to lead us to conclude that iron exceeds 12% when it is less than 12%, for example 11% in the standard notation of hypothesis testing we are testing $\mu \leq 12$ against $\mu > 12$.

p. 346   It should be emphasized that the approach of Section 12.2 is valid only if N is large, say $N \geq 20$. (For, the Central Limit Theorem is implicitly used, as discussed in the remark above for page 343.)

Section 12.2

p. 349   It should be noted that Section 12.2 is really an outgrowth of Section 12.1 where instead of simulating many samples to obtain $\bar{X}$, we use the theoretical fact that the distribution of $\bar{X}$ is approximately normal with mean μ and standard deviation $\sigma/\sqrt{N}$. This is the only difference from the approach of Section 12.1.

Section 12.3

p. 355   A very common error made by practicioners of statistics is to follow hypothesis-testing rules that have a very large probability of Type II error, (usually because the sample size is modest). In such situations, we should merely report that one fails to reject the hypothesis, rather than the stronger statement that one <u>accepts</u> the hypothesis. Thus we would avoid making a Type II error. Only if both Type I and Type II errors have small probabilities (say 0.10) is legitimate to "accept" a hypothesis.

p. 356   Strictly speaking t is <u>not</u>, as we claim, a statistic. <u>This</u> is because, when the mean μ is unknown, it is <u>not</u> computable from the data since we cannot substitute for μ. However in hypothesis testing applications (see Step 5 of the example of Section 12.6), we compute: $t = (\bar{X} - 50)/(S/\sqrt{N})$ which <u>is</u> a statistic.

<u>Notes</u>:   (1) All the hypothesis testing treated in Chapter 12 consists of one-sided hypotheses vs. one-sided alternatives, either of the form:

$$H_0: \mu \leq 6 \text{ vs. } H_1: \mu > 6,$$

or

$$H_0: \mu \geq 6 \text{ vs. } H_1: \mu > 6.$$

There is a third important case, the so-called two-sided case:

$$H_0: \mu = 6 \text{ vs. } H_1: \mu \neq 6$$

This will be treated in Chapter 13.

(2) Hypothesis testing concerning whether the underlying population has a normal distribution is possible using the theory of the chi-square distribution. We did not include this case.

(3) A very important case is the comparison of two population means. For example, "which of the two teaching methods produces the greater improvement in test scores?" leads to the comparison of two population means. Formally, if μ_1 denotes mean test score with method #1 and μ_2 with method #2 then one considers

$$H_0: \mu_1 = \mu_2 \text{ vs. } H_1: \mu_1 \neq \mu_2$$

or

$$H_0: \mu_1 \leq \mu_2 \text{ vs. } H_1: \mu_1 > \mu_2$$

Unfortunately, we simply could not cover this important application.

CHAPTER

13

Advanced Topics

1.   PREAMBLE.

In any statistics class, there is likely to be a wide range of interests and abilities. This chapter provides an opportunity for students to explore in greater depth, perhaps on an individual basis, topics from earlier chapters that have generated a particular interest. One of the aims of the authors has been to stimulate an interest in statistics, which requires the provision of a range of subject matter. Not all of this material will interest all students and it will be an unusual class that covers all the material in this book.

The material of this, and the next, chapter will probably find its greatest use in the context of a term project at the end of the course. Many teachers have found this to be one of the most important features of a successful statistics course. During such a project, many important research skills are developed and the ability to draw on the students' particular interests make this a most rewarding experience. Students will often pursue an interest to a deeper level than has been reached in the earlier chapters in the book, and the topics developed here have been selected in the light of experience with such students.

2.   LEARNING OUTCOMES.

Students will be able to:

(a)   apply the chi-square test to problems where the expected frequencies are unequal;

(b)   use the chi-square test to test for independence of certain variables or ways of classification;

(c)   use binomial probability theory to compute certain probabilities;

(d)   recognize two-tailed hypothesis-testing in situations and apply the correct procedure for testing;

(e)   recognize in a more formalized manner certain characteristics of randomness.

3.   TEACHING COMMENTARY.

The topics in this chapter comprise extensions of the content covered in the earlier sections of the book. The wide range of ability that so often occurs in statistics classes at this level requires the availability of material that can be given to those students who require more challenging investigations. The topics covered here are likely to arise during the weeks, at the end of the course, that are devoted to individual final projects. Students will frequently come up with an idea for a project that demands a technique covered in this chapter. In such cases, it has been found that students learn this material more effectively because it is NEEDED for their project.

Section 13.1   Chi-square: unequal expected frequencies

The treatment of chi-square earlier in the book was restricted to situations in which the outcomes occurred with equal probability. Such situations are not the most frequent.

More often, the expected value of the outcomes are not all the same value. This requires more careful calculation of the chi-square statistic since

$$\frac{(O - E)^2}{E}$$

must be calculated for each outcome and before summing to obtain the value of chi-square.

Apart from this, there is no difference between this section and the earlier chapters.

Section 13.2   Chi-square: Independence

One of the most common and most fascinating applications of chi-square is in the analysis of data presented in the form of a 2-way table, otherwise known as a contingency table. The example used to illustrate the application concerns:

A.   a child's order of birth (oldest, in-between, youngest, only child)

B.   delinquent (yes or no)

A child belongs to one of the four categories A and to one of the two categories B. The question asked is "Does membership in categories A affect membership in categories B, or is such membership independent?" The study of this question brings together earlier work on independent events (chapter 4), chi-square (chapter 6) and the framework for decision making (chapter 12).

Membership in the two groups is assumed to be independent, and hence the product rule and

$$p(X \text{ and } Y) = p(X) \times p(Y)$$

can be applied to the calculation of the expected numbers in each of the categories.

The concept of degrees of freedom will require some elaboration. A good method is to make use of the calculations of the expected values. To begin these calculations we start with the following information:

| | DELINQUENT | | |
	YES	NO	TOTAL
OLDEST			474
IN-BETWEEN			341
YOUNGEST			246
ONLY CHILD			93
TOTALS	111	1043	1154

Now using the assumption of independence between the 4 categories, we calculate the expected number in the OLDEST/YES box by saying that since 474/1154 of the girls are oldest children, then we would expect $111 \times 474/1154 = 45.6$ of the 111 delinquent girls to be OLDEST/DELINQUENT. So 45.6 is entered in the appropriate box.

| | DELINQUENT | | |
	YES	NO	TOTAL
OLDEST	45.6		474
IN-BETWEEN			341
YOUNGEST			246
ONLY CHILD			93
TOTALS	111	1043	1154

Now note that it is possible to fill in the OLDEST/NO box without using the product rule. We know that there are 474 oldest children, so that if there are 45.6 in the OLDEST/YES box, there must be $474 - 45.6 = 428.4$ in the OLDEST/NO box. This is written into the table using normal type. The complete table is shown below with italicized numbers used for those requiring the rule of independence and ordinary Roman type for those that can be inferred without using the rule. The degrees of freedom are the number of italicized entries.

| | DELINQUENT | | |
	YES	NO	TOTAL
OLDEST	*45.5*	427.4	474
IN-BETWEEN	*32.8*	308.2	341
YOUNGEST	*23.7*	222.3	246
ONLY CHILD	8.9	84.1	93
TOTALS	111	1043	1154

Newspapers and other sources are full of data where chi-square tests of independence suggest themselves.

THE KEY PROBLEM - background, use and development

The data collected by Mendel's assistant for his classical experiments on pea breeding, is a most interesting set of figures. The point in this example is an unusual one. The chi-square value for this data is 0.51, which is an unusually low value. In fact the probability of getting as low a value as this is 0.08. The suggestion has been made that the data fit Mendel's model rather too well, and suspicion has been cast on the reliability of the results. Some have suggested that Mendel's assistant, who collected the data, was anxious that Mendel's theories be substantiated, and so selected data that fit the model! But there is another equally unlikely example of a closely fitting model. These are the data concerning the number of deaths per corps that resulted from horse kicks in the Prussian Cavalry between the years 1875 and 1894. Such data are believed to be described by a model known as the Poisson model. Here are the observed and expected values.

Deaths/yr	0	1
Frequency	109	65
Expected frequency	108.7	66.3

Deaths/yr	2	3 or more
Frequency	22	4
Expected frequency	20.2	4.8

The value of chi-square is 0.32 for 3 degrees of freedom, and the probability that chi-square is as low as this is 0.04. But one doubts that the deaths were organised in a way that makes the data fit the model. The entire subject of fitting models to data can be used in this chapter to reinforce earlier topics, particularly those investigated in the chapters on probability and simulation.

Section 13.3   Binomial   probability

The concept of a YES-NO population was introduced in chapter 5. The expected frequencies for a yes-no distribution can be calculated using a BINOMIAL PROBABILITY MODEL. The conditions for this model and its connection with the binomial expansion of

$$(p + q)^N$$

are developed in this section. This is an important theoretical model and students intending to proceed in mathematics beyond the high school level should certainly make themselves familiar with the development contained in this section. The most capable students will be able to develop the results

mean = Np   variance = Npq

for the binomial distribution. This exercise provides beneficial reinforcement of the work on the binomial expansion for those students enrolled in a Grade 12 Functions course.

Section 13.4   Two-tailed tests

So far in this book, all of the tests have been one-tailed. That is, only one tail of the statistical distribution that is produced in the experiment, or referred to in the statistical table, is used in making a decision about the obtained statistic. Now, two-tailed testing situations are introduced. This requires careful reading of the problem and sketching of the sampling distribution that is being used.

Section 13.5   Randomness

The concept of randomness is subtle. It has, for example, psychological overtones. Ask the class to write down 10 digits "at random." Then, have the students circle any "double digits," that is, two digit numbers such as 77 or 33. It will likely be found that the class tended to avoid repeating a digit, since, somehow, "it had its turn already."

In this section, methods are presented for producing random digits. The mid-square method (page 396) lends itself particularly well to use with a hand calculator.

The special interest feature in the next chapter (page 411) provides some novel aspects of randomness.

4.   STATISTICAL   COMMENTARY.

Section 13.1

p. 372   The data set in #2 is very famous. It is quite interesting statistically, since the fit of the data is almost "too good to be true".

Section 13.3

p. 385   More generally the probability of k heads in n tosses of an <u>unfair</u> coin that has probability p of heads is given by:

The derivation of this uses the assumption of independence of tosses together with a counting argument. Good mathematics students can handle this formula and even understand its derivation.

Section 13.4

p. 388   Some formalism may help in understanding and/or presenting the fact that P (number correct is greater than 8 or less than 2) = 0.08. Let A = (8 or more correct), B = (2 or less correct)

Note that $A \cap B = \emptyset$. In such cases, it is a property of probabilities that $P(A \cap B) = P(A) + P(B)$. Thus 0.08 is correct.

Section 13.5

p. 395   The digits of the decimal expansion of pi could be used as pseudo-random numbers. This is a particularly dramatic example where the digits clearly <u>are</u> <u>not</u> random, but even after exhaustive statistical investigation, appear to be random.

CHAPTER

14

Monte Carlo Methods

1.   PREAMBLE.

The comments in the preamble to chapter 13 of the resource manual apply equally well to this chapter. The difference lies in the fact that where chapter 13 is devoted to further development of some of the statistical techniques introduced earlier in the book, Chapter 14 examines a number of different applications of one of those techniques, namely simulation and the Monte Carlo method. There will be a number of students interested in the application of computers to the contents of the course and this chapter provides a number of ideas that could be developed as a term project at the conclusion of the course.

The Monte Carlo method is a most interesting example of the change in approach to mathematics caused by the advent of the computer. Problem solving techniques are not confined to algebraic formulations but include any approach that sheds light on the problem. Such are the approaches to the problems presented in this chapter.

2. LEARNING OUTCOMES.

Students will be able to:

    (a) use BASIC to produce random numbers with certain properties;

    (b) find areas of given geometric figures by "target practice" (Monte Carlo method);

    (c) do a Monte Carlo simulation of an atomic reaction;

    (d) use Monte Carlo methods to find resistances of certain electrical circuits;

    (e) use Monte Carlo methods to find reliabilities of certain systems given reliabilities of the system's individual components.

3. TEACHING COMMENTARY.

The simulation techniques that have been widely used in this book are a part of a class of techniques known as Monte Carlo methods. The six sections in this chapter present five different applications of these methods. They each make very useful investigations, particularly for those students who have experience with computers.

Section 14.1   Welcome to Monte Carlo: Computer style

All the investigations in this chapter require the use of random digits. For most students this will mean that they will use the BASIC RND( ) function on their computer. The method of using RND is given here for those students who may not already have used it.

Section 14.2   Finding areas: Easy as pi

When the term Monte Carlo method is used, many people think of the example described in this section, namely that of estimating the area of a circle. It makes a straightforward exercise for any student. This is, however, not a very accurate method of estimating the value of pi. The method known as Buffon's needle takes many thousands of trials to reach reasonable levels of accuracy.

Section 14.3   Radiation

The subject of radiation and radioactive decay is a random process. Simulating the process of neutron diffusion is yet another area where the techniques of statistics and probability reach into another subject. And once again, the process of setting up the model, designing the simulation, and learning from the results is an effective way of reviewing material covered earlier in the course. A good way of evaluating a student's progress in this section is to expect an explanation, and modification, of the program listed. The modification might include such things as rewriting in Pascal, or adding graphics, or a version in LOGO.

Section 14.4   Electrical circuits

The study of electrical resistance circuits provides useful knowledge of the importance of errors. Resistances have a manufacturer's "tolerance." Care in selecting appropriate tolerance levels is an important part of the design of a circuit. Simulation is used to reinforce the effect of error in a circuit.

Section 14.5   Genetics

The topic of genetics is taught in many high school biology classes. The foundations of the subject are based on ideas of probability, which means that the topic lends itself to exploration by means of Monte Carlo methods.

Section 14.6   Reliability of systems

The reliability of systems make an interesting investigation for students interested in engineering. It is also an important aspect of the design of Very Large Scale Integrated chips (VLSI). The manufacture of integrated circuits requires there to be NO impurities in the silicon wafers used. This is difficult to achieve. But if 400 chips are constructed on a single wafer the probability of an impurity on any one chip can be made quite small, and maybe 80% of the chips will be satisfactory. But there may only be 4 VLSI chips on a single wafer. In such cases the impurities would create many more defective chips. So the designers build several duplicated circuits in the VLSI chips so that if an impurity occurs in one circuit, there may be another available to take over.

Underlying the work on reliability are the basic laws of probability for independent and mutually exclusive events. Hence, the technique of simulation is an effective way to teach your students something about this important topic.

4. STATISTICAL COMMENTARY.

Section 14.3

p. 413   The "simplifying" assumptions are rather extreme. Thus, it is quite possible that predictions made by applying the model will not agree with reality. The dilemma of the applied mathematician is that there is always a dynamic tension between producing realistic models (i.e. those that do not seriously distort reality) and tractable models (i.e. those that can be solved mathematically). The use of simulation to solve models for probabilities of interest allows the use of models that otherwise would be intractable. The simplification in Section 14.3 is for pedagogical reasons only. That is, Monte Carlo simulation could be used even if the model were much more complex and hence more realistic.

Section 14.4

p. 418   Assuming a uniform distribution from 90 to 110 is probably not the best model. In reality, the distribution is probably more like a normal distribution with mean 100 and a variance small enough so that it is rather unlikely to have resistors with values less than 90 ohms or greater than 110 ohms.

Section 14.5

p. 421   Clearly the theoretical probability is 3/4 here. But more complex genetics problems are not so easily solved.

Section 14.6

p. 423   If three events are independent then $p(A \cap B \cap C) = p(a) \times p(B) \times p(C)$ for these events. Thus, the theoretical answer on p. 423 is $(0.9)^3 = 0.729$. Again, answers to more complex problems are not so easily arrived at.

p. 424   The correct theoretical answer is $1 - p$ (both fail) $= 1 - (1/4)^2 = 15/16$.

More Random Data

1. Tosses of a fair coin
2. Rolls of a 4-sided die
3. Rolls of a 6-sided die
4. Rolls of an 8-sided die
5. Rolls of a 10-sided die
6. Rolls of a 12-sided die
7. Spins of a 3-spinner
8. Spins of a 5-spinner
9. Spins of a 9-spinner
10. Birthday problem digits

1. COIN TOSSES

ROW

1	HTHHT	THTTH	THTHT	HHTHT	TTTTT	HHTHT	HHHTH	HTTTT	TTHHT	HTHTH
2	TTHHH	HTHTH	HHHTH	HHHHT	THTTT	TTHHH	HTTHH	THTTT	TTHTH	HTTTH
3	THTHT	HHHHH	HHTTT	HTTHT	HTTHT	THHHT	HHTHH	THTHT	HHHHT	TTHHT
4	TTHTT	HHTTT	THTHH	TTHHH	HHHTH	HHTHH	HHHHT	HHTTH	THTTH	HHTTT
5	HTHTH	HTTHH	HHTHH	TTTTH	HTTHT	HTTHH	HTHHT	HHHTH	THTHH	HTTTT
6	HHTTH	HHHHT	TTHHH	HTHHT	HHTHH	HTTHT	HHTTH	THHHT	HTTTT	HTHTT
7	HHHTT	THTHH	THHTH	THTHH	THTHT	THHHH	THHTH	HTTTT	HHTTT	HTTTH
8	HTHTH	THHHT	THHHH	TTHTT	THHHH	HTTTT	THTTH	HTTTT	TTTHT	THHTH
9	HHTHT	HHHTT	HTHHT	HHTTH	HTHTT	HHTTH	THTHH	HTHTH	TTHTH	HHTTT
10	THHTT	THHHH	HHHTH	HTTTT	HHHTH	HTHTH	THHHT	HTHTT	HHHTH	HTHHT
11	HHHHT	THHHH	TTTTH	THHTT	THHTT	TTHTT	THTTT	THHTH	HHTHH	HHHHT
12	HTHHT	THTTT	HTHTH	THHTH	HTHHH	TTTTT	HTTHT	HHTTH	THTHH	THHTT
13	HTHTH	HTHHH	HHTTT	HTTHT	THHTT	HHHHT	HTTHT	HTTTH	HHHTH	TTTHT
14	HHTTH	HTHHT	HTHTH	HHTTH	TTHTH	HHHHH	HTTTH	THTTH	TTHTT	HTTTH
15	TTHHH	TTTTT	HTHHH	HHHHH	HHHHT	TTTHH	TTHTH	TTTTT	HTHHT	TTHHH
16	HTTTT	HHHTT	HTHHT	TTTTH	HHTTT	HTTHH	HTHTT	TTHHH	TTHTT	HHHTT
17	HHHTH	HHTHT	HHTHT	HHTTH	TTHTH	TTHHT	THHTH	HHHHH	HHTTH	TTHTH
18	TTTTT	HHHHT	HHTTT	TTHTH	HTTHT	THTTH	HHHHT	THHHT	HHHTH	TTTHH
19	THTHT	TTHTT	HTHHH	HTHTT	TTHHH	THTTH	HTHTH	HTTTT	TTTHH	TTTTT
20	HHTHH	HHTHT	TTTTT	HHHHH	HTHTT	HHTHT	THHTT	HHTTT	THHHH	HHHTT
21	HTHHT	HHTHH	THHTT	TTHHT	HHTHT	HHTTT	HTTHT	THTTH	HTHTH	HHHTH
22	TTHHT	HTTHH	THTHH	TTHTT	HHTHT	HHTTH	HTTTH	HHTTH	TTHHT	HHHHT
23	HHTTT	HHHHT	HHHHH	TTTHT	HHHHH	HHTHH	TTTTH	HHHTT	TTHHH	TTHHT
24	THTHT	TTHHH	TTTTT	HHTTT	THTTT	THTTT	TTHHH	HHHTH	HTHTH	TTTHT
25	HTTHT	TTTTH	HTTHH	HHHHT	TTTHT	HTTHT	THTHT	HHTTH	TTHHT	THHTT

ROW

26	THTTH	THTTT	HHHHT	HTHTH	TTTHT	TTHTT	HTTHT	TTTTT	TTTTT	HTHTT
27	TTTHH	HHTTT	HHTTT	HTHTH	HHTHH	THTHT	HHTTT	HTTHH	HTHTH	THHHH
28	HHHHH	THTTT	THHTH	HTHTT	TTTTH	THTHH	TTHTH	HHHTH	HTTHT	HTTHH
29	HTTHT	HHHTH	HHHHT	TTTTT	TTHTH	THTHH	HTHHT	HTHHT	HHHTH	HTTTH
30	HTTTT	THHTH	HTTTT	HHTHH	THHTT	HTTTT	THHHH	HHTHT	HHTTT	HTHTT
31	HHTHT	TTHHH	HHTTT	HHTTH	TTHHH	THTHH	HTTHT	THTHT	HTTHT	HTTHH
32	THTTH	TTHHH	TTTTH	HHHHH	TTTTT	THTHH	HTTTT	HTHTT	TTHTT	HHHHH
33	HTTHH	TTHHH	HTHHT	HTTHT	THTTT	THHHT	HTTHT	THTTH	HHTTH	TTHTT
34	HHHHT	TTTHH	HTTHH	HHTTH	HHTHH	TTHTT	HTTTT	HTTHT	HTHHT	HTHHH
35	TTHHH	TTHTH	TTTHH	TTHHH	THHHT	HTHHH	TTHTH	THTTH	HTTTH	TTTHT
36	HHHHT	THHTH	TTHHT	HTHHT	HTHTH	THHTT	TTHHH	HTTHH	TTHTT	TTTHH
37	THTHT	HTHTT	THTHT	HTTTH	THHHH	HHHHT	THTHH	HTTHT	HTTTH	HTTTH
38	HHHHT	HTHTT	THHHH	THTHT	HTHHT	THTHT	HTTHT	HTHHH	HHTTH	TTTTH
39	HHHTT	TTHTH	HTHTH	TTTHH	HHHTH	THTHT	HHHHH	HHHHH	HTHTH	TTHTH
40	TTTHH	HTHTT	HHHTT	TTTTT	HTTHT	HTTHH	TTTTT	THHHT	THHTT	HHHTT
41	THTTH	HTHHH	THTTH	HHHHH	TTTHT	HTTHH	TTHHH	HHHTH	HHHHT	HTHHT
42	TTHTT	TTTHT	HHHTT	TTTHT	HTHTT	THTHH	THHHH	THHHH	HTTHT	HHHHH
43	TTHHT	THHHT	HHTTH	HHTHH	HHTTH	THTHH	HTTTT	TTTHH	THTHT	HTHTT
44	TTHHH	HHTTT	THTTH	TTTHH	HTTTT	TTTHH	THTTT	HTTHT	TTTHT	TTTTT
45	HHTHT	HHTHT	THTHH	HTTHT	HTTTH	TTHTT	TTTHT	HHTHT	TTHHT	HHHTT
46	THTHH	HTTTH	TTTTH	TTTHT	TTTHH	HHHTT	HTHTH	THTTH	TTTHH	TTHTH
47	TTHTH	HHHHH	HHTHH	HTHTT	HTHTH	THHTT	THTTT	THHHT	HTTHT	THTHH
48	HTTTH	TTHTT	HHHTH	TTHHT	TTTTH	HHTTT	TTTTH	HTTTH	TTHTT	TTTHT
49	HTHHH	TTHHT	HTHTT	HHTHT	HTTHH	HTHHH	TTTTT	HTTTT	HTHHT	THTTH
50	THTHT	HTHTH	TTHTT	THTHH	HTHTT	HTTTT	HHTTH	HHHTH	HHTTH	TTTHH
51	TTHHH	TTHTT	HHTHH	TTHTH	HTHHT	TTTTT	HTTHH	TTHTH	HHHHT	HTHHT
52	TTTTT	HTTTH	HTTHH	HTHHH	HHHHH	THHTT	TTTHH	HHTHH	THTHT	TTHHH
53	HHTHH	TTHTT	TTTHH	HTHHH	HHHTH	HTHHH	HHTHT	TTHTT	HHHTT	TTTTH
54	THHTH	TTHTT	TTHTT	THTHH	THHTT	HTTTH	HHHTT	THTTT	HHHHH	THHHT
55	TTTHT	THHHH	HTHTT	HHTHT	THHHH	HHTTH	TTHHT	HTTTH	HTTTH	HHHTH
56	THHTH	HHHHH	THTTH	TTHTT	TTTHH	THHTH	HHTHT	THTHH	HTHTT	TTTHH
57	TTTTH	HTTTT	HTHHT	HTTTT	THTTT	HHHHT	TTHHT	HHHTT	HTHTT	TTHTT
58	THTHT	HTHHT	THTTT	HTHTH	HTHHT	HHTTH	THTTT	TTHTT	TTHTT	THTTT
59	HTHTH	HTHHH	HHHTH	TTHTH	HHHHH	HHTHH	HHTHH	HTHHT	THTTH	TTTTT
60	TTHTH	TTHTT	HTHHT	THHHH	TTTHT	TTHTT	HTHTH	HTHTT	HHHHT	HTTHT
61	HHHTT	HHTHT	HHTTH	HTTHH	THTHT	THHHH	HTTHT	TTHTH	HTHTT	TTTTT
62	TTTHT	TTTTT	HTHHH	HTTTT	HHTHH	HHHHT	HTHHH	HTHHH	HTTHT	THHTH
63	HTHHT	TTHTH	THHTH	HHTHH	HTHHT	HHTHT	HTHTT	TTHTT	THTHH	TTHHH
64	THHHH	THTTT	TTTTH	HHHHT	TTHHH	HHTTT	HTTTT	THTHH	THTHH	TTHTT
65	THTHT	TTHTT	THTHT	HHTTT	HHHHH	HHHTH	HTHHH	THTHT	THTHH	HTTHH
66	TTHTT	HHHHH	TTHTT	TTTTT	TTTHT	HTTHH	HHTTH	THTTT	HHHTH	TTHHT
67	THHTT	HTHTT	THTHH	TTHTH	THHHT	HTHHH	TTTHT	TTTHH	TTTHT	HTHHH
68	THTHT	HHTHH	HHHTH	TTTTT	TTTTH	THTHH	THHTH	HHHHT	THHHH	HHTTH
69	HHHHH	TTHTT	HTTTT	HHHTT	HHHTT	THTHH	HTTTT	THTHT	HHHHH	TTTTH
70	HHHHH	THTHT	HHTTT	THHTT	TTHHT	HTHHH	THTHH	THHTT	HHHTT	HHHTT

ROW

71	TTHHT	HTHTT	THTHT	THTTH	HTTTT	THTHH	THTHH	TTTHT	THHTH	HTTHT
72	HHHHH	HHTTT	HHHTH	TTHHH	HTTTT	HTHHH	HTTTH	HHHHH	HTTHH	TTTTT
73	THHHT	TTTHH	TTTHT	THHHH	TTHTH	THHHT	TTHTT	HTHTH	HTTHT	TTHTH
74	THTHT	TTTTT	TTTTT	HHHTH	THTHT	THHHT	TTHTT	TTTHH	HTHHH	HTHTH
75	HTHHH	HHHTT	THTHH	TTHTH	HTHTT	TTTHT	HTHHT	TTTHH	HTHHH	HTHHH

76	HHTTH	HHHHTH	TTTTH	THTHT	TTTHH	HTTTH	THHTH	THTHH	TTHTT	THTTT
77	HTTTH	HHHHH	HHHTH	HTTTT	HHTTT	HTTTT	THHTH	HHTTH	THTHT	THTHH
78	HHTTT	THHHH	HTTHH	TTHTT	HHTHH	HHHHT	TTTHT	THTHT	HTHTH	THTTH
79	TTHHH	TTTTH	HTHHT	HHHTH	TTTHT	HTTTT	THTHH	HTHTH	HTHTT	HTHTT
80	HHHHT	THHTH	HHHHH	HHHTH	THTTH	THTHH	HHTHT	HTHTH	HTHTT	HTHTT

81	TTHTH	HHHHT	TTHHH	TTTHH	HHHTH	HTHHH	TTTHT	HHHTT	THHTT	TTTHT
82	HHHHT	HTTHT	THHTH	HTTTT	HTHTT	THHHT	TTHHT	TTTTT	THHTT	HHTTT
83	TTTHH	HTTHT	TTHHH	TTTHT	HHTHH	HHTTT	TTHHT	THTHH	HHHHH	THHHT
84	HHHTH	TTTHT	HTHHH	HTHTT	HTHTT	TTHTH	HHTHT	HTHHT	HHTTT	THHHT
85	THTHH	HTHHT	TTHTH	HHTTH	HTHHT	HHTHH	HHHHT	THTTT	HTHHH	THHHH

86	HTHHT	TTTHT	THTHT	HTTHT	HHTHT	THTHH	HTTTT	HHHTT	HTHTT	HHTHT
87	HTTHH	TTHHT	THHTH	TTHHT	HHTHH	HHHTT	TTTHH	HTHHH	HTHHT	HTHTH
88	THHTT	HHHTT	HHHHH	HHHHH	THTHT	HTTHH	HTTHH	THHHT	THHTH	HHHTH
89	TTTHH	TTTTH	THHHT	THHHH	TTTTT	HTTTT	TTHTT	TTHHT	HTHTT	TTHTT
90	HHTTH	TTTHT	HHTTT	HTTHH	TTTHH	HTTHT	HHHTT	HTHTT	THTTT	TTHHT

2 . ROLLS OF A 4 - DIE

ROW

1	44441	32231	24343	32222	44234	34313	41414	21241	41324	12323
2	42424	32334	41134	14142	23431	34124	22132	44331	11422	21432
3	34122	22222	13111	23422	34112	24442	43132	24411	21243	21132
4	14244	32224	32113	14312	34443	43132	41344	22442	13321	23232
5	44142	23314	34433	32411	43213	14314	21434	14114	44242	33342

6	22224	13242	32243	24443	24121	13133	31232	12423	13114	24442
7	44213	33344	32414	31424	11132	43444	34222	11422	32143	42421
8	14131	44111	24221	14124	13211	43342	43443	42422	12144	33322
9	31234	44124	11341	12233	42432	14132	12314	13423	41443	12142
10	24323	21111	31222	12221	44242	31131	11323	44432	23122	41322

11	31342	13422	24114	33123	43121	13141	13311	42231	33331	24411
12	24143	23144	23434	34322	12424	23344	42222	14111	11434	43341
13	42223	22133	21343	34123	22234	44333	14212	11124	44131	31221
14	33242	42124	11124	12133	12332	33121	21431	32411	42242	12213
15	21423	14212	41441	22432	42411	14334	41334	12443	31222	34213

16	34421	31422	43413	44442	11244	12422	32132	22421	21111	13331
17	24313	42114	24231	22241	14113	42423	42211	12121	33443	41223
18	43224	41143	44221	42312	21221	42334	44412	34233	22122	24411
19	23123	11333	44342	21133	14234	41141	14132	13333	21442	23422
20	22142	14414	44222	13211	22121	14431	33413	41141	24134	24314

ROW

21	32221	31241	12441	24223	11221	33113	24234	34443	11333	13423
22	41221	21141	31213	44223	22342	23123	44123	21411	22144	33443
23	21422	14421	33312	33343	34323	34132	24414	12323	32312	42342
24	33222	33223	12132	24121	13433	44244	42123	33412	42243	11111
25	32212	44334	34212	23443	32433	13211	24124	42242	43411	34223
26	33421	14323	33121	23113	22423	12211	13433	23324	13233	23214
27	41111	31243	31114	44443	14444	13444	12214	32221	22233	13324
28	11314	12121	34112	13232	44323	31114	21132	34233	43141	21443
29	14213	21344	24122	14134	24441	41322	14423	34331	34331	34233
30	14132	33414	11431	34343	41144	31214	13432	14434	43112	21221
31	24114	31111	34243	24343	13144	23112	23432	11422	14114	41324
32	12344	22412	22114	24241	44321	13323	41331	34432	41313	34442
33	12123	23322	11441	44131	23223	34332	11233	22211	24221	31241
34	23344	21421	33343	24131	14421	32113	23321	32214	11441	14311
35	24423	22432	33314	11114	14244	14324	21114	42323	21231	13241
36	42334	32341	31223	21424	44133	33121	33222	12221	33114	33313
37	22112	14433	31443	43111	12443	13412	31232	23433	33332	21424
38	11113	14122	14214	13134	24413	21342	11333	24442	11411	34312
39	34142	11342	32133	21122	22323	24141	21433	34214	32232	13134
40	11221	12431	34233	11133	24121	12423	11434	24414	13123	43224
41	24124	24133	11243	44241	12211	42433	24234	24441	42412	24243
42	23412	22123	41341	24114	22124	14423	42213	33242	12322	24121
43	12132	42334	22433	21242	43322	14411	21224	13333	31134	41311
44	13142	24341	44234	43443	31211	42344	13321	22242	24233	12432
45	32121	13242	42322	14142	34423	13244	11434	21443	33341	12134
46	42231	33431	22114	33122	41131	13231	12342	33421	44433	33432
47	34344	34222	32241	23242	21444	23331	24323	31123	33234	34442
48	43411	41412	31214	22413	11123	22212	11424	32224	23112	24334
49	41334	41343	11431	11144	21221	11243	42134	44443	33142	13333
50	21243	32422	34212	14112	14123	42314	34112	23344	43431	11143
51	43113	23133	14321	23443	34424	12431	42432	33121	22343	12313
52	32331	33213	42313	34231	32431	31241	23331	42134	42212	21243
53	24314	42424	13324	11121	34441	22444	34433	41234	43134	14133
54	23121	33331	31323	33211	34221	22141	33413	21143	13122	14344
55	22113	44313	43224	24114	33234	11232	44314	41142	14442	21111
56	12131	14242	34444	43343	22342	12121	33133	42133	22331	33124
57	14214	42133	31111	43412	11111	32312	42132	42433	22342	43334
58	44412	34311	32212	43342	22443	14332	22314	11321	32124	24413
59	43112	43442	13414	33314	44422	42244	13441	32244	11332	11233
60	41134	23213	32343	34211	32444	13243	42432	42332	43131	41234
61	14143	34243	44314	34423	43211	31232	41314	34224	11313	31231
62	43431	24123	43142	24124	43313	33424	43114	42224	24214	14411
63	24343	13241	23434	33443	43212	23112	31441	41312	12421	31144
64	31124	23121	43441	21323	21231	12224	11342	44223	44141	32123
65	32442	44411	34111	44422	32442	14231	33124	33321	43244	32134

ROW

66	23212	14233	32313	24112	43314	32343	24232	44422	21424	43323
67	23242	12211	12442	13331	21332	23132	44322	24431	44234	24213
68	13121	13312	42432	12443	22144	31421	32412	32121	33321	23331
69	42343	31211	43123	41434	24144	14333	23113	24424	23141	11234
70	14144	42142	23431	14112	14124	14313	44321	22341	13233	33123
71	22424	33242	32144	23132	22143	41422	43341	23413	44411	44132
72	11414	43434	13213	13412	14311	41112	43234	12121	22123	24331
73	44131	31224	21133	14414	41443	21442	44132	21213	24141	24323
74	22244	44223	12321	34331	33122	32114	41131	21234	32414	33112
75	41121	14222	12242	22111	23132	44221	21231	34441	24334	44234
76	31413	33124	31313	22334	34221	31433	42122	23333	33224	14422
77	41212	44231	11433	33121	34234	44141	21343	14321	11333	22422
78	32113	43144	44113	14343	41321	41343	12324	23214	14231	42344
79	34423	31332	43121	13112	21431	44234	41444	31223	32131	11432
80	41413	22212	11231	42221	22332	21222	33323	43413	34421	42212
81	31144	43322	22413	31131	33224	14334	12414	34111	23331	13143
82	22314	11144	33412	32233	41112	44312	12333	42323	23244	41421
83	12432	33433	42231	42424	41241	23121	11113	31344	31412	41441
84	34244	43124	43311	33424	23443	22331	43343	23442	42232	42241
85	43411	44241	23232	41121	24422	42232	43324	21441	14231	34241
86	34431	11423	24121	44143	11413	41233	42324	12144	23413	11341
87	33211	23434	11113	13432	34433	21244	21222	11432	43224	13224
88	11122	12432	23421	31443	32134	41322	32414	23443	44314	31344
89	24322	13343	23133	41423	41342	22324	24434	32423	21333	22214
90	24244	34213	44442	44324	42221	23211	44333	34242	22123	43223

3 . ROLLS OF A 6 - DIE

ROW

1	31441	24135	24526	13255	32141	46554	13626	66363	64131	23435
2	66436	23354	61423	31616	45221	44254	15442	64562	22251	32165
3	26215	24543	64245	32654	35432	36525	21124	15214	41412	13461
4	35435	41245	25162	24215	26555	25313	64656	61112	26646	13263
5	21646	65212	23361	35161	33154	63134	54531	31433	32321	24214
6	22115	66463	25113	54246	41252	14325	34113	63632	35316	43433
7	26412	15264	51513	13356	53212	16345	14112	24531	55213	35365
8	42542	31662	44462	56236	41211	64634	45544	23424	24455	33113
9	63442	61264	45364	54224	53645	65551	23446	54214	21526	22354
10	56613	34214	24133	11631	22414	61313	43222	33265	26141	65534
11	35411	41116	35156	11424	11122	23623	36361	13654	26326	41535
12	66165	65614	51122	41122	61232	21355	31434	31625	41314	26611
13	43563	23613	62615	13423	32651	21141	43424	22464	51146	53664
14	25624	64342	53666	66263	22161	54254	45234	62563	42261	64521
15	12552	23226	12514	36452	45454	66232	54246	12515	42541	33323

ROW

16	55662	51624	22163	54546	11335	62263	23232	43632	63616	14434
17	52251	21624	13143	31136	54332	52621	45313	33161	41342	16461
18	16343	36244	32233	45115	11541	45332	36546	21451	62625	16643
19	45642	25161	23356	21245	54655	15423	53363	51531	36346	63122
20	52424	12255	16626	52413	62233	35513	22651	11166	22463	54264
21	64244	22231	52656	64424	23252	52532	54354	33422	14263	64325
22	34654	56212	21462	31245	23361	36222	31643	42461	46156	25451
23	62522	22215	64166	13214	24636	24535	65263	54151	34421	43135
24	54664	22332	26126	42663	24434	45443	24162	36235	33225	13164
25	63361	52433	25316	33266	34132	44263	34533	51412	16215	31144
26	14422	35562	34251	15211	52132	13624	62214	44665	51362	31465
27	21211	42235	54612	64416	66155	56626	51116	25224	13411	31241
28	53516	12212	14644	65414	56612	46155	25461	14451	41662	36336
29	12611	43511	52664	51443	36143	63121	62632	44464	52411	54555
30	34453	55233	25343	51132	54214	66523	42543	12456	54432	23364
31	21222	34232	61314	66151	26664	63543	12642	11526	51121	13242
32	32461	46235	43245	64323	55626	25414	66612	56463	14461	26655
33	63315	42243	62352	62164	23516	26252	51354	33135	63133	31321
34	54214	51226	61551	36621	52635	63544	26114	13141	61421	35633
35	16146	13536	33333	23365	51461	51543	42266	42443	64434	63664
36	36234	44315	43112	45456	43624	56455	14335	23115	34626	13435
37	16355	45254	13223	53624	45363	22444	11635	25352	53126	61215
38	62353	61144	22365	26333	42125	46264	32165	56255	54652	11455
39	55364	26616	56351	55311	22431	43311	15113	62254	43664	24422
40	51266	54452	42354	43352	53211	13145	43214	32346	43162	12256
41	22263	46645	62354	14435	24556	46465	42213	53555	36166	12414
42	44641	53523	34264	64352	55236	63555	43255	56116	41156	21635
43	22122	15651	13542	45332	42366	63351	22155	36126	34251	24233
44	26111	16555	36222	63565	15166	25661	13641	25524	51333	61263
45	12225	25311	51123	44136	34555	16551	54454	62431	46314	11426
46	24514	23435	51152	21236	14433	15144	52665	45561	25365	51245
47	36125	32532	11421	61665	45324	63354	66566	34346	66221	55444
48	62611	13544	66331	26133	32554	33516	66552	11345	41365	26124
49	44534	12523	65365	22623	16361	36421	62615	53331	32353	61116
50	44343	13663	31224	13546	64324	46522	14144	52461	63534	34252
51	55432	43246	32242	53523	16522	42353	33331	41312	52542	46245
52	14325	53311	31212	46135	52316	22263	21254	56166	36635	36565
53	55124	22625	61426	43616	61345	51125	44365	54425	46513	16114
54	44143	33561	51144	46335	55643	23626	42342	51543	14356	11553
55	13236	36143	25632	56632	42556	54656	43252	66236	63514	32153
56	42151	34466	23514	56321	33232	16514	35642	22524	44232	24465
57	62225	44352	65132	34261	14224	41665	21144	26625	16521	26414
58	53456	12362	22432	53552	24654	55313	15365	12636	31431	41361
59	43265	31264	32534	31446	45212	41365	26542	64352	62413	21634
60	36146	44514	53121	14362	21651	12552	12534	45236	24545	26421

ROW

61	24643	63566	24551	62122	53431	32366	51114	21325	32315	44312
62	24415	36152	35413	16541	62155	45512	54166	21164	35433	64542
63	55126	42152	41536	36435	54433	41446	65554	56223	65456	42455
64	56215	61351	43534	43515	54542	46615	24265	41421	36465	23123
65	45661	13445	41515	16365	64321	44461	63616	34125	63253	66412
66	41655	23131	62656	52653	22562	14426	63533	63441	26455	53215
67	42322	43542	31151	51231	64635	56321	56621	13621	15354	24542
68	24342	34153	64216	45455	46652	63322	45326	16355	24132	51566
69	14516	33134	14262	36122	25435	26442	45162	35645	16554	16145
70	44215	54454	31126	25455	41643	51143	61636	36252	43125	52264
71	12611	45612	43615	45541	23663	34616	34341	11412	61445	14233
72	15514	51415	26555	36225	24621	21433	26155	11623	11414	66442
73	13426	61415	51266	41654	53361	16324	62441	45625	44133	13115
74	33346	55541	25363	26335	65555	15534	61263	52211	66555	21645
75	26261	15425	16416	46555	34262	55535	16566	46113	41641	65461
76	66561	34646	11242	43662	26564	63153	62622	12642	22626	53424
77	64341	51166	42221	35111	65145	63162	45365	11643	36635	24536
78	13442	13133	41442	51234	42626	13435	65663	34531	52312	25435
79	14544	63366	56324	11325	64621	65336	63551	31253	54116	23256
80	12115	65262	62441	24525	66246	11346	32125	66662	53314	24265
81	64322	12412	66535	44141	42362	12564	61512	24322	53613	45552
82	63115	53625	63661	12636	64456	31364	11133	33551	34466	66111
83	12551	54246	13111	24536	34141	24343	53634	46153	34261	21436
84	21134	26465	44254	66333	41433	35254	52166	66341	25653	43651
85	62414	31365	13143	51442	62621	21655	61361	26234	14542	33642
86	11143	51355	22622	33553	64463	11146	12612	33262	34361	25334
87	12624	53634	41414	56326	63353	45462	44153	22344	46251	53523
88	62551	36624	15624	45122	23542	32623	15364	25441	15432	53321
89	16641	32554	25452	53662	15452	36323	66145	11352	26112	24355
90	21365	63365	55333	36413	64454	42366	43135	12553	35135	22114

4 . ROLLS OF AN 8 - DIE

ROW

1	15742	77872	81486	51766	68253	68546	21664	77751	85441	61586
2	35447	63387	17625	61362	75416	63774	22727	32731	84321	46325
3	81788	36636	33248	42261	51735	81877	48226	74346	25753	56448
4	55574	13212	54375	62526	81586	26234	18177	84781	22727	15588
5	43285	61882	72135	53544	36535	11165	13533	46764	74588	72788
6	84585	61115	17267	71876	84826	83385	47451	43483	73684	46467
7	78775	63162	72884	77281	21338	81416	32848	86668	41641	36288
8	74321	63122	78517	83834	55461	51361	13411	47628	62528	45153
9	47255	51323	15174	45741	15656	64168	32766	74672	76888	78152
10	82448	27541	44282	11213	13623	83415	38631	27525	11676	61185

ROW

11	46376	34783	78221	83586	11181	16144	54368	28327	85571	11466
12	14721	51434	24146	85283	54681	12833	84822	12636	45256	55151
13	24261	38318	25113	84662	22634	62255	16468	73684	28321	81744
14	22773	86243	83525	86617	23544	61682	31771	44265	35585	74472
15	45237	66161	35754	85211	67684	68715	74883	47174	56674	17145
16	11268	55687	85338	85575	61232	57838	62785	28142	57151	61686
17	37152	57785	18665	71137	14622	57378	46887	27238	71234	52443
18	87241	66558	46777	18171	61781	16131	88527	33764	65758	83441
19	42514	82632	44573	75467	78827	42177	34464	13422	16433	63316
20	23668	53722	58688	48243	75378	57248	36774	27528	77811	17487
21	58356	76648	21337	23852	36616	12547	78821	14672	36851	84783
22	38753	82752	14786	17457	26634	72854	61374	54372	71545	76138
23	38616	55558	73655	38448	14348	35324	67878	15744	33276	55788
24	42384	18536	68548	22443	58487	36841	58726	75565	23564	18331
25	73815	21568	73674	14817	38711	76462	17458	27775	33342	77657
26	83242	73524	32362	73134	64114	78861	67241	75221	58212	13361
27	57852	18371	54311	36245	31442	16382	37386	56717	35325	34451
28	68832	54487	64564	54324	67332	75618	13414	33351	88665	26283
29	45188	56467	23451	51873	78476	48426	27761	56872	18476	38171
30	34257	31237	25225	45753	88523	65172	36323	71362	31458	48471
31	68738	14447	84756	64288	66363	36383	47553	68557	17251	87418
32	78622	38888	23783	24641	61828	41662	41865	24127	12122	44537
33	17381	84851	66143	17574	41566	88427	68887	77682	26435	54782
34	73816	58316	27826	33454	33226	38171	57213	77325	71866	11334
35	84526	14644	27255	33134	48875	42321	81174	31381	32642	31581
36	24314	26384	41631	55358	48116	62688	31334	41783	13782	35651
37	27723	44822	46125	44777	81788	25158	13756	63877	38447	17254
38	28467	16625	42665	88315	82565	62338	33158	53834	87826	73287
39	86215	47225	54652	76528	33383	86513	44654	25135	12533	37861
40	87678	83337	54467	76588	78458	28748	52371	48348	38783	81384
41	41244	62356	71834	77138	84812	74288	26887	25756	55886	26212
42	51336	77332	15335	65854	51784	65721	82424	81557	73315	68812
43	57443	74426	61568	77136	74871	65532	76527	67334	44688	43472
44	23171	31776	47487	67263	74514	52348	28868	13646	58658	85521
45	66126	57868	78681	27241	86116	12562	68381	22835	66373	62835
46	56758	66436	37358	85722	45147	53853	27183	76211	74734	28623
47	31432	83882	36221	52473	62561	64716	56654	81874	33762	41838
48	64261	27471	86463	53862	82735	56248	18755	17482	85436	87217
49	34145	74584	26214	45257	71415	16665	53845	85682	38568	76755
50	11488	28234	12814	85581	12761	24482	85842	86634	47184	53156
51	45835	72817	26544	22428	13587	51716	38624	87518	25387	27381
52	31613	23384	67161	51425	62364	32666	56668	51716	81328	51778
53	18562	76843	81582	11524	35656	27755	34122	13265	58348	36322
54	74417	33151	65272	63484	11577	32567	88322	66355	44844	12223
55	82373	34152	44657	83548	23428	24135	35363	68138	48235	38167

ROW

56	63153	52246	84176	71738	42117	21452	64434	57812	44116	63773
57	27412	52585	71865	14812	44558	76428	74168	52362	64281	64753
58	88618	38813	48337	14581	81553	55763	74287	88584	68825	87776
59	28375	11458	18723	21336	62811	61385	17256	53614	65551	16457
60	53861	15854	11172	17585	37467	78814	64644	54634	25464	22888
61	71444	78454	54736	14655	51523	51335	13777	38246	58268	34517
62	47716	16771	12217	65648	63316	37346	15361	61788	44732	42773
63	31371	46124	18864	71165	51354	41824	11654	62131	85527	54553
64	51522	71141	72153	83615	31687	15772	56818	33642	53445	18114
65	22343	31823	17662	63646	53753	14777	88143	22511	78271	31138
66	55617	72457	66282	15452	63851	25144	17232	28473	32271	24771
67	52445	33574	84145	73357	54381	14476	67866	12512	12384	83813
68	48177	88312	41585	71623	28828	65448	64568	23464	65523	16162
69	51757	13237	52782	25546	64564	35136	74478	82657	85342	62637
70	33668	51466	43478	57873	41128	57543	27432	73138	51341	41251
71	47444	88537	33485	77848	22536	86418	16238	75587	78151	36256
72	41831	55566	34448	56173	68232	87837	17282	76276	11637	45586
73	38732	27428	26428	14615	78738	41456	55273	58286	76618	54864
74	83365	22317	55563	12243	64244	88713	67688	74386	78537	64387
75	38167	13253	77152	47655	67183	31454	11653	14523	82674	52342
76	31672	74822	78656	47685	35653	85146	73636	55166	45418	41873
77	37153	21657	77332	38376	51245	58176	26153	63514	32168	16518
78	73272	64374	64243	28864	41712	61262	87388	31533	65371	88135
79	57326	11276	71423	86848	74246	66371	63526	36418	51786	34274
80	71561	35384	81487	65373	55817	52122	82338	21271	71527	64155
81	46124	82288	72338	28623	74476	82573	64811	81524	87735	25185
82	23534	87438	36186	71738	22642	55161	77371	31365	86683	11314
83	63462	57266	27227	42861	73568	17712	77575	21641	83222	34851
84	18721	86636	51556	76415	66318	32265	25837	66474	76558	23236
85	76826	38875	56641	11882	17531	62857	44335	24836	48545	43755
86	67186	47585	53511	87235	21845	18751	18487	23547	74123	24851
87	67872	45187	28371	11878	17262	42383	33614	32658	78346	24636
88	18615	47552	47718	76437	63715	85427	27323	86445	63643	37717
89	57476	33253	31218	31815	66353	88476	42548	22417	45662	81361
90	26123	35237	76782	73586	56256	55544	87123	21361	41871	12462

5. ROLLS OF A 10 - DIE

ROW

1	06197	10224	25612	30455	80263	37921	09326	77331	46783	89967
2	11480	30482	02719	92255	10587	60371	18369	16222	70280	74334
3	26328	84438	39460	11362	72944	49395	30947	12557	11921	80765
4	89835	53382	91553	98780	29537	05272	92200	27721	07783	72170
5	67581	56828	55077	82830	02588	50840	11896	93356	31840	04336

ROW

6	16168	68249	95835	89494	06019	42043	47829	66526	50243	58391
7	73538	69929	34285	36000	90443	02736	37818	50917	12978	16966
8	98686	20691	20698	01913	22709	74521	40847	16782	86566	00493
9	22060	44969	47026	30308	43806	43722	43781	01582	51789	95579
10	37798	51305	68627	55249	74324	12457	13989	10794	49029	64360
11	73137	30914	90151	01690	61017	46700	42461	18589	50859	73090
12	19582	06548	69732	81017	49861	33997	95103	11297	61686	09650
13	29257	51567	94245	66505	78849	78698	47002	75185	13481	35535
14	82279	25887	85037	56220	99136	05187	28747	17840	89096	75760
15	05058	08626	56070	39379	98674	67380	25822	84482	17651	39617
16	36787	92378	92854	56789	03346	54067	45536	17213	90534	60281
17	32595	56455	36985	58183	65138	04062	78769	84034	58940	99536
18	47215	68552	16124	74144	05685	35326	15748	42873	82114	43108
19	17032	96690	74402	15613	68961	24698	54272	31940	82587	83389
20	62737	69031	40955	91532	27724	36235	33951	12319	02981	73792
21	48056	32617	89238	40711	33956	80220	41217	25921	15857	33519
22	28979	18811	37713	29401	02404	59174	54010	04211	39460	73320
23	89733	86763	63026	66825	60061	46566	07647	32170	72180	86008
24	12241	37833	96201	37029	69299	70986	31051	87583	42089	36467
25	73400	92361	73198	53060	12257	99977	17413	00348	13154	45408
26	12208	16599	13938	66179	99522	17876	86209	84333	17854	47820
27	26248	50374	80639	39028	24210	39406	48420	33714	74754	54194
28	70343	71219	61675	82517	60205	15235	79277	68365	22252	50554
29	18331	80841	22185	24693	09762	55196	44322	75324	53808	66704
30	01131	42140	29661	48573	84204	66532	71316	33074	76399	20242
31	62883	57026	26100	05516	62836	19049	74115	10895	81913	72672
32	88678	83052	18384	65912	41150	94457	47783	40794	63543	53577
33	89723	72430	22721	83428	98222	25340	10865	48873	90520	93247
34	01258	43478	06369	22582	20184	96347	22060	81335	78795	62499
35	29240	16652	90278	02057	71715	44202	73139	63340	46860	20658
36	94746	47122	43436	51522	04560	03675	12852	00323	82794	47393
37	13351	02263	87447	60809	31430	56778	76695	64658	79783	02311
38	45054	03366	57142	28537	99006	75668	93408	86911	53599	16696
39	57054	33621	75795	60878	66041	37835	54427	71854	84432	09754
40	01380	13152	73136	23414	80907	20377	33677	71816	17628	58630
41	59114	14644	34936	31445	70358	88219	69307	25001	15792	39304
42	21907	48437	73516	07750	81007	78317	79213	01135	05689	76044
43	54762	11295	77408	37008	52598	98634	40407	02739	59822	95214
44	76201	27508	39549	29471	35499	86472	48608	24847	40718	11943
45	76735	80690	60274	25590	19235	25445	37775	15118	66458	45816
46	00734	21225	93348	62507	92133	45350	72652	54743	03537	52416
47	11995	80427	29761	22660	13643	69713	29985	01347	40898	32319
48	26095	38532	09399	72241	21614	65393	38249	56491	73695	76398
49	08957	08194	39477	14779	54594	12902	54075	66473	43311	76556
50	17426	22174	67222	77888	26447	97022	69920	04822	30506	55136

ROW

51	48273	42912	37802	71129	32808	55640	78486	22481	91355	08265
52	85760	78867	47605	26545	10575	18106	20558	91650	17043	04157
53	11448	41711	74543	24555	80609	96425	99028	46046	92444	36696
54	94955	35224	42963	53914	77570	31387	06767	38135	71087	74522
55	68250	51704	77308	01150	84140	10431	74954	88206	19513	51639
56	48159	97961	07339	86045	99262	84583	63000	25718	10603	79205
57	06177	39797	78019	45682	64635	87846	39874	02777	14472	54132
58	47735	58342	91276	12418	17617	59519	34242	98405	38709	46086
59	44928	98804	49899	82970	09790	66576	42222	57370	96975	09039
60	52287	76547	49677	96933	53522	20844	78709	31303	52936	43423
61	30068	97069	49996	25811	28645	28982	21449	78353	10648	18064
62	06707	58371	98299	69011	39338	22046	24909	52163	21927	43964
63	65481	59761	64490	82825	33233	36858	68628	57010	43766	98769
64	37157	48581	14382	48504	13978	82685	57243	27452	40698	21393
65	62618	54430	29365	09804	16357	28381	02654	96838	34454	06705
66	48443	88282	60847	70682	62912	11234	59971	99501	58322	10212
67	10180	41294	05905	04188	77033	43293	65815	06450	97400	99396
68	16406	77533	55814	70119	52217	87603	03562	42990	87597	51376
69	36836	62626	81313	52056	93046	72039	72060	08011	27647	51999
70	28395	88360	97286	39221	68440	13626	83420	07523	90348	97465
71	21558	68449	83369	33135	71103	13971	78628	78622	36712	35210
72	99091	89563	08141	05995	15533	16679	79949	37627	11310	04922
73	12330	12683	29879	79751	09218	53161	99494	52212	78907	08705
74	43203	58656	64387	59120	24006	19608	82611	19491	89654	45370
75	79506	73865	44158	88734	21950	21095	92255	81712	67756	72059
76	02836	92484	94533	50444	02001	98545	03299	67692	36674	09845
77	80547	24368	28928	67894	22954	31270	35764	62547	50466	06187
78	98401	56792	15244	31155	95561	25955	18039	64558	59296	68707
79	68450	20285	59827	40940	37465	27182	86189	43839	18996	42019
80	96886	57079	96396	50401	26763	24778	04550	00241	21997	53652
81	78256	77302	88683	37369	59263	76097	72414	57385	24973	83708
82	48339	99711	60203	25472	23024	57175	87907	96799	01374	57252
83	53912	92319	33193	54871	56287	17297	40082	43688	34563	50426
84	69670	21524	81166	88459	03883	63987	93946	82204	14718	07715
85	11320	68090	55952	38984	81738	30867	58789	60439	30431	69277
86	06141	27163	11637	39327	69765	34305	77507	04284	07684	91691
87	89197	87454	57020	10870	99167	30737	94631	45884	55254	98344
88	83965	81858	64805	06316	64133	89333	59856	58429	54718	20705
89	63528	07204	04384	84870	53003	30541	03214	68177	72120	14762
90	20568	33661	67019	39297	69467	05546	13587	55702	74599	21137

```
6 . ROLLS OF A 12 - DIE
Note:  0 = ten, E = eleven, T = twelve
```

ROW

1	26036	60954	79676	23077	02812	39804	487E4	894T4	176T0	02086
2	6803T	5E618	80T41	45229	T1E61	11248	6881T	5T345	63641	2ET44
3	35788	1182E	688T3	05033	99661	E4T09	19T93	T4911	49531	48TE4
4	61562	17197	8807E	18755	13689	2E35E	8194T	05TT8	54T85	E0570
5	2EE1E	76T96	430T9	30198	6T012	0068E	03E83	E5517	73302	91642
6	15004	71829	T0T69	T9660	E3452	9T222	66535	4TE0T	1816T	965E7
7	9811T	53830	460EE	7535T	725ET	T0E17	579E5	34442	T5753	842E1
8	97496	24796	46743	15646	5334T	23984	1256T	1T07T	04120	T00E9
9	2E947	188E8	2477T	08231	24T71	32332	5801T	66230	T581E	20947
10	344ET	78726	85TEE	1T42T	89T42	E8142	6T077	8400E	018T6	95953
11	650T2	57376	7E236	02E53	T632T	13969	T685E	760T9	T1532	371TE
12	03116	28605	T61T2	887T7	294E7	E00T0	7T173	046T5	1E705	81T87
13	0E3E6	5T516	46043	6E342	4E402	094ET	2ET10	731EE	80730	2TE8E
14	8T166	420E5	E7530	75E63	94TE1	8920T	10476	81E54	07972	006T5
15	95001	819T4	60T39	004E2	28E03	T7ET8	08744	EE1ET	3994T	30E75
16	3986E	66770	92284	2603E	3162E	96757	5973E	481T4	7E103	69153
17	77150	468T4	ET30E	6981T	057E0	368E9	446T5	9438T	78069	80742
18	ET856	75975	15698	37174	69206	T5379	T8567	28168	E6588	356TT
19	81646	64613	367E2	E1906	96166	42E8E	E7591	89T42	79295	68T97
20	10EE5	13616	41561	051E5	E565T	38232	10T45	10604	82605	56029
21	08762	13544	11975	6E381	06T30	57715	56630	75303	66860	5ET04
22	66057	16543	E543E	98781	07926	16E57	89812	TE916	77372	26E19
23	5T938	113E7	00784	2T213	97587	44350	01EE7	3T027	53151	1975T
24	74044	43944	26160	T9TE9	63948	5T3E7	10301	269T3	74344	18T2T
25	E48EE	61386	57TT6	47486	3EE07	3E516	685T2	3T48E	23E17	61370
26	T5575	98241	44768	TT030	7965T	2052E	313E3	T93TT	36613	72E68
27	053T9	2081T	73441	28630	61159	01873	42013	52464	33335	5TTE3
28	52008	11553	9E030	E6096	T0T54	941E9	0E329	7T7TT	E073E	710T3
29	E8489	82107	32384	67458	83297	30746	64462	5261E	E7734	66T85
30	93400	05740	1E368	94975	62548	19940	31659	77454	79696	T0940
31	10206	769E7	75701	95746	560E3	1996T	31EE9	034E2	1899E	0E267
32	14906	232T5	40905	69995	58318	E1932	E7759	2948T	1T92T	9T42T
33	44212	E3261	6T552	T5448	T7777	37917	E04E8	22717	49595	33899
34	57486	08391	14232	118E9	48192	20049	01TE1	28016	75E28	49E61
35	25558	07E9E	14T28	51446	507E2	0E871	1E46E	77T09	27928	8745E
36	0166T	1T441	12T10	35546	0T748	50049	E2670	56266	78537	ET559
37	92424	50814	T2389	09667	556E5	E44T5	75051	82T34	84891	E69TE
38	T6243	3T2E4	68449	T079E	117E6	00362	83027	T34T6	25694	T8741
39	4059E	76318	739E1	67297	3E00T	347T0	7E95E	5E6E0	TT393	577TE
40	68564	44870	E2779	0030T	47280	17878	T603T	45611	EE852	20856
41	E6117	82106	3157E	7E08T	TET18	13331	1T510	E1T34	51E49	031TE
42	32098	1T149	EE0E0	0598T	767T7	70TE7	48682	95E07	59492	37421
43	410T8	58948	407T1	00T6T	41179	683T9	3066E	30903	49679	93499
44	E467E	20748	E9838	0T279	6T756	8T430	60344	316ET	E1E43	981T4
45	1E4E5	16E10	9T7T9	T9978	E24E0	2169E	TT9E2	TT007	00668	69783

ROW

46	35485	905ET	6231T	22E02	4516E	36023	T6930	4T835	02591	84080
47	0E48E	17727	5090T	84028	76E9E	7881T	61843	19732	11159	90755
48	41E7E	11340	3622T	E8E85	12688	41733	22265	55784	86587	E38F3
49	T5160	8431T	28483	7E607	75159	359T9	5243E	628T9	T3701	126ET
50	0E669	28632	4518E	1527E	1543T	82885	29465	1T780	9338E	T2E35
51	46752	9257E	433T1	04328	9E55E	47T8E	55T31	27698	T8379	28919
52	91802	29E1T	86028	38024	E4064	79199	3951T	EE662	4T028	50727
53	24036	7437T	19ETE	17570	51E38	4E551	70315	6E76T	41E7T	7E278
54	31E48	88597	687T7	385T1	27734	54035	ETT99	TE578	T3237	06319
55	E9T50	55277	61546	26980	43202	0408E	353T4	75TE4	2764T	83242
56	3E9T1	07EE4	TE215	25T72	31T83	658T5	0E92T	91251	6T5E5	54766
57	989E6	4T163	93341	776T5	E5320	00080	79E8T	E0398	774E2	12710
58	6E9T8	8687T	02680	225T3	26483	29419	6T61T	0TE28	21002	15744
59	07389	10613	83629	27021	E6247	E83E4	E3154	48901	74719	120E6
60	08552	8397E	8253E	79264	96077	7932T	E29E5	36950	09732	ET812
61	8E500	7880T	2273E	43ET9	0T695	72E26	E9729	8TE85	66927	57T46
62	95990	E7413	T118T	50611	20580	6622T	63E93	20144	04396	99T95
63	05631	T13E2	E4032	38854	7T274	07550	6TT35	2T033	T1ET9	93TT7
64	44157	93539	1ET0T	79261	7EETT	T9TT5	533E6	3E99T	23994	22275
65	73268	7E503	65116	12675	T51E5	2560T	1E108	96117	27766	T023E
66	94311	T4419	46355	24302	14477	5T1E9	26654	720E0	E7593	40491
67	3T35E	T70E9	219E3	8503E	52179	2819T	8ET16	55876	T66E3	649E2
68	1T869	01501	99007	E1115	667TE	70571	71647	80525	E34E5	69318
69	T6E27	E0486	3909E	52187	138ET	5473E	86815	E6358	18ETE	44292
70	1ET26	96311	T583T	95957	25T24	E1551	41483	220T6	218E7	5436E
71	T2263	5ET75	88E05	9ET54	41246	E8612	48T1E	317T1	68T5T	95910
72	23966	62989	8T6E2	30970	12054	7T4T7	7E56E	898TT	18EE8	08190
73	E3592	7E453	6E9EE	7T243	0977T	445EE	07374	04383	959T0	18694
74	E9124	64271	07T15	5ET2E	622E7	E2T13	42985	52ET9	62411	11311
75	14T87	69835	24661	E0E15	53196	356E6	274EE	8T201	T0E29	86EE8
76	19E60	11294	94288	88638	3TT1T	797E3	T11T4	30039	38632	67897
77	69957	3084T	81217	39411	4E265	EE15E	13TT3	0TE36	8585T	21T82
78	250T5	45126	03005	39527	T5EE4	T0366	25206	32296	8269E	10297
79	86389	94932	83501	810E7	84287	E4609	E4745	91330	11149	3T61E
80	2839T	62343	T6TE2	2054E	88993	2T064	6TTE5	67267	T362T	E871E
81	4744T	201E8	T43E9	97591	797E5	39354	53017	26780	7T182	82067
82	7E171	85608	ETE97	8T6E0	57166	89586	3T718	50395	83T2E	18221
83	76599	17459	E5954	265E2	8189E	E5108	07795	7E056	09TE0	55832
84	07966	61272	91T4T	TE710	78E44	25T6E	06475	57806	3TE61	9T552
85	08056	T8471	9E231	3ET88	0T3T6	62998	2T097	E0TT9	T7ETT	04397
86	4TE97	654T4	6570T	041E2	4906T	58E01	5T131	5322T	8T4EE	63150
87	20953	E8260	E2134	8488E	ET742	40171	E487E	95T5T	250T8	2TT60
88	14223	21E15	58944	42E0T	94895	27133	T2523	T1548	47393	6T49E
89	48EEE	46472	9541T	597E2	89T38	T6406	63005	79E57	97E1E	88395
90	11E09	6TT48	T70T9	29559	90128	51762	E99E4	10250	E8ET5	T1E52

7. SPINS OF A 3 - SPINNER

ROW

1	31221	33332	31221	13123	11312	12122	32131	22231	23231	13121
2	22132	33111	11121	33221	23123	13222	13112	12221	22311	11312
3	33333	12213	21332	22222	33222	12212	33323	22311	22331	13212
4	22231	32312	21323	32131	33323	33133	32233	33311	21322	12311
5	32311	31333	12123	32123	22211	22233	12223	13313	31321	11223
6	23311	13132	31311	31321	22313	11133	13211	31312	22112	21233
7	12311	32112	31113	31231	22223	23213	12123	11323	33232	11331
8	11111	32331	33232	33123	22311	13131	21113	22231	13112	11213
9	13112	12332	12123	12122	23331	22121	31123	33122	12222	33121
10	32333	21312	22311	13332	22211	23111	21321	33231	13121	12222
11	12223	12121	11132	32332	31131	13121	23133	22232	13113	12223
12	23213	21222	23132	33312	13211	23332	12232	12113	32131	33222
13	21232	13313	12131	21323	12323	12133	33311	33332	13123	23232
14	21121	13321	23312	22212	21313	31333	32121	32112	33111	32222
15	21313	11331	31213	32232	22312	11322	12121	11213	32322	23321
16	32212	33233	11132	13123	12331	22322	22231	23132	11113	21233
17	11332	23233	32233	32323	33231	12311	12122	31331	33323	22312
18	21321	11113	33221	12132	12212	12311	22311	21133	31222	11321
19	33131	31332	11231	13132	33211	33322	23222	22232	11322	13131
20	23233	31231	32333	22132	33221	11122	22133	13131	11321	21313
21	31133	31333	31312	23212	31213	22211	11233	32221	33221	11123
22	22313	33211	31113	23322	23211	33121	11231	11332	12211	33221
23	33331	32323	33321	21321	31221	11312	13123	11211	21111	33322
24	31333	33323	32212	31222	32323	11333	12333	21212	12133	22321
25	31131	22221	13221	12113	23221	11311	13213	32121	33221	33232
26	21332	31333	22323	12222	21123	31233	13212	22133	11333	11222
27	12233	23132	23322	33322	13233	21322	12221	33331	23131	32123
28	33111	12133	32222	22333	21222	11221	31213	31232	11223	33111
29	13313	11112	32232	32311	21111	31223	33233	12313	11121	32333
30	31131	31222	21232	23223	21221	23323	12112	32223	23132	32123
31	33122	33122	13131	33313	11133	13122	32121	13322	21113	33321
32	22133	33222	32132	31312	22212	31132	22333	11113	31131	12333
33	22333	33332	22233	12332	11332	31131	11221	12221	13131	23213
34	32223	23113	21223	13223	21313	11113	33311	12133	31111	11331
35	31213	32323	31332	22223	32111	21313	22112	22222	22112	22111
36	12323	21112	11313	31111	11112	13131	21331	23311	21231	23213
37	22122	21122	33321	11111	31111	21313	11231	23223	13121	31222
38	32122	23113	22333	31322	13132	32321	21313	23322	11233	31133
39	33131	22332	32212	31222	32322	33232	11131	32121	12223	21113
40	12212	21112	33222	33113	31133	11232	23122	33322	32212	13312

ROW

41	32322	32222	12222	12133	12311	21312	32233	12111	33133	12311
42	22212	32121	12322	11232	31323	21321	11332	33231	33111	13212
43	22121	33311	12333	12213	11233	12312	33121	33311	32123	33213
44	11132	32313	22233	13223	31312	23211	32222	22321	11122	31321
45	23331	23312	32131	32313	31223	33321	23322	21133	23112	11121
46	12121	23321	11211	23132	23211	12231	21232	11322	12321	31311
47	31211	11313	31123	12121	23321	13213	11311	22312	23333	23133
48	23311	21222	23211	23113	12131	22222	11111	13223	21312	23132
49	21222	21123	32131	23132	12113	21221	32321	33313	12322	21133
50	12221	21122	23231	32211	33222	13133	13322	22212	33331	23231
51	32323	13113	13323	12311	21231	31223	23221	33233	23132	12122
52	32122	12311	31333	12221	33131	22322	33111	13232	33211	22331
53	31311	23311	33232	31323	33121	12312	22113	21333	33312	12231
54	13132	23313	23133	12312	33213	11312	13121	32322	33311	13231
55	13333	11221	32311	23222	13311	22312	22231	31132	21131	31332
56	13322	21123	13111	22131	33221	13212	23323	11323	23121	31133
57	31333	33322	23221	33332	22132	33111	13133	32231	11131	33112
58	21321	12132	21321	21223	22313	33321	23232	33323	13211	32321
59	21132	23113	31113	21332	32213	31332	23123	11322	22132	23223
60	33223	23233	21112	11111	13213	33321	12231	32211	33333	23133
61	23232	23132	33313	33212	22133	13332	13111	31133	11223	13231
62	22313	23322	33231	33331	32112	13333	32332	13323	12232	33133
63	13121	21312	31322	33112	12331	22212	33323	22222	23222	13222
64	21322	12333	22231	21233	31223	12323	32231	23321	32222	32122
65	12233	21131	22112	13323	31213	13323	13233	31332	32133	11323
66	22233	22211	23311	33113	11133	32112	12311	13222	33322	11323
67	23113	31123	31313	22113	21113	23213	23123	33122	21331	12231
68	12121	32121	21123	13212	11313	13122	11232	32213	13233	31123
69	12223	31213	21311	22133	31313	12231	13331	21333	11212	23121
70	11221	11132	12121	32213	11312	12131	11331	21231	22113	11123
71	13332	32111	31211	32112	12132	13232	23312	11222	32212	13123
72	23233	21323	13213	13111	12331	32123	11312	33331	31123	32312
73	12312	23131	33222	32211	23213	22113	13322	13313	11311	13212
74	13132	12132	13222	21323	33212	12132	22123	22112	22313	12223
75	22223	13313	21311	32111	32311	31333	23331	11212	11222	13323
76	22131	13123	32211	23133	33333	21212	22221	23113	23331	23321
77	11331	23212	31121	31232	31311	31312	31222	22222	33231	13213
78	11233	32233	22322	33232	22312	21132	32131	23133	31221	33211
79	32231	12222	13132	13122	13232	11211	23131	21231	12112	13331
80	23123	21212	31333	12111	21322	13332	13331	22113	11113	11323
81	21312	31331	11231	13123	21311	31332	12113	33111	32123	12322
82	33212	21331	13113	13233	21223	33122	31123	22312	11232	33132
83	13312	32131	32222	32121	21332	22333	11121	31131	11311	23222
84	31232	22123	31221	21122	33131	11231	12332	32213	13323	32233
85	22322	13331	13112	32231	23312	31113	21313	31111	23112	33212

ROW

86	22132	23111	33332	12112	13113	33233	21113	22322	11222	33211
87	11131	33213	33132	31223	12133	22323	23331	21231	33122	13212
88	12313	22113	21223	13331	11132	13111	32233	23322	31131	11321
89	23232	22313	13323	32132	21313	23121	22223	33123	22112	12212
90	22222	11121	11112	22232	11222	12233	31122	23322	12133	31132

8 . SPINS OF A 5 - SPINNER

ROW

1	42423	45314	55454	55234	55121	34521	32415	11445	23431	53331
2	14412	51523	24324	14445	13513	54321	12344	43211	31324	43134
3	42331	52342	25232	41214	31114	42233	35342	42343	41143	31345
4	12132	24125	14514	43221	52332	21224	12223	55231	41512	41121
5	25225	11112	41331	42212	41123	33352	41142	14251	11212	53454
6	11214	52511	25441	52455	31221	53453	32521	52215	11132	31415
7	12553	34551	15252	11212	54545	55342	51532	51531	51452	25542
8	13544	22352	13312	23122	53513	11512	13431	42211	21333	42335
9	34342	41531	12444	45521	32525	24345	12524	34555	32245	14325
10	35523	12244	24351	42514	51451	51413	33222	44444	44233	55335
11	12441	34243	51522	24435	14542	51435	43423	52145	35111	13245
12	34113	32141	24545	53323	52153	23255	24425	44151	22443	23545
13	22515	34232	54152	42321	22434	53323	42543	14455	25541	13241
14	35332	21442	44311	35324	41151	35513	12214	15525	23454	14445
15	45553	53544	21331	24321	24123	25241	32411	51154	43153	52425
16	35112	42214	22313	23325	34454	11442	14412	14114	21331	22124
17	52123	52245	15424	31144	22311	24415	33553	53125	23351	41115
18	32553	12514	14514	23212	31452	53453	42125	22552	43423	22445
19	21124	54212	33252	53451	45352	43145	55121	22215	31132	52532
20	51153	34252	34352	54434	45452	14451	43414	21153	21144	24422
21	42221	43413	15254	44145	14335	41142	13143	35135	21252	11334
22	31221	33454	53423	35255	43225	32334	32354	45515	41145	42332
23	41213	34412	45153	23121	11333	41311	41355	55414	44144	35325
24	22214	11434	24154	15152	52554	55522	45454	31542	24145	25551
25	22422	21225	13443	51211	23413	41323	12254	54222	23122	25215
26	24522	22333	35131	31224	24233	14324	21115	12433	32134	52123
27	41524	55312	54434	14155	32342	25321	35332	31415	23252	55344
28	13445	25512	55222	24114	15354	22342	21541	51523	23453	12245
29	23532	24524	51233	22533	33541	12155	24155	15542	33523	21354
30	21454	35525	31233	12134	31524	14125	14121	52511	41522	42434
31	52214	43431	45324	23345	12532	51433	21455	41451	44252	51135
32	24525	22423	11335	11152	14345	31411	34412	23211	23512	23343
33	11531	55452	11544	11255	21152	31454	33324	14255	42445	21131
34	31144	15434	12425	44152	44234	43551	44241	14133	11533	44451
35	41423	14414	35111	55324	44555	24145	24125	15215	54525	25211

ROW

36	25235	31454	51114	23243	34414	31542	13134	21232	45451	15252
37	25233	42215	25232	41121	15142	12113	33121	22311	51114	41433
38	43535	22433	41324	44431	53543	45225	43221	22313	52145	32242
39	51315	24531	14424	12545	52543	41513	32254	21215	34122	53232
40	22343	24452	42153	32133	31433	12211	32511	35241	44331	25313
41	11323	13454	31325	34525	25133	35521	43111	24521	33231	43423
42	22545	33342	22213	23432	44531	34351	21354	15514	42234	42122
43	21513	22313	42141	11253	25234	42251	15455	22454	15325	45225
44	25353	25224	44353	44423	42254	42525	23234	53433	21152	33424
45	11352	45243	51145	52535	32314	23523	23545	33113	45213	43544
46	22153	45333	42235	32141	52252	15534	55531	54322	42325	14534
47	13454	41241	54451	43455	25544	24455	33121	54315	13544	41313
48	23243	24143	55112	34144	44443	45345	21352	34222	42351	55411
49	45453	23152	22541	11344	21131	51553	12333	14252	53331	52213
50	25452	31115	55513	24553	52113	13553	54435	43313	11125	45415
51	12513	52124	43545	44314	51232	54414	25431	51343	14554	33213
52	41313	31342	51425	25222	15442	22541	25521	32214	15534	43433
53	51215	34155	54354	44342	11111	15235	12455	15412	52214	43255
54	54452	34524	31554	31245	25155	45241	11335	55312	24551	21241
55	25552	21515	41431	12351	11112	32133	25121	51115	31414	11423
56	13354	42234	23435	55312	25324	43532	51313	25434	42244	24235
57	45544	42542	22153	12421	54142	11311	11314	41155	15453	41451
58	54342	13541	22143	31454	53523	41531	52252	14411	53123	51224
59	35311	23534	15411	51511	11124	24522	12521	53531	31321	33531
60	12231	43123	43431	52122	55432	41232	12431	13315	41312	23545
61	54124	55154	15553	45541	52121	35541	11334	21353	51113	45315
62	11133	32345	45255	45445	34324	32434	24435	13344	13123	44211
63	44454	23453	44211	12434	51333	35215	11335	25323	23411	13531
64	13115	22131	11341	15432	21335	33315	35253	15352	33543	53254
65	45431	43541	52111	35552	31315	34511	24332	53435	21531	42453
66	52225	44355	14421	54414	55534	13415	43453	22454	51121	35512
67	44211	41311	55122	34524	32542	54415	52355	11335	31333	22542
68	11334	13422	33525	24244	44541	53445	52454	33552	54221	52242
69	32413	53355	34233	14433	55331	35524	11552	31144	44432	32112
70	21114	53125	44212	44421	12124	13343	13321	21241	55455	53324
71	13311	43145	54415	35555	25241	35334	23213	15253	13513	32235
72	41433	24423	32153	14454	12124	41152	55443	12441	24515	15352
73	34334	15253	35431	55242	25523	11531	31232	34244	22123	35413
74	15415	42252	51455	42115	55122	43541	14114	44532	21212	32115
75	43142	14534	54133	25555	23415	25135	42341	44332	15325	42233
76	35533	14533	34455	44413	43555	32242	52541	42543	42253	11432
77	55411	44142	25423	22425	41325	54523	41253	25521	15223	54142
78	52411	31415	21214	22335	53543	43441	13353	23541	53153	35541
79	54223	53334	23251	43544	42112	43353	14145	52523	55125	13521
80	13333	55425	25122	41353	41453	14531	22135	41115	12132	35423

ROW

81	14215	23154	41121	52523	35415	34342	54221	21531	14114	13325
82	15335	22324	54233	43123	22112	24511	35551	32241	43112	55335
83	25431	42522	24225	11411	24254	54245	54544	35131	14145	43422
84	31333	52332	41434	42323	52122	42121	24342	12531	54242	23324
85	31314	21211	43133	24334	53121	43511	54141	15214	32554	43231
86	42531	32351	51122	25212	14535	51111	45545	25415	15125	14542
87	21532	34554	12222	44512	53541	32551	44232	11253	42434	14144
88	44313	35323	23135	24335	54354	43431	41254	33231	42131	25554
89	13453	24222	33535	35541	54125	51332	43114	54432	14145	43412
90	31455	14253	11121	22525	45415	52544	43423	15423	52541	55244

9. SPINS OF A 9 - SPINNER

ROW

1	68397	23367	51962	17269	47469	58359	76173	97667	93635	99346
2	41895	49353	88198	96172	75633	62329	98764	13936	93362	77689
3	31287	29379	47515	96257	41169	39229	73777	13899	84712	26924
4	83412	82272	44534	12434	78883	67679	65979	54432	77285	72631
5	75227	39923	51465	86129	61421	73346	34317	73272	62459	92878
6	87671	49243	21377	15391	22756	29769	64838	75692	81147	87214
7	72626	55661	41937	26461	57656	18328	65928	35834	72117	69556
8	88196	54326	46258	19148	78926	85885	17174	99581	47774	12513
9	39531	36418	11154	11391	88345	19495	26196	59622	84472	15928
10	98516	93194	51643	17919	14328	37166	16882	94165	98413	56127
11	79891	14845	79834	74216	68598	44957	68919	63366	91498	48514
12	14332	13674	63629	23958	58987	73715	96957	34377	22968	78381
13	98535	46895	53149	25784	15754	88274	79282	79742	39129	16271
14	78164	68751	18884	54954	76688	88958	22429	57248	83363	78513
15	29653	23833	43264	22296	15564	61551	74362	27161	44639	54666
16	31315	21316	13776	49175	98951	88352	38513	64693	92275	67554
17	83443	39962	94973	53759	87332	18281	36949	69415	61411	32998
18	21395	73659	73832	23395	17394	84385	56745	28729	61421	98579
19	27335	28314	78481	68946	66898	11713	17611	61523	53531	71819
20	59774	37734	52159	17742	38788	62378	77369	88161	92312	58699
21	38747	88379	67429	56248	24328	86952	13882	75682	89969	56495
22	58299	76566	57567	23587	56528	79719	61337	29179	28366	63173
23	93742	85481	75774	61721	51342	81856	98558	37469	56895	45856
24	47832	79192	73813	59626	59663	48273	68463	22684	93852	91544
25	77873	24299	49333	62859	82137	84964	16855	97717	58479	91216
26	44263	41188	92822	11526	49592	97728	32661	18213	39784	38628
27	36543	54253	15223	44271	57462	88765	83997	79948	55531	23434
28	22953	23183	41851	46718	63832	64593	62964	81621	48566	62586
29	44739	56834	77778	67372	98499	34198	64413	16537	84152	27547
30	43236	68499	42264	42941	87818	78317	94622	35179	29389	92277

ROW

31	52821	46168	96466	67714	84365	83215	92123	47348	66528	96987
32	43343	78564	46687	82219	34319	42791	72315	23454	82242	57586
33	89118	94698	34978	53867	68426	93739	66515	98477	59924	87525
34	32786	16654	39355	18834	87926	36779	93718	53192	59388	92773
35	53873	48844	87413	53519	12434	11485	88767	98754	45434	82796
36	35467	54645	91461	93857	93877	22297	71624	59289	29368	37745
37	76915	45492	57653	14155	11696	22593	43442	25217	78742	94318
38	76529	14892	99434	45236	22293	16617	81166	93995	28397	23828
39	87141	69737	28652	21669	19334	56489	37111	74914	61195	18857
40	76961	77749	31671	17192	16114	94974	32323	57856	17362	24539
41	88856	75167	38162	86794	19994	78732	44749	58824	59742	49623
42	37549	11113	29591	75648	49733	76513	32563	22726	22656	45225
43	49738	35542	74293	47324	83337	82376	53678	73483	45219	37766
44	38151	99731	83458	42761	22724	92835	13576	23453	56776	62612
45	98127	64338	85382	38565	47567	11758	38715	83162	12345	42987
46	14841	86415	58856	38686	54658	59374	47165	41615	36747	58911
47	64922	34581	97219	33481	42631	73436	58828	92972	42754	37766
48	74515	25588	82317	85424	37323	33551	48835	78983	76859	98228
49	56416	42537	96754	12139	48475	96938	26295	75974	87253	98131
50	43866	67311	19592	15345	68819	53479	74155	88714	84487	83611
51	89744	44913	97125	55589	62643	21652	67557	16859	91898	58364
52	94888	65456	44253	62553	22686	47467	26649	79171	72313	93455
53	12124	47629	93821	39183	95287	12733	24924	51414	55216	89188
54	47472	45264	56314	44469	72747	79859	25652	56575	85247	67231
55	36968	38525	99499	89551	75866	78865	74584	31536	82252	65517
56	82448	42838	51585	36517	18783	66676	52243	57248	12282	57642
57	19352	57247	56683	63329	99732	27732	25144	26965	74958	54654
58	25594	67921	18254	86552	28776	55832	35132	76929	91585	34874
59	76994	93352	53725	11165	68771	62948	55143	38853	49439	48763
60	23586	53629	82233	73678	43594	46612	69722	98748	45113	91126
61	51253	26921	95398	31389	36738	69866	62299	63768	46869	53697
62	94175	65848	25434	75196	55629	59892	72419	44211	93759	63668
63	59697	97445	27622	21973	93217	14648	95168	71379	85631	93732
64	74435	66217	39237	72467	25975	34151	96573	89474	31841	94364
65	54174	59372	59849	72911	61667	81256	98626	35192	79626	94114
66	88979	63614	79639	18396	34517	53253	76322	98395	74131	66971
67	94784	29535	53363	83163	49736	63942	21483	93612	94912	63517
68	77136	81337	41681	13524	19175	77492	53322	76299	67441	42538
69	75415	41745	77718	63654	67596	44941	47821	94231	42455	29786
70	14499	39983	44255	57935	41632	12221	71999	79221	45996	79493
71	81296	49688	43594	24966	22752	28176	44115	72455	99231	75651
72	35121	11566	39913	77745	21231	36819	73813	19493	46286	46164
73	29878	55118	87133	49514	97714	81419	23877	28931	92692	17587
74	89369	75573	46698	18648	44424	58886	21474	78457	92921	68342
75	97927	48995	52746	87211	11777	27848	42288	32939	88417	68953

ROW

76	81479	13681	34472	42772	15912	66587	27291	94112	62551	85843
77	56429	13223	54536	37512	35133	11748	11181	84641	27641	52178
78	96926	27287	57313	66893	63716	34359	19114	74845	36536	39834
79	14986	35452	24221	26652	79581	51999	19886	53858	59935	76242
80	93184	94552	54813	53117	58523	67749	37543	16959	79787	42848
81	54593	72264	81548	57248	45435	38959	47651	94481	41157	58258
82	42486	97815	42796	52735	27732	15377	25773	32337	33164	91444
83	65831	79377	36159	12355	11134	54599	97369	29759	55416	36546
84	79882	45577	13563	88121	87144	58646	67854	39659	28915	49149
85	26686	92845	35583	25786	13582	85524	34671	85557	76973	66945
86	72969	15357	15131	87427	13833	86454	76889	88386	54496	22783
87	19938	26295	79353	73492	93668	25237	39742	55545	35549	44858
88	16751	35352	44667	37969	77231	41117	85815	75851	45663	85553
89	92772	57732	93169	99344	36823	59119	22313	94515	59794	21414
90	85689	66341	96554	97842	46556	96735	13733	52228	74972	48364

10. BIRTHDAY PROBLEM DIGITS

ROW

1	51	313	211	104	111	212	292	34	117	138
2	159	241	301	75	165	167	110	3	183	88
3	82	143	211	335	81	126	178	30	141	247
4	151	322	23	69	189	37	188	244	220	100
5	149	277	316	147	80	11	272	330	248	12
6	260	349	364	293	27	132	277	157	120	181
7	185	58	112	310	134	37	211	206	50	291
8	120	25	208	112	279	44	111	197	333	137
9	196	273	164	220	119	15	196	92	308	51
10	97	324	339	28	43	208	233	327	245	172
11	9	181	242	78	178	204	60	336	334	272
12	293	84	323	151	248	262	331	267	210	42
13	72	242	261	282	30	316	30	219	98	264
14	70	13	10	73	118	34	325	104	39	23
15	125	350	338	299	39	95	272	339	44	35
16	185	312	176	25	204	136	274	1	4	124
17	190	161	270	359	37	100	250	185	316	179
18	47	337	175	19	66	224	45	286	84	299
19	309	191	289	140	335	358	9	193	65	19
20	17	98	99	296	234	250	121	239	183	241
21	118	99	16	138	146	288	44	28	77	136
22	229	283	77	283	184	174	39	42	322	39
23	220	299	352	346	154	22	98	81	328	38
24	233	143	235	193	9	265	125	113	288	94
25	188	110	295	298	91	288	309	319	3	246
26	328	327	77	233	1	263	360	298	55	172
27	338	20	318	235	178	200	359	21	46	254
28	27	47	73	28	105	151	175	33	261	222
29	28	220	230	355	187	266	98	62	309	136
30	327	61	108	33	263	55	287	158	85	46
31	363	238	227	237	112	60	102	106	150	295
32	116	206	220	255	180	209	51	255	242	113
33	62	125	322	343	126	9	123	135	331	143
34	172	255	317	111	111	213	97	17	202	77
35	354	117	306	105	73	218	45	155	23	47
36	135	181	195	240	285	125	191	208	164	240
37	353	330	13	143	8	33	80	5	28	240
38	35	269	310	177	47	6	172	215	18	214
39	87	107	324	29	247	338	309	315	340	241
40	118	242	129	264	176	364	71	286	92	230
41	61	65	202	2	286	179	172	341	307	120
42	239	273	240	351	221	296	344	55	10	339
43	299	121	293	352	142	274	157	102	39	220
44	62	267	340	65	177	160	265	117	139	255
45	213	135	159	15	311	121	339	345	150	298
46	309	317	356	90	137	342	63	283	267	98
47	152	165	102	353	337	49	147	180	358	302
48	165	55	359	216	203	112	287	20	346	38
49	246	118	39	329	23	303	112	312	225	18
50	336	12	26	89	221	295	266	103	227	126

APPENDIX

B

Class Projects

APPENDIX B
Class projects

Preamble

Most teachers of statistics courses at this level put a lot of emphasis on practical project work. A key ingredient of such projects is the collection and interpretation of data. It is a good idea to start work on this activity early in the course. If data collection becomes an integral part of each chapter, then there is a much wider body of experience available when it comes time for the students to decide on the subject for a term project. In the first chapter, very little groundwork has been laid for an extensive project to be possible, but one activity can be a useful source of data for later projects, the collection of articles from newspapers and magazines illustrating the use of statistics. For the sports minded, making a collection of the summary reports of the various professional games is often a vital prerequisite for a major project in that area. A number of teachers make the compilation of a scrapbook of clipping the principal activity of the first chapter. From this collection, at least one clipping is taken from each student and displayed on photocopies, together with appropriate questions. In more than one case, unit tests for this chapter have been built around newspaper cuttings obtained in this manner.

This activity lays the groundwork for students to acquire the habit, when seeing a numerical argument, to analyse it rather than dismiss it. Such a habit is not acquired in the space of a single chapter, but requires frequent practice and reminders, throughout the semester.

PROJECTS
descriptions and development.

1. Testing for randomness in a set of random digits.

A uniform frequency distribution of the digits is but one test for a series of random digits. Clearly the series 123456789012345 67890123456789... if continued far enough will produce a uniform distribution, but clearly the digits are not randomly produced. But conversely, a method that does not give a uniform distribution over a long series of digits can hardly be uniform.

Students should select a method of generating random digits and use the chi-square statistic to see if the assumption of equally likely digits gives unusually high values of the χ^2 statistic. Some suggestions are:

(a) the last digits of telephone numbers in the residential white pages;
(b) the last digits of telephone numbers in the yellow pages;
(c) ask 100 people to give the first digit that comes into their head;
(d) the digits in a table of logarithms or trigonometric functions;
(e) the digits of a state or provincial lottery;
(f) the digits on the license plates in the school parking lot.

2. Testing for other uniform distributions.

Any data that might be considered to give a uniform distribution can generate an interesting project. Some newspapers publish the births at the local hospital. Is a child equally likely to be born on any of the 7 days of the week, or are there fewer births on the weekends?

3. Testing for nonuniform distributions.

If it is true that the probability of a child being born a boy is 0.5, then the probabilities of a three-child family having 0,1,2,3 boys are 0.125, 0.375, 0.375, and 0.125. This model can be tested using χ^2.

4. Obtain the number of students absent on each school day of a week. Is it equally likely that a student will be absent on each of the school days of the week?

5. Examine age distributions in different parts of the country and for different years (present time and 30 years ago) to see if there are differences in the distribution of ages.

Although these are classified by chapter, the classifications are very rough. Teachers are encouraged to "sort through" the projects and select those most suitable for the goals of the lesson or chapter at hand.

Chapter 1

OPTICAL VARIABILITY OF QUASARS.
A study of the optical variability of near and distant quasars, to see if there is any pattern to the short-term variabilities.

DO COMPOSERS HAVE FAVORITE KEYS?
Frequency distributions of the keys used in piano sonatas by Beethoven, Mozart and Haydn. Look for differences between the distributions.

GROWTH OF RETAIL SHOPPING SPACE IN YOUR TOWN.
An investigation into the amount of new retail shopping space and the revenue needed to keep all the new shops in business.

BIORHYTHMS AND DATE OF DEATH.

Search for patterns in the biorhythm readings for prominent people at the time of their death.

POPULARITY OF DANCE BANDS AT A JUNIOR HIGH SCHOOL.

A survey showed that there were differences between popularity for listening or for dancing. The results are used to plan the programs for forthcoming dances.

TIME TAKEN TO DELIVER A LETTER.

An investigation of the distributions of the time in days between posting letters in various parts of North America and their delivery in your town.

DRAWING POWER OF TEAMS IN THE NATIONAL HOCKEY LEAGUE.

On the basis of the attendance at all the games in the 1979-80 season, box-and-whisker plots were made of the attendance at each arena. Showing the popular teams on the plots gave an indication of the drawing power of each of the teams.

WORLD VETERANS GAMES.

A study of the distribution of countries of origin of participants in the 3rd World Veterans Games held in 1976.

BIRTH MONTH AND DEATH MONTH.

Repeat the investigation described in Statistics, a Guide to the Unknown (pages 52-65).

DELAYS ON BUS ROUTES.

The school bus always seemed to be late. A survey showed a consistent difference between the arrival time and the published schedule, except at the first few stops. Investigation showed that the school board had forgotten about a large new apartment complex which had opened during the summer. The school bus routes were altered.

WEEKLY ATTENDANCE AND OFFERINGS AT A CHURCH.

The teacher had the data for attendance and offerings at church. Students graphed the data each week and were able to pick out Mother's Day from the graph, but not Father's Day.

STYLE ANALYSIS.

There are many projects under this heading. They include:

doing an investigation of the distribution of sample variances of logs of sentence length;

finding a statistic that measures the variety of noun used in a passage;

Identifying a mystery author by looking at sentence length and noun variety distributions;

investigation of the Fog index and other readability formulae.

For further details see Teaching Statistics, Vol 2, #1.

THE DISTRIBUTION OF PROFESSIONAL SPORTS TEAMS ACROSS NORTH AMERICA.

An investigation into attendance, stadium capacity, and percentage of different ethnic groups in cities that have professional sports teams.

DISTRIBUTION OF TIMES TAKEN TO GET OUT OF THE SCHOOL PARKING LOT.

Before a reorganization of the student parking lot went into effect, the times taken to get onto the road from different areas of the lot were collected. After the reorganization, the distributions were compared.

Chapter 2

CHIPPING ABILITY (GOLF).

An examination of a student's ability to chip onto a green from a distance of 20 meters. 50 balls were chipped each day and their distances from the pin recorded. The student wanted to see if his accuracy improved over a two-week period.

EARLY MORNING GOLF.

The student hit 50 balls at the green from a distance of 50 meters, and measured the distance of each ball from the pin. This was repeated each morning (6:30 a.m.) and evening (4:30 p.m.) for a week. A comparison of the morning and evening distributions was made.

PRICES OF USED FIREBIRDS AND CAMAROS.

A survey of the prices of used Firebirds and Camaros as found in the used car ads in several newspapers across the country. Which car kept its value better in different cities?

TRANSPORTATION ENERGY CONSUMPTION.

Two sets of bicycles were prepared, one set with the tires properly inflated, and the other set with 10 lb. less air in the tires. Each student rode bicycles from each set around a half-mile course. The times were recorded, along with the rider's pulse rate at the end of the course. The distributions were compared.

MR. AND MRS. AVERAGE??

A description of the average married couple in your town.

Chapter 4

FIRST GOALS IN THE NATIONAL HOCKEY LEAGUE.

An investigation to estimate the probability of winning an NHL game, given that the team scored the first goal.

CLAIRVOYANCE WITH A DECK OF CARDS.

Testing for clairvoyant ability in predicting sequences of 10 cards drawn at random from a deck of cards.

PROBABILITY OF A WIN IN BASEBALL.

An estimate of the probability that a team will win a major league game given that the team scores the first run, or given that the team scores a home run.

Chapter 5

LEGAL DRIVING AGE.

An opinion survey concerning the desirability of raising the minimum legal age for driving a car.

ATTITUDES TOWARDS SMOKING CIGARETTES.

An opinion survey among smokers and nonsmokers concerning such things as health, ability to stop smoking, family smoking habits.

USE OF AN OPEN-AIR SWIMMING POOL.

A survey of the use of an open-air pool and opinions about the desirability of converting the pool for winter use.

DISTRIBUTION OF JAPANESE AND DOMESTIC CARS IN A TOWN.

An investigation of the origins of cars owned by the residents in different areas of the town.

Chapter 6

ATHLETIC ABILITY AND ASTROLOGICAL SIGN.

The distribution of astrological signs for 220 professional athletes.

Chapter 7

EMERGENCY TREATMENTS AND THE WEATHER.

Look for connections between the number of people treated each day at the emergency ward of the local hospital and various weather factors, mean atmospheric pressure that day, mean daily temperature, daily rainfall.

RENT AND VACANCY RATES OF APARTMENTS IN YOUR TOWN.

A survey of vacancy rates and the rents in those apartments that were vacant in a given month.

TIME SERIES ANALYSIS OF 5 STOCK PRICES.

A study of the variations in prices of five stocks and Federal Bank interest rates in a certain period.

TRENDS IN THE TIMES OF THE OLYMPIC 100M FREESTYLE.

Fit a curve to the data of the Olympic records for the mens' 100 m. freestyle, and the year in which the record was broken.

Chapter 8

DEPTHS OF SUCCESSFUL OIL AND GAS WELLS 1959-1974.

An investigation into the drill depth necessary to strike oil and gas in Canada between 1959 and 1974. Fit a curve to the trend.

Chapter 10

AGE DISTRIBUTION OF ROOKIES AND PLAYERS IN THE NATIONAL AND AMERICAN LEAGUES.

A comparison of the distributions in the two baseball leagues.

Chapter 12

REACTION TIMES.

An investigation of the distribution of reaction times of the writing and non-writing hands, when a graduated card is dropped between the thumb and first finger.

CHECKING ADVERTISING CLAIMS.

Students picked an advertisment and ran checks:

(a) Several types of ketchup were compared for thickness. A fixed amount was poured into a small kitchen strainer and the time taken to land on a plate 8 inches below was recorded. It was assumed that the longer it took the thicker the ketchup.

(b) Tests were made on the amount of different oils that was absorbed by french fries. A fixed amount of frozen french fries was cooked in a fixed amount of oil for a predetermined time, then left to drain for a fixed time. The remaining weight of oil in the pan showed how much oil had been absorbed by the fries.

(c) A gourmet brand of popping corn was compared with other brands to see how many unpopped kernels remained after a fixed time of heating.

PATTERNS OF STUDENT SPENDING.

A survey was commissioned by the student newspaper. The paper wanted the information to convince local merchants to place ads in the paper because the students were spending so much in the local stores.

VARIETY OF NOUN DISTRIBUTION IN FRENCH AND ENGLISH NOVEL.

Examining the distribution of statistics that measure variety of noun usage and sentence length in a French novel and comparing it with the distributions for its English translation.

MEMORIZING WORDS USING LEFT AND RIGHT EYES.

A comparison of memorizing ability by left eye reading with right-eye reading.

MAZE TEST.

A maze was constructed from strips of balsa wood. The maze was memorized by tracing the arrangement of the strips with a finger while blindfolded. The end of the maze was indicated by a piece of sandpaper. Each person was timed to see how long it took before he/she was able to negotiate the maze without making a mistake. The student (an older individual) timed two groups of people in a beer parlor, those who had just come into the pub, and those who had been there for over 2 hours. He then compared the distributions.

Chapter 13

AIR BRITISH COLUMBIA.

The student worked for AIR BC. He conducted a survey to gain information about the attitudes of frequent passengers towards the airline, service fares, and schedule and compared these attitudes with those of people who had never flown with the airline, or who flew only if they had no other alternative.

TESTING A RANDOM NUMBER GENERATOR.

Test the random number generator on a microcomputer. . . the runs test, the poker test, and distribution of digits.

WEATHER PATTERNS IN YOUR TOWN.

An investigation of patterns in the weather data for the past 30 years.

PERSONALITY CHARACTERISTICS OF SCIENCE FICTION READERS.

Scores on a standard personality test were compared for students in the Science Fiction Club, and students who had no interest in science fiction.

ATTITUDES OF STUDENTS TOWARDS THE STUDY OF FRENCH.

A survey of students at a high school was taken to find their attitudes toward the study of French and also their attitudes to seven possibly related factors. A regression technique was used to analyse the results.

FACTORS AFFECTING A HIGH SCHOOL COUPLE'S RELATIONSHIP.

A study of the factors that affect the strength of the relationship between couples in a senior secondary school.

TESTING COLA DRINKERS.

A repetition of the well known Coca-Cola and Pepsi-Cola challenge - do students have the ability to tell the difference?

BUTTER - MARGARINE TASTE TEST.

An investigation of the question - can students tell the difference between the taste of butter and margarine?

COLOR SENSITIVITY OF FINGERS.

An investigation based on the material in Statistics by Example - Detecting Patterns: "Sensitive fingers and defective TV tubes."

APPENDIX C

Solutions to Exercises

When referring to the answers, please keep in mind that in many cases the obtained solutions are the result of random outcomes. In such cases, the values given in the answer key will not be exactly those obtained by the student. (Student answers should be "close" to those provided here, however). The more important aspect of the solution to be regarded is the method or procedure followed (model used, how trial is defined and so forth).

1. Infant Mortality

   Better medical treatments
   More concern about nutrition
   Better prenatal care

2. Life Expectancy

   Better health care
   Nutrition
   Physical fitness awareness

Year	Value		Year	Value
1980	73		2050	84
1990	75		2060	86
2000	76		2070	87
2010	78		2080	88
2020	79		2090	90
2030	81		2100	91
2040	83			

   (Answers will vary; this is an illustration only)

3. Millionaires

   Many large ranches in state.
   CA, NY, IL all have large urban areas.

4. Have students bring in articles. Put up on a bulletin board.

5. Same as #4.

6. Discuss how to interview.
   List questions to be asked.
   Interview school personnel.
   (Could use as a mini project)

7. 93 million;
   better equipment for measuring.

Chapter 1   Section 1.2

1. Statistics scores

Stem	Leaf	freq
2	7	1
3	7, 9, 1, 5, 7, 3, 6, 1, 6, 2, 3, 5, 8, 2, 7, 6, 8, 6	18
4	6, 2, 3, 9, 8, 6, 7, 3, 8, 4, 2, 7, 2, 7	14
5	1, 4, 5, 1, 1, 6, 1, 0, 7, 1, 2, 2, 0, 7, 8	15
6	8, 5	2

2. Stems for rats' weights
    18, 19, 20, 21, 22

3. Rats' weights

Stem	Leaf	freq
18	2, 8	2
19	2, 4, 1, 0, 3, 7, 6, 1, 8, 0, 2, 6, 0, 5	14
20	6, 2, 5, 0, 6, 8, 1, 7, 5, 2, 3, 4, 6, 3	14
21	0, 6, 5, 0, 1, 1, 5, 5	8
22	0, 0	2

4. Stopping distances (meters)

    64, 68, 60, 61, 64
    75, 71, 73
    82, 80

5. Final statistics scores

    73, 75, 72, 74, 79
    87, 80, 84, 84, 85, 83, 82, 88
    96, 93, 96, 95, 92, 90, 91

6. Lowest and highest scores
    a) 72
    b) 96
    c) 24

7. Inaug   Death

					Inaug		Death	

```
Inaug                                              Death

                              2, 3     4
                     9, 8, 6, 9, 7     *    9, 6
        4, 1, 0, 2, 4, 0, 4, 1, 1, 4, 1    5    3
  7, 7, 7, 8, 7, 7, 6, 5, 5, 6, 5, 5    *    6, 7, 8, 7
                           1, 4, 0, 2    6    4, 3, 0, 0, 3, 4
                              8, 5     *    7, 8, 5, 6, 7, 7
                                        7    3, 1, 4, 0, 1, 1, 2
                                        *    8, 9, 7, 8
                                        8    3, 5, 0
                                        *    8, 0
                                        9    0
```

More variation for ages at death.

8. Diff

```
10,  29,  26,  28,  15
23,  21,  25,   0,  20
 4,   1,  24,  16,  12
 4,   0,  17,  16,   0
 7,  24,  12,  16,   4
18,  21,   9,   2,   9
36,  12,  28,  16,   3
11
```

```
0    0,  4,  1,  4,  0,  4,  2,  3
*    7,  9,  9
1    0,  2,  0,  2,  1
*    5,  6,  7,  6,  6,  8,  6
2    3,  1,  0,  4,  4,  1,  2
*    9,  6,  8,  5,  8
3
*    6
4
```

Shortest is 0
Longest is 36 years - Hoover

9. British monarchs

AC	stem	DE
1, 3, 4	0	
	*	
0, 2	1	3
8, 8, 5	*	6
1, 3, 2	2	
8, 5, 7, 6, 5	*	
1, 2, 2, 2, 3, 1, 2, 0	3	2, 4
9, 5, 7, 7, 9, 7	*	5, 7
4, 4, 2, 1	4	3, 2, 3, 1, 3
	*	9, 9, 7, 8
4, 4, 4	5	4, 0, 3, 1
8	*	6, 6, 9, 5, 9, 5, 7
0	6	0
5	*	7, 5, 8, 9, 7, 7, 5
	7	0, 1
	*	7, 7
	8	1, 1
	*	6, 8
	9	

10.   Years lived after becoming monarch

Diff

21,	12,	35,	19,	35,	10,	18,	26,	35,	20
50,	22,	15,	11,	48,	22,	0,	4,	25,	38
6,	6,	44,	22,	23,	5,	32,	25,	51,	12
5,	12,	13,	33,	59,	9,	6,	63,	8,	26
35,	16,								

Stem	Leaf
0	0, 4
*	6, 6, 5, 5, 9, 6, 8
1	2, 0, 1, 2, 2, 3
*	9, 5, 6
2	1, 2, 0, 2, 2, 2, 3
*	5, 5, 6
3	2, 3
*	5, 5, 5, 8, 5
4	4
*	6
6	3

Range is 63
Least number is 0
Greatest number is 63

11.   Home runs

AL			NL
2,4	2		3,1,3
	*		7,8,8,9,8
3,4,2,3,2,2,3,2,2,2	3		0,1,1,4,3,1,4,0,3
9,6,5,7,6,9,7,7,7,6,9	*		9,8,5,6,7,9,6,6,8,8,8
1,1,4,3,3,2,2,2,0,4,4,4,1	4		2,1,3,3,0,2,3,4,1,4,4,0,4,0
6,7,6,9,6,8,9,9,6,8,5,9,9,9,6,5	*		7,7,9,7,6,6,9,7,5,5,8,8
4,2,2	5		1,4,1,2,2
9,8,8	*		
0,1	6		

AL has larger range and also more home runs

12. Battery time

Stem (original ÷ 10)

5	18, 51, 76, 90, 03, 55, 41
6	32, 32, 36, 34, 32, 46, 42, 85, 62, 14, 44, 11, 01 41, 53, 59, 48, 41, 06, 49, 81, 21, 40, 63
7	45, 10, 84, 94, 52, 62, 34, 79, 09, 03, 13, 42, 43 47, 75, 42, 18, 45, 92, 49, 16
8	97, 16, 68, 23, 18, 46, 33, 38

13. Copper bar

Divide stem by 10 to obtain original

347	9
348	6, 7
349	5, 5, 3, 5, 3, 5, 9, 3
350	1, 8, 6, 2, 2, 7, 1, 0, 0, 4
351	2, 0, 3, 5, 0, 4, 1
352	0, 0

Section 1.3

1.

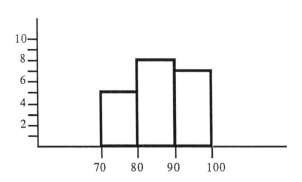

2.

	short	long
Carry on	48	10
Flight attendant	31	34
Beverage service	8	--
Food service	7	39
Other	6	10
Entertainment	--	7

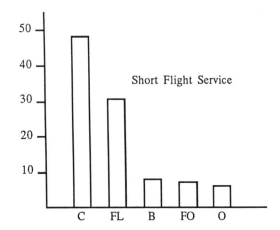

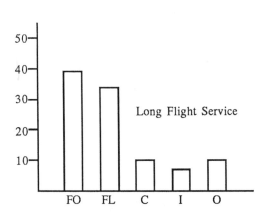

3. Cases of polio
    1952;   60,000

4. Cases of polio
    1938;   2,000

5.

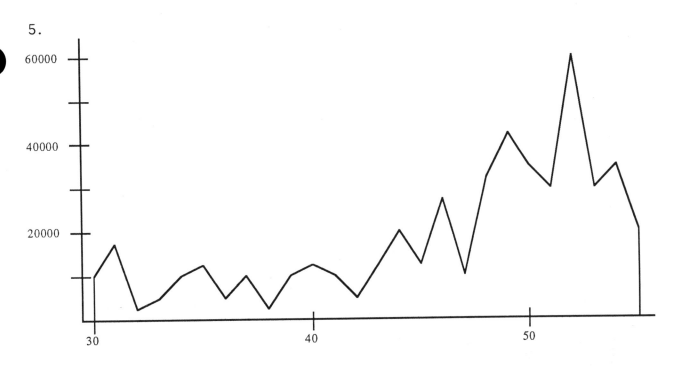

6. Example - answers will differ

T H H T T   H H H T H   H H T H H
T H T T H   T H T H T   T T H H H

H   17
T   13

H   T

7. Example - answers will differ

H   26
T   24

H   T

8. P(H) = 17/30 for example in 6; answers will differ

9. Example - answers will differ

side	frequency
1	5
2	7
3	4
4	4
5	3
6	7
	30

10. For Example

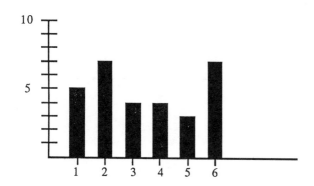

11. For Example

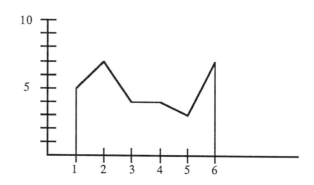

12. Thumb tack

    point up   17

    point down   23

    Prob (up) = 17/40
    Prob (down) = 23/40

    (discuss different types of tacks and what results might occur)
    Could introduce notation P (up), P (down)

13.

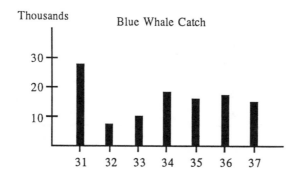

14.

Thousand

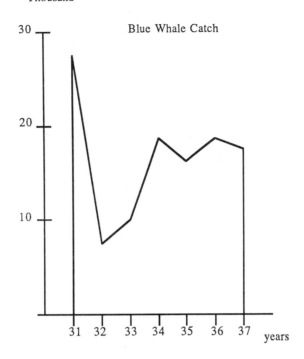

15.

stem	leaf						frequency
18	9,	6,	1,	9,	5,	8	6
19	2,	4,	8,	2			4
20	7,	5,	1,	5,	7		5
21	3,	0,	3,	5,			4
22	0						1

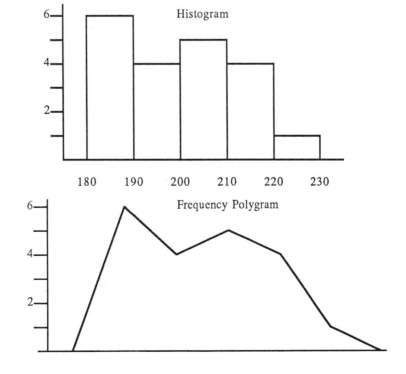

Section 1.4

1. P (Heads) = 103/200 or .515
    P (Tails) = 97/200 or .485

2. Six-sided die roll
    P (1) =   12/120 or .10

    P (3) =   15/120 or .125

    P (6) =   30/120 or .25

    P (even) = $\dfrac{12 + 18 + 30}{120}$ or $\dfrac{69}{120}$ or .575

    P (odd) = $\dfrac{12 + 15 + 24}{120}$ or $\dfrac{51}{120}$ or .425

3. True die roll
    about 50 ones;
    about 50 sixes

    p (1) = 1/6
    p (6) = 1/6
    p (even numbers) = 1/2

4. Answers will differ
    Example

    | T H H H H | H H T H T | T T T H T |
    | H T H T H | T H T T T | T T H H T |
    | T H T T H | T T H H T | H H H H H |
    | | H H T H H | |

    P (H) = 27/50 or .54
    P (T) = 23/50 or .46

    Discuss differences

5. P (lift off) = 35/40

6. Total   3,967,005,000

    P (woman) =   1987049000/3967005000 or .5009
    P (man)   =   1979956000/3967005000 or .4991

7. a) Prop. indicating terrible   2/50

    b) Est. prob. for fantastic   3/50

    c) P (OK) = 20/50

8. P (Heads) = 3009/6000 or .5015

9.

side	freq.
1	13
2	10
3	10
4	12
5	5
6	$\dfrac{10}{60}$

$P\ (1) = 13/60$

$P\ (3) = 10/60$

$P\ (\text{odd}) = \dfrac{13 + 10 + 5}{60} = \dfrac{28}{60}$

$P\ (\text{even}) = \dfrac{10 + 12 + 10}{60} = \dfrac{32}{60}$

10. Coin Toss
  a) $P\ (\text{heads}) = 44/100$
  b) $P\ (\text{tails}) = 56/100$ (approximately)

11. $P\ (1) = 15/60$
   $P\ (4) = 11/60$ (approximately)
   $P\ (6) = 3/60$

Section 1.5

1.

N	freq	proportion	c.P.
0	3	3/50 or .06	.06
1	8	8/50 or .16	.22
2	26	26/50 or .52	.74
3	10	10/50 or .20	.94
4	2	2/50 or .04	.98
5	0	0/50 or 0	.98
6	$\dfrac{1}{50}$	1/50 or .02	1.00

c)

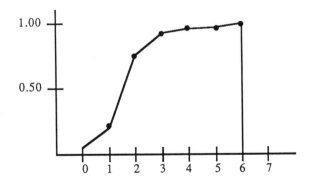

d) $P\ (2\ \text{or less}) = .74$
   $P\ (4\ \text{or less}) = .98$

2. Length of phone call to doctor

Min	freq	Proportion	c.P.
1	18	.18	.18
2	29	.29	.47
3	23	.23	.70
4	15	.15	.85
5	8	.08	.93
6	2	.02	.95
7	1	.01	.96
8	3	.03	.99
9	1	.01	1.00
	100		

a)

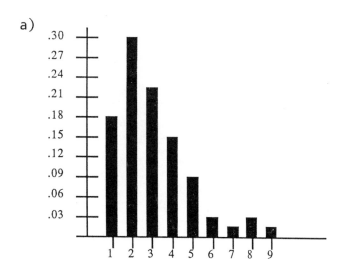

b)

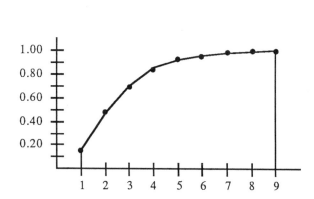

c) (i) P (3 min or less) = .70
 (ii) P (4 min or less) = .85
 (iii) 2 min
 (iv) Average length - lead question - What do we mean by average?
   (Mean is 2.97; median is 3; mode is 2)

3.

Outcome	freq	prop.	c.P.
1	15	.125	.125
2	21	.175	.300
3	23	.192	.492
4	19	.158	.650
5	17	.142	.792
6	25	.208	1.000
	120		

(a) see prop column
(b) see c.P. column
(c) see graph
(d) (i) prop of 3 or less = .492
  (ii) prop of 5 or less = .792
  (iii) prop of more than 3 = .158 + .142 + .208 = .508
  (iv) prop of odd = .125 + .192 + .142 = .459

4.   Six-sided die 120 rolls

    (a) P (3 or less) = .492
    (b) P (5 or less) = .792
    (c) P (more than 3) = .508
    (d) P (even number) = .541
    (e) P (1 or 2) = .425

Section 1.6

1.   Graph A is more accurate in the portrayal of the situation.
Vertical units are equal.

Graph B is more dramatic. Observer must note that vertical units begin at 180,000.

2.   Bring in news clips or use those already handed in.

Note: a bulletin board of students' findings is helpful.

Add to or change weekly.

3.   Get comments from students.

Graphic misinterpretation.

What "average" means (nice lead to next chapter).

Chapter 2   Section 2.1

1. $\bar{X}$ = 1/6 (60 + 63 + 62 + 68 + 60 + 62)
       = 375/6
       = 62.5¢ for milk

2. $\bar{A}$ = 1/8 (3 + 2 + 0 + 2 + 5 + 0 + 1 + 2)
       = 15/8
       = 1.875 accidents

3. $\bar{D}$ = 1/5 (1 + 3 + 0 + 0 + 7)
       = 11/5
       = 2.2 defectives

4. $\bar{P}$ = 1/8 (21 + 10 + 14 + 5 + 8 + 19 + 19 + 12)
       = 1/8 (108)
       = 13.5 Points

5. $\bar{T}$ = 1/20 (15 + 17 + 14 + 14 + 16 + 19 + 18 + 15 + 15 + 15 + 14 + 12
              + 13 + 16 + 16 + 17 + 15 + 15 + 16 + 14)
       = 306/20
       = 15.3 degrees C

6. $\bar{T}$ = 1/15 (1 + 3 + 2 + 2 + 1 + 9 + 4 + 6 + 1 + 10 + 1 + 4 + 5 + 10 + 1)
       = 60/15
       = 4 min. mean response time

    median   Arrange in order and find 8th team
              1   1   1   1   1   2   2   3   4   4   5   6   9   10   10
              3 min. median response time

7. Median score is 6
    $\bar{X}$ = (9 + 9 + 8 + 6 + 5 + 4 + 4)/7
       = 45/7
       = 6.43 mean score

8. Arranging points in order
    5, 7, 8, 10, 10, 11, 11, 12
    median is 10

9. Ages of grandchildren
    Arranging in order
    1, 3, 4, 5, 5, 5, 10
    mode is 5

10. Home runs
    29, 36, 37, 39, 58, 71, 76, 89, 93, 94

    median $\dfrac{58 + 71}{2} = \dfrac{129}{2}$ or 64½

11.   Bowling
         190, 199, 201, 205, 220
      median is 201

12.   Coins
         0, 1, 1, 1, 1, 2, 2, 2, 3, 3
      median 1.5
      $\bar{H}$ = 16/10
      mean is 1.6

13.   (Answers will differ)

Example

Heads	Tally	freq.
0	//	2
1	////	4
2	///	3
3	/	1

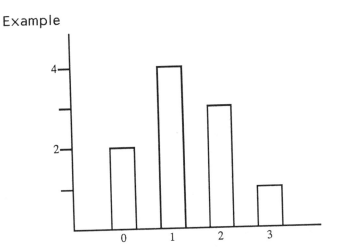

$\bar{H}$ = 1/10 (0 + 4 + 6 + 3)
    = 13/10
    = 1.3 Heads
median number   1

14.   Baskets
         17, 18, 21, 21, 24
         mode is 21

15.   Test scores
         29, 31, 31, 31, 33, 33, 40, 45
         mode is 31

16.   Fire Response time
      mean is 4
      median is 3
      mode is 1
      Reporting mode--the lowest--would indicate they were very good.
      Median would indicate middle and might be the fairest here.
      Mean is highest; might indicate they need more training, newer
      equipment

17.   Hair cuts --
      Mode is Duck Cuts -- the most fashionable at that time

18. | Heads | freq. | prop |
      |-------|-------|------|
      | 0 | 1 | .05 |
      | 1 | 5 | .25 |
      | 2 | 10 | .50 |
      | 3 | 3 | .15 |
      | 4 | 1 | .05 |
      | | 20 | |

      mode   2
      median 2
      mean   38/20 or 1.9

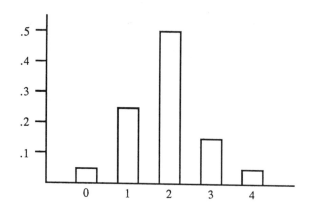

19. Answers will differ
    Example

Heads	freq
0	2
1	4
2	8
3	6
4	0

so

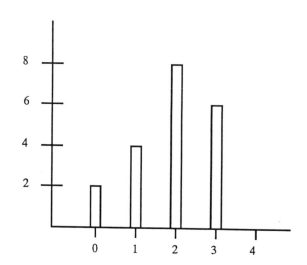

Section 2.2

1. $\bar{A}$ = 1/4 (10 + 15 + 20 + 25)   Median
      = 1/4 (76) $17\frac{1}{2}$
      = 17.5

   $\bar{B}$ = 1/4 (10 + 15 + 20 + 2500)   Median
      = 1/4 (2545) $17\frac{1}{2}$
      = 636.25

   Median unchanged; mean dramatically changed.

2. $\bar{A}$ = 1/5 (100 + 110 + 120 + 130 + 140)

       = 1/5 (600)

       = 120

Median
120

    $\bar{B}$ = 1/5 (0 + 110 + 120 + 130 + 140)

       = 1/5 (500)

       = 100

Median
120

Median unchanged; mean lowered by 20 points

3. Wages

    $\bar{W}$ = 1/7 (5.50 + 17.50 + 22.00 + 28.00 + 30.00 + 30.00 + 32.50)

    $\bar{W}$ = 1/7 (165.50)

    $\bar{W}$ = 23.64

Median is $28.00

4. Earnings for mowing lawns
    mode $30.00
    median   28.00
    mean   23.64

Discuss "better" in
terms of problem.

Each average gives "different picture", not better

5. mode   1
    median 3
    mean   4

6. Salaries ($)

    5,000 6,500   7,000   7,000   10,000   30,000

Without 30,000, mean is $7,100
With 30,000, mean is $10,916.67

Median or mode could be used--discuss.

7. $20.50 × 110 = total
    $2,255.00

8. 85 -- Intuitively! or
    80 (3) = 75 + 80 + X

        85 = X

X is score needed

9. 80 or better

10. Heads   freq.
    2   5
    1   7
    0   0

Modal number is 1

11. Heights

	Tally	Freq	
50	/	1	Bimodal -- 54 and 56
51		0	
52	/	1	
53	//	2	
54	////	5	55 is median
55	////	4	
56	////	5	
57	///	3	mean is $\frac{1384}{25}$ = 55.36
58	//	2	
59	/	1	
60	/	1	Average height is about 55 in.

12.

0	1	2	3	4	5	6	7	8	9	10	11	12
40	15	5	2	1	1	1	0	1	1	3	10	20

$$\text{Mean} = \frac{1}{100}(0(40) + 1(15) + 2(5) + 3(2) + 4(1) + 5(1) + 6(1)$$

$$+7(0) + 8(1) + 9(1) + 10(3) + 11(10) + 12(20))$$

$$= \frac{1}{100}(443)$$

$$= 4.43$$

Median is 2 magazines

Mode is 0 magazines

Depends upon what effect you want.

Good effect - Report mean

Bad effect - Report mode

13. Mean is used in the ad. Jane would find median or mode a more descriptive value.

Section 2.3

1. Least calories lowfat milk and plain lowfat yogurt 119
   Most calories: strawberry whole milk yogurt 211
   Range is 211-119 or 92

2. Tokyo $144
   Chicago $98
   Range $144-98 = $46

3.

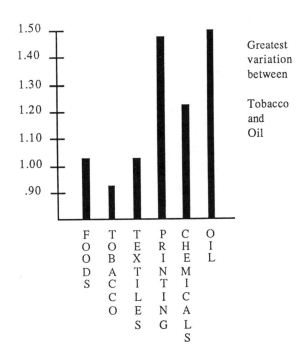

Greatest
variation
between

Tobacco
and
Oil

4.

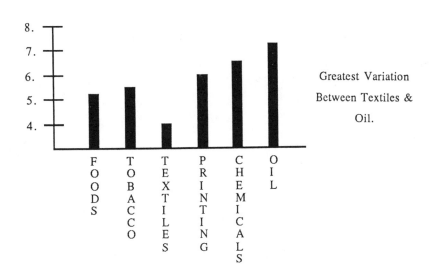

Greatest Variation
Between Textiles &
Oil.

Discuss impressions given by various graphs.
Discuss appropriateness of each kind.

5. Oil   7.27 - 1.50 or 5.77 inc   (Therefore the greatest.)
    Textiles   3.97 - 1.04 or 2.93 inc   (Therefore   the   least.)

6. 522 - 261 = 261 (range)

7.

City	H	L	Range
Anchorage	61	48	13
Denver	68	51	17
Flagstaff	78	39	39
Louisville	78	55	23
Edmonton	80	48	32

8. Anchorage had smallest range.
    Flagstaff had largest range

9. Raiders   78-72 = 6
    Bullets   77-74 = 3   Bullets had smaller range

10. Last year 89 - 43 = 46
    This year 121 - 32 = 89

    More consistent last year
    Discuss - Is that better?

Section 2.4

* <u>Note</u>:   To obtain consistency in answers, Q_1 and Q_3 are given as the largest and smallest values in the middle half. (This is merely a convenient convention.)

1. Home runs (15)   (leaves in order)

stem	leaf
3	2, 2, 3, 7
4	0, 2, 2, 2, 3, 5, 8, 9
5	2, 2
6	1

    $Q_1 = 37$ Median 42
    $Q_3 = 49$

2. Salary data (9)

Stem	Leaf
500	0, 0, 0, 0
600	0
700	0, 0
800	0
.	
.	
.	
6000	0

    Median = 6000

    $Q_1 = 5000$
    $Q_3 = 7000$

3. Manitoba Temperatures (12)

Stem	Leaf			(In order)
-2	2			
-1	8	7	0	
-0	8			
0	0	3	9	
1	0	5	7	8

$Q_1 = -10$ Median $1\frac{1}{2}$
$Q_3 = 10$

4. Dogs' trials to jump (30)

Stem												
0												
*	5	5	6	6	7	7	7	8	8	8	9	
1	0	0	1	1	1	2	2	3	3	3	3	3	4
*	6	6	7	7	8							
2	4											
*												

$Q_1 = 08$ Median 11
$Q_3 = 13$

5. Camelot   (12)   Eldorado   (12)

	1	5
9	2	0, 0, 2
0, 0, 5, 8	3	0, 2
0, 2, 2	4	5
0, 8, 9	5	8, 8
0	6	0
	7	7, 8

Median   41   Median   38.5

$$\frac{40 + 42}{2}$$ $$\frac{32 + 45}{2}$$

$Q_1 = 35$ $Q_1 = 22$
$Q_3 = 50$ $Q_3 = 58$

She would prefer Camelot.

6. Alpha   (10)   Beta (10)

9	7	
7	8	
1, 5, 5	9	7, 8, 8, 9, 9
3, 3, 5, 5, 6	10	1, 1, 2, 3, 3

Median 99   Median 100
$Q_1 = 91$ $Q_1 = 98$
$Q_3 = 105$ $Q_3 = 102$

Recommend Beta - less spread

Section 2.5

1.

City	°F	Deviation
Atlanta	42	- 3
Bismark	12	-33
Great Falls	27	-18
Miami	77	32
El Paso	67	22

$\bar{T}$ = 1/5 (225)

= 45   Atlanta was closest to mean

2.

Ht.	Dev.	Ht.	Dev.
78	2.6	77	1.0
77	1.6	76	.0
77	1.6	76	.0
72	-3.4	74	-2.0
73	-2.4	77	1.0

$\bar{R}$ = 377/5 $\bar{B}$ = 380/5

75.4   76

3.

Conf	Winner	Dev.	Loser	Dev.
Ivy	30.6	3.9	11.0	.3
Big Eight	22.2	-4.5	7.6	-3.1
Southeastern	25.7	-1.0	9.4	-1.3
Mississippi Valley	25.8	- .9	10.6	- .1
Big Ten	23.9	-2.8	12.0	1.3
Western Athletic	33.7	7.0	15.5	4.8
Pacific Eight	24.7	-2.0	8.6	-2.1

$\bar{W}$ = 186.6/7 $\bar{L}$ = 74.7/7

or 26.7   or 10.7

4. Example

2, 2, 3, 3, 4, 6, 10, 10
Sum is 40   40/8 = 5

```
- 3        1
- 3        5
- 2        5
- 2       11
- 1
-11
```

Sum is 0

Proof:

X_1 X_2 ... X_n are scores.

Mean is $(X_1 = X_2 = ... X_n)/n$

so deviations are

$$X_1 - (X_1 + \ldots X_n)/n$$
$$X_2 - (X_1 + \ldots X_n)/n$$
$$X_n - (X_1 + \ldots X_n)/n$$

and sum of deviations is

$$X_1 + X_2 + \ldots X_n - n(X_1 + \ldots X_n)/n = 0$$

Section 2.6

1.

	score	deviation
Bill	3	-3
Jane	7	1
Mary	6	0
Pat	5	-1
Phil	9	3

$\bar{S} = 30/5$
     $= 6$

Mean dev = 8/5
            = 1.6

2.

	wind speed	deviation
Juneau	8.4	-1.28
Chicago	10.3	.62
Boston	12.5	2.82
Nashville	8.0	-1.68
Miami	9.2	- .48

Mean   = $(8.0 + 8.4 + 9.2 + 10.3 + 12.5)/5$
        = 48.4/5 or 9.68

Median   9.2

Range is 12.5 - 8.0 or 4.5

Mean dev. 6.88/5 or 1.376

3. Temp = 856/20
          = 42.8 or 43 degrees

4. Waterfall Vibration

Waterfall	vibrations	dev
Lower Yellowstone	5	-10.7
Yosemite	3	-12.7
Canadian Niagara	6	- 9.7
American Niagara	8	- 7.7
Upper Yellowstone	9	- 6.7
Gullfoss (lower)	6	- 9.7
Firehole	19	3.3
Godafoss	21	5.3
Gullfoss (upper)	40	24.3
Fort Greeley	40	24.3

(a) mean = 157/10 or 15.7

(b) median = 8½ or $(\frac{8 + 9}{2})$

(c) They differ by quite a bit; wide range of values; mean is affected by extreme values

(d) See deviation column

(e) Mean dev. = $\frac{114.4}{10}$ or 11.44

5.

	Cam	Dev.	El	Dev.
Jan	29	-13.75	15	-27.91$\bar{6}$
Feb	30	-12.75	20	-22.91$\bar{6}$
March	35	- 7.75	22	-20.91$\bar{6}$
April	40	- 2.75	30	-12.91$\bar{6}$
May	42	- .75	45	2.08$\bar{3}$
June	58	15.25	58	15.08$\bar{3}$
July	60	17.25	78	35.08$\bar{3}$
Aug	59	16.25	77	34.08$\bar{3}$
Sept	50	7.25	60	17.08$\bar{3}$
Oct	42	- .75	58	15.08$\bar{3}$
Nov	38	- 4.75	32	-10.91$\bar{6}$
Dec	30	-12.75	20	-22.91$\bar{6}$

Mean = 513/12   515/12
42.75   42.92 or 42.91$\bar{6}$

Mean dev =   Mean dev =
112/12   237/12
9.$\bar{3}$ 19.75

Recommend Camelot

6.

Alpha	Dev.		Beta	Dev.
95	- 1.9		99	-1.1
91	- 5.9		103	2.9
105	8.1		101	.9
103	6.1		98	-2.1
- 95	- 1.9		99	-1.1
87	- 9.9		102	1.9
106	9.1		103	2.9
105	8.1		97	-3.1
79	-17.9		101	.9
103	6.1		98	-2.1

Mean = 969/10
     = 96.9

Mean = 1001/10
     = 100.1

Mean dev = 75/10
        = 7.5

Mean dev = 19/10
        = 1.9

Beta is better - less spread.
Same conclusion as 2.4.5

Section 2.7

1.

		dev	$(dev)^2$
Bill	3	-3	9
Jane	7	1	1
Mary	6	0	0
Pat	5	-1	1
Phil	9	3	9

Mean = 30/5 or 6   Var = 20/5 or 4

Mean deviation is 1.6; smaller than variance.

2.

	temp	dev	$(dev)^2$
Juneau	8.4	-1.28	1.6384
Chicago	10.3	.62	.3844
Boston	12.5	2.82	7.9524
Nashville	8.0	-1.68	2.8224
Miami	9.2	- .48	.2304

VAR = 13.028/5
      = 2.6056 = 2.61

3.   Var of 5, 5, 5, 5 is 0.   Mean is 5; each deviation score is 0.

4.   Spelling errors

errors	dev	$(dev)^2$
12	5	25
7	0	0
5	-2	4
4	-3	9

Mean = 28/4   Var = 38/4
     = 7   = 9.5

5.

error	dev	$(dev)^2$
8	5	25
3	0	0
1	-2	4
0	-3	9

Mean = 12/4   Var = 38/4
     = 3   = 9.5

Mean decreased but variance did not.

6.

Defectives	dev	$(dev)^2$
4	2	4
2	0	0
0	-2	4
1	-1	1
3	1	1

Mean = 10/5   Var = 10/5
     = 2   = 2

7.

Camelot dev	$(dev)^2$	Eldorado dev	$(dev)^2$
-13.85	189.0625	-27.92	779.5264
-12.75	162.5625	-22.92	525.3264
- 7.75	60.0625	-20.92	437.6464
- 2.75	7.5625	-12.92	166.9264
- .75	.5625	2.08	4.3264
15.25	232.5625	15.08	227.4064
17.25	297.5625	35.08	1230.6064
16.25	264.0625	34.08	1161.4464
7.25	52.5625	17.08	291.7264
- .75	.5625	15.08	227.4064
- 4.75	22.5625	-10.92	119.2464
-12.75	162.5625	-22.92	525.3264
	1452.7500		5696.9168

Var = 121.06   Var = 474.74

8.

Alpha dev	(dev)^2		Beta dev	(dev)^2
- 1.9	3.61		-1.1	1.21
- 5.9	34.81		2.9	8.41
8.1	65.51		.9	.81
6.1	37.21		-2.1	4.41
- 1.9	3.61		-1.1	1.21
- 9.9	98.01		1.9	3.61
9.1	82.81		2.9	28.07
8.1	65.61		-3.1	9.61
17.9	320.41		.9	.81
6.1	37.21		-2.1	4.41
	748.90			42.90

$$Var = 74.89 \qquad\qquad Var = 4.29$$

Beta is better

9.

Accidents	dev	(dev)^2
4	-1	1
0	-5	25
6	1	1
10	5	25
5	0	0

Mean = 5   Var = 52/5   SD $\doteq$ 3.22
                    = 10.4

10.

Defectives	dev	(dev)^2
2	-2	4
4	0	0
0	-4	16
10	6	36

Mean = 16/4
     = 4

Range = 10 - 0 = 10

Mean Dev = 12/4 = 3

Var = 56/4 = 14
SD = 3.74

11. Quiz Scores
Var = 1/5 (9 + 1 + 0 + 1 + 9)/5
    = 20/5
    = 4

SD = $\sqrt{4}$ or 2

12. Waterfall data
Var = $((-10.7)^2 + \ldots (24.3)^2)/10$
    = 1788.10/10
    = 178.81

SD $\doteq$ 13.37

13. Camelot Var $= 1/12 \; ((-3.75)^2 + \ldots)$
   $= \underline{121.96}$
   SD $= \sqrt{121.96}$ or 11.0

   Eldorado Var $= 1/12 \; ((-27.91\bar{6})^2 + \ldots)$
   $= \underline{474.74}$
   SD $= \sqrt{474.74}$ or 21.7

14. Fire Alarms

	Dev	$(Dev)^2$
1	-3	9
3	-1	1
2	-2	4
2	-2	4
1	-3	9
9	5	25
4	0	0
6	2	4
1	-3	9
10	6	36
1	-3	9
4	0	0
5	1	1
10	6	36
1	-3	9

Mean $=$ 60/15 or 4
Var $=$ 156/15 or 10.4
SD $= \sqrt{10.4}$ or 3.22

15. Data 10, 15, 20, 25

	Dev	$(Dev)^2$
10	-7.5	56.25
15	-2.5	6.25
20	2.5	6.25
25	7.5	56.25

Mean $=$ 70/4 $=$ 17.5
Var $=$ 125/4
   $=$ 31.25   SD $=$ 5.59

Data 10, 15, 20, 2500

	dev	$(dev)^2$
10	-626.25	392189.06
15	-621.25	385951.66
20	-616.25	379764.06
2500	1863.75	3473564.06

Mean $=$ 2545/4   Var $=$ 4631468.74/4
   $=$ 636.25   Var $=$ 1157867.2

                         SD $=$ 1076

16.   Set A   Mean dev = 20/4 or 5

       Set B   Mean dev = 3727.5/4 or 931.875

       Mean deviation is more robust;
       it is less affected by extreme values

Chapter 3   Section 3.1

1.   12 tosses;   100 trials
      M = (12+44+80+80+150+147+144+36+11)/100
        = (624)/100
        = 6.24

2.   12 tosses;   50 trials
      M = (12+24+50+72+56+56+18+10)/50
        = (298)/50
        = 5.96

3.   Heads meant "had rain", so 6.24 cities (on the average) had rain.

4.   Tails meant "no rain", so 12-6.24 or 5.76 had no rain. or
      Using heads for "had rain", then 6.24 cities (on the average) had
      rain.

5.   Example - Answers will differ.

      Model - Coin
      Heads — Rain
      Tails — No Rain
      Results of 2 students   Days before rain

2	2
3	3
2	1
0	1
1	0
4	2
2	0
0	0
0	1
2	0
4	0
0	0
1	6
0	0
0	2
3	2
1	0
0	0
0	2
5	3
Todd's	Susie's

              D = 30/20   D = 25/20
                = 1.5   = 1.25

Section 3.2

1.   Model: Coin
              Head — Girl
              Tail — Boy
     Trial: Toss 3 coins - one for each child.
     Stat. of Int.:   Record the number of heads - girls
     Repeat
     Mean Value = _____

2.   Model: Coin
              Head — Girl
              Tail — Boy
     Trial: Toss Coin 4 times, once for each child.
     Stat. of Int.:   Record the number of tails (boys).
     Repeat
     Mean Value = _____

3.   Model: Die   odd number - boy
                    even number - girl
     Trial: Roll die 4 times - once for each child.
     Stat. of Int.:   Record number of odd numbers - boys
     Repeat
     Mean Value = _____

4.   Model: Deck of cards
              Red — girl
              Black — boy
     Trial: Select card, return, select next card.
     Stat. of Int.:   Record number of red cards - girls.
     Repeat
     Mean Value = _____

5.   Model: Cards   OR   Die
              Club a hit   1 hit
                                   2, 3, 4 no hit
                                   5, 6 ignore
     Trial: Select a card 20 times - once for each time at bat or roll a
     die 20 times - once for each time at bat.
     Stat. of Int.:   Record the number of hits.
     Repeat
     Mean Value = _____

6.   Theoretical value is .250 (20) = 5

7.   Model: Cards
              Ace to 10 ignore J, Q, K
              Let A, 2, 3 — hit
     Trial: Draw a card, record, return to deck, shuffle; continue 20
              times (once for each time at bat).
     Repeat
     Mean Value = _____

8.   Model: Coin
             Head — girl
             Tail — boy
     Trial: Toss coin until head (girl) occurs.
     Stat. of Int.:   Record number of tosses needed to obtain head - girl.
     Repeat
     Mean Value = _____

9.   Model: Die   OR   Cards
             1 — Rain   Heart — Rain
             2, 3, 4 No Rain
             5, 6 Ignore
     Trial: Toss die until 1 (rain) occurs.   OR
             Select card, record, return, shuffle, until a heart (rain) occurs.
     Stat. of Int.:   Record number of tosses before the 1.   OR
                     Record the number of cards before the heart.
     Repeat
     Mean Value = _____

10. (a) Model: Cards
                  Heart — hit
         Trial: Select card (return) until a club, diamond or spade
         appears.
         Stat. of Int.:   Record number of hearts (hits).
         Repeat
         Mean Value = _____

     (b) Model: Cards
                  A, 2, 3 hit
                  4, to 10 no hit
                  Ignore J, Q, K
         Trial: Select card, return, continue until a 4 to 10 occurs.
         Stat. of Int.:   Record number of aces, twos and threes (hits).
         Repeat
         Mean Value = _____

11. Model: Cards
             Club, Diamond, Heart - rain
             Spade - no rain
     Trial: Draw a card until a spade (no rain) occurs.
     Stat. of Int.:   Record the number of cards (days) before the spade
     (no rain) occurs.
     Repeat
     Mean Value = _____

12. Model: Coin
             Heads — hang up
             Tails — talk
     Trial: Toss coin until tail occurs (a talker).
     Stat. of Int.:   Record number of tosses (calls) before a tail (talker).
     Repeat
     Mean Value = _____

Section 3.3

1. A trial consists of tossing 2 coins 10 times. Possible outcomes are 0 to 10. 10 tosses of the 2 coins made up a trial. 50 trials were requested.

2. A trial consists of tossing 3 coins 20 times; 100 trials were obtained.

3. $M = (0(4)+1(12)+2(21)+3(30)+4(22)+5(8)+6(2)+7(1)+8(0)...)/100$
   $= (12+42+90+88+40+12+7)/100$
   $= (291)/100$
   $= 2.91$

4. $M = (0(26)+1(127)+2(250)+3(253)+4(184)+5(104)+6(46)+7(7+)8(2)+9(1))/1000$
   $= (0+127+500+759+736+520+276+49+16+9)/1000$
   $= (2992)/1000$
   $= 2.992$

5. Model: 2 coins; Penny SJ; Nickel Chi
              Head — rain
              Tail — no rain
   Trial: Toss 2 coins 20 times once for each day.
   Stat. of Int.: Record the number of times 2 heads (rain in both) occurred.
   Repeat 60 times.

   Mean Value = $\dfrac{\text{Sum of Stat. of Int.}}{60}$

6. Model: Coins
              Head — green
              Tail — not green
   Trial: Toss 2 coins (one for each light) 10 times (once for each day).
   Stat. of Int.: Record the number of times HH (2 greens) occurred.
   Repeat
   Mean Value = _____

7. Model: Coin
              Head — green
              Tail — not green
   Trial: Toss 2 coins (one for each light) 10 times (once for each day.)
   Stat. of Int.: Record the number of TT (no green).
   Repeat
   Mean Value = _____

8. Model: Coin
              Head — rain
              Tail — no rain
   Trial: Toss 3 coins (one for each city) 12 times (once for each day).
   Stat. of Int.: Record number of HHH.
   Repeat
   Mean Value = _____

9.   Model: Coin
            Head — correct
            Tail — incorrect
Toss coins 10 times (once for each question).
Stat. of Int.:   Record number of heads (corrects).
Repeat
Mean Value = _____
<u>or</u>
Take test - then correct.
Model: Coin
            Head — True
            Tail — False
Trial: Toss coin 10 times (once for each question). This determines Robert's answers.
Toss coin 10 times (once for each question). This determines correct answers.
Stat. of Int.:   Record number of corrects (matches).
Repeat
Mean Value = _____

Section 3.4

1.   Trials for introvert extrovert couple.   Answer will vary.   Theoretical answer is 4.

2.   Trials for bubble gum problem.   Answers will vary.

3.   Model: 8 sided die
Trial: Roll die until each side has occurred at least once.
Stat. of Int.:   Record the number of rolls necessary to obtain all 8 sides.
Repeat
Mean Value = _____

4.   Model: 6 sided die
            side 1 represents correct key
            2 to 6 represent incorrect key
Trial: Roll die until side 1 (correct key) occurs.
Stat. of Int.:   Records the number of rolls necessary to obtain the side 1 (correct key).
Repeat
Mean Value = _____

5.   Theoretical answer to number of rolls necessary to get <u>all</u> the numbers.
For 12

$$\frac{12}{1} + \frac{12}{2} + \frac{12}{3} + \frac{12}{4} + \frac{12}{5} + \frac{12}{6} + \frac{12}{7} + \frac{12}{8} + \frac{12}{9} + \frac{12}{10} + \frac{12}{11} + \frac{12}{12} = 37.2$$

For 50-trial experiment, answers will vary.

6. Model: 6 sided die
                1-4 Win for NL
                5-6 Loss for NL
    Trial: Toss die until 4 wins or losses occur.
    Stat. of Int.: Record the number of tosses (games) needed.
    Repeat
    Mean Value = _____
    (Assumption of independence of games is made.)

Section 3.5

1. Epidemic - 6 hermits
    Answers will differ.

2. Model: 8-sided die
                1 side for each hermit
    Trial: Roll die to obtain 1st hermit infected. Roll die to determine
    next hermit visited. Continue until an immune hermit is visited. (Ignore
    successive repetitions).
    Stat. of Int.: Record number of rolls before repeat occurs (Immune is
    visited).
    Repeat
    Mean Value = _____

3. Model: Coin and 6-sided die
                1H, 1T, 2H, 2H, etc.
    Trial: Toss coin and roll die to determine first hermit infected. Roll
    die to determine hermit visited. Continue. (Ignore successive
    repetitions).
    Stat. of Int.: Record numbers of rolls necessary to obtain a repeated
    number (visit an immune hermit).
    Repeat
    Mean Value = _____

Section 3.6

1. Collect data from students for average distance for walk of 10 steps.

2. Die - even number East
            odd number West

3. Answers will vary.

4. Answers will vary.

    Example of 1 trial.

```
Coin Tosses        Dir.

     H  T            S
     T  T            E
     H  H            N
     H  T            S
     T  T            E
     T  H            W
     H  H            N
     H  T            S
     T  T            E
     T  T            E
```

Shortcut EW EEE and NNSS S   EEE EW is equivalent to 3E
            3 E + IS   NNSS S is equivalent to IS
                                    d = 9 + 1 or 3.162
                                    so final destination is (3,-1)

5.   Answers will differ.

6.   (a) (1,3)
          Example - Results of 20 class trials.
               3°   13
              15°   4
              30°   0
              45°   3

     so T = (39+60+0+135)/20

          = 234/20

          = 11.7

     (b) (2,4)
          Answers will differ.

     (c) (3,1)
          Answers will differ.

Chapter 4   Section 4.1

1.   (a) P(H) = 44/100 or .44

     (b) P(H) = 255/500 or .51

     Yes - proportion hovers around .5 which is theoretically correct and intuitively obvious.

2.   P(up) = 27/500 or .054

     Tosses are independent. Tosses are made in same manner.

3.   P(hit) = 24/92 or .261

4.   Find stats from newspaper.

5. P (Ace) = 14/100 or .14

6. Answers will differ.

7. Answers will differ.

8. Answers will differ.

9. Probability of certain kinds of weather; probability of winning in any athletic contest; probability of obtaining a particular grade.

10. P (white Christmas) = 34/90   or   .378

11. We can expect rain 25 times in 100 (or 1 in 4) when conditions are similar.

12. Over the long run, Casey Jones has had 250 hits out of 1000 times at bat.

13. Probability (show up) = 1850/2000 or .925
    Probability (no show) = 150/2000 or .075

14. Location favors the home team - usually.
    Palmer is stronger than Gentry.
    Students will provide other interesting points.

Section 4.2

1. Answers will differ - Example

Heads	freq
0	3
1	23
2	19
3	5

   P(3) = 5/50 or .1

2.
Heads		freq
0	6 + 3	9
1	20 + 23	43
2	16 + 19	35
3	8 + 5	13
		100

   P (2 or more) = $\frac{35 + 13}{100} = \frac{48}{100}$

   Interesting - the same! (Not always)

3. Model: Coin
            Head — girl
            Tail — boy
   Trial: Toss coin 4 times - once for each child.
   Successful trial: Occurs if 2 or more tails (boys) appear.
   Repeat
   P (2 or more boys) = $\frac{succ}{trials}$

4.   Models: Coin
                    Head — girl
                    Tail — boy
      Trial: Toss coin 3 times - once for each child.
      Successful trial: Occurs if 1 or more heads appear.
      Repeat
      P (at least one girl) = $\dfrac{\text{succ}}{\text{trials}}$

5.   Model: Cards
                    Club — rain
                    Others — no rain
      Trial: Draw 3 cards 12 times and record the # of times 2 or more clubs occurred.
      Successful trial: Occurs if 2 or more clubs (rainy days) appear.
      Repeat
      P (2 or more rainy cities) = $\dfrac{\text{succ}}{\text{trials}}$

6.   Model: Die
                    1-2 hit
                    3-6 no hit
      Trial: Toss die 10 times (once for each time at bat).
      Successful trial: Occurs if 5 or more tosses are 1 or 2 (hits)
      Repeat
      P (5 or more hits) = $\dfrac{\text{succ}}{\text{trials}}$

7.   Model: die
                    1 - strep
                    2-6 no strep
      Trial: Toss die 4 times, once for each child.
      Successful trial: Occurs if at least one toss results in a 1 (strep)
      Repeat
      P (1 or more strep throats) = $\dfrac{\text{succ}}{\text{trials}}$

8.   Model: Coin
                    Heads - correct
                    Tails - wrong
      Trial: Toss coin 8 times (once for each question).
      Successful trial: Occurs if 6 or more are heads (correct).
      Repeat
      P (at least 6 correct) = $\dfrac{\text{succ}}{\text{trials}}$

9.   Model: Die
                    1-2 — saw ET
                    3-6 — did not see ET
      Trial: Toss die four times, once for each person.
      Successful trial: Occurs if 2 or more tosses result in 1 or 2 (people who saw ET).
      Repeat
      P (2 or more people have seen it) = succ/trials

10. Model: Usual aim   Careful aim
                 1 coin   2 coins
                 H — hit   HH, HT, TH — hit
                 T — no hit   TT — no hit
     Trial: Toss coin 40 times - once for each shot. Use appropriate
              model as described in the problem.
     Stat of Int: Record the number of bull's eyes.
     Repeat
     Mean Value = _____
     Note: This is a mean value (not a probability) problem.

Section 4.3

1.   Answers will differ.

2.   Answers will differ.

3.   (a) Model: 1-digit RN — (RN represents Random Number)
                    1-2 burst
                    3-9 & 0 not burst
          Trial: Read six RN (one for each bag).
          Successful trial: Occurs if one or more are 1 or 2 (burst).
          Repeat
          P (at least one bag bursts) = succ
                                         ―――――
                                          trials

     (b) Change
          Successful trial: Occurs if 2 or less are 1 or 2 (burst).
          P (two or less burst) = succ
                                  ―――――
                                   trials

4.   Model: 1-digit RN
               1-2 burst
               3-9 & 0 not burst
     Trial: Read 6 RN - one for each bag.
     Successful trial: Occurs if no 1 or 2 appears.
     Repeat
     P (more bursting) = succ
                        ―――――
                         trials

5.   Model: 2 digit RN
               1-33 hit
               34-99 & 00 no hit
     Trial: Read 10 RN (one for each time at bat).
     Successful trial: Occurs if 4 or more are in 1-33 interval.
     Repeat
     P (4 or more hits) = succ
                          ―――――
                           trials

Example - Using average of .283.

6.   Model: 3-digit RN
               1-283 hit
               284-999 & 000 no hit

Trial: Read 10 RN (one for each time at bat).
Successful trial: Occurs if 4 or more are in 1-283 interval.
Repeat
P (4 or more hits) = $\dfrac{\text{succ}}{\text{trials}}$

7.   Model*:   2-digit RN
             01-95 developed
             96-99 & 00 not developed
Trial: Read 12 RN (one for each picture).
Successful trial: Occurs if 2 or more are in 96-99 & 00 interval (not
      developed).
Repeat
P (2 or more not devel) = $\dfrac{\text{succ}}{\text{trials}}$
* Other assignments of RN are possible.

8.   Model: 2-digit RN
             01-06 below
             07-99 & 00 ok
Trial: Read 20 RN (one for each capsule).
Successful trial: Occurs if 2 or more are in 01-06 interval.
Repeat
P (2 more more below strength) = $\dfrac{\text{succ}}{\text{trials}}$

9.   Model: 1-digit RN
             1-2-3 correct
             4-9 wrong
             0 ignore
Trial: Read 12 RN (one for each question).
Successful trial: Occurs if 6 or more are 1 or 2 or 3 (correct).
Repeat
P (6 or more correct) = $\dfrac{\text{succ}}{\text{trials}}$

10.   Model: 2-digit RN
             01-18 no show
             19-99 & 00 show
Trial: Read 42 RN (one for each reservation).
Successful trial: Occurs if 2 or more are in 1-18 interval.
$\overline{\text{or}}$
Successful trial: Occurs if 40 or less are in 19 to 99 & 00 interval.
Repeat
P (2 or more no shows) = $\dfrac{\text{succ}}{\text{trials}}$
P (40 or less shows) = $\dfrac{\text{succ}}{\text{trials}}$

11.   (a)   Model: 1-digit RN
                   1-7 quartzite
                   8,9 and 0 none
      Trial: Read 10 RN (one for each pebble).
      Successful trial: Occurs if 8 or more digits are in the 1-7
      interval (contain quartzite).

Repeat

P (8 or more containing quartzite) = $\frac{succ}{trials}$

(b) Change

Successful trial: Occurs if 6 or less are in the 1-7 interval (contain quartzite).

P (6 or less containing quantite) = $\frac{succ}{trials}$

Section 4.4

1.

Trial	1-6 SJ Rain	1-4 Chi Rain	Succ
6	3 yes	6	
7	0	3 yes	
8	1 yes	5	
9	9	9	
10	9	1 yes	
11	0	6	
12	5 yes	8	
13	7	2 yes	
14	0	0	
15	4 yes	1 yes	yes

2.   P (RR) = 26/80 or .325

3.   P (R in SJ) · P (Rain in Chi) =

$\frac{42}{80} \cdot \frac{50}{80} = \frac{2100}{6400}$ or .328

4.   Model: 1-digit RN

   1-3 green

   4-9 not green

   0 ignore

Trial: Read 2 RN (one for each light).

Successful trial: Occurs if both are in 1-3 interval.

Repeat

P (green, green) = $\frac{succ}{trials}$

p (green, green) = $\frac{1}{3} \cdot \frac{1}{3}$ or $\frac{1}{9}$

5.   Model: 1-digit RN

   First 1-5 Green; 6-9 & 0 not

   Second 1-3 Green; 4-9 not 0 ignore

Trial: Read 2 RN one for each light (if digit is 0 read again).

Successful trial: Occurs if first digit is in 1-5 interval and second digit is in 1-3 interval.

Repeat

P (G, G) = $\frac{succ}{trials}$

p (G, G) = $\frac{1}{2} \cdot \frac{1}{3}$ or $\frac{1}{6}$

6. Model: 2-digit RN
             01-75 fire
             6-99 & 00 no fire
    Trial: Read 2 2-digit RN (one for each engine).
    Successful trial: Occurs if both RN are in 01-75 interval.
    Repeat
    P (lift off) = $\frac{succ}{trials}$

    p (lift off) = .95 (.95) or .9025

7. Model: 1-digit RN
             0 failure
             1-9 success
    Trial: Read 2 1-digit RN (one for each engine).
    Successful trial: Occurs if at least one number is in 1-9 interval.
    Repeat
    P (safe flight) = $\frac{succ}{trials}$

8. Model: 1-digit RN
             0 failure
             1-9 success
    Trial: Read 4 1-digit RN (one for each engine).
    Successful trial: Occurs if 2 or more RN are in the 1-9 interval.
    Repeat
    P (safe flight) = $\frac{succ}{trials}$

9. Model: 1-digit RN
             odd 1, 3, 5, 7, 9 girl
             even 2, 4, 6, 8, 0 boy
    Trial: Read 3 1-digit RN (one for each child).
    Successful trial: Occurs if at least one digit is an odd digit (girl).
    Repeat
    P (at least one girl) = $\frac{succ}{trial}$

10. Following hint in text:
    Model: 1-digit RN
             1, 2, 3 Choice A
             4, 5, 6 Choice B
             7, 8, 9 Choice C
             0 ignore
    Trial: Read 2 sets of 10 1-digit RN (ignoring zero) first for student
    answer and second for correct answer.
    Successful trial: Occurs if corresponding RN's (answers) match.
    Repeat
    P (5 or more correct) = $\frac{succ}{trials}$

Example of 1 trial

9	7	2	4	5	7	3	8	2	1
C	C	A	B	B	C	A	C	A	A

5	1	7	5	3	4	1	3	9	7
B	A	C	B	A	B	A	A	C	C

Only 2 correct, so this trial is a failure.

11. Model: 1-digit RN
            1-7
            ignore 8, 9, 0
              1 — M
              2 — T
              3 — W
              4 — Th
              5 — F
              6 — Sat
              7 — Sun
Trial: Read 2 RN (one for each accident).
Successful trial: Occurs if both are 6 or 7.
Repeat
P (2 accidents on weekends) = $\frac{succ}{trials}$

12. Model: 12-sided die
Trial: Roll die twice (once for each wheel). Roll again twice.
Successful trial: Occurs if both pairs of numbers are identical.
Repeat
P (matching wheels) = $\frac{succ}{trials}$

13. Model: 2-digit RN
            01-65 win
            66-99 & 00 lose
Trial: Read 3 2-digit RN (one for each game).
Successful trial: Occurs if all three are in the 01-65 interval.
Repeat
P (winning 3 in a row) = $\frac{succ}{trials}$

Section 4.5

1. Tossing a coin
Rolling a die
Drawing a card
Selecting a random number

2. Tetrahedral die
$p(1) = 1/4$ $p(e) = 2/4$ or $1/2$
$p(2) = 1/4$ $p(\text{number less than 4}) = 3/4$
$p(3) = 1/4$
$p(4) = 1/4$

3. Spinner
   p(each digit) = 1/10
   p(0) = 1/10 = p(1) = p(2) =....
   p(odd) = 5/10 or 1/2

4. p(being selected) = 1/20
   (don't forget yourself!)

5. Cards
   p(black) = 26/52 or 1/2
   p(heart) = 13/52 or 1/4
   p(ace) = 4/52 or 1/13
   p(king of diamonds) = 1/52

6. Find census material.

7. p(valve pos) = 1/12
   p(valve pos two times) = (1/12) (1/12)
        or 1/144

8. p(odd) = 3/6 or 1/2

9. p(prime) = 3/6 or 1/2   (2, 3 and 5 are prime)

10. 2 dice

	1	2	3	4	5	6		Sum	freq.
1	2	3	4	5	6	7		2	1
2	3	4	5	6	7	8		3	2
3	4	5	6	7	8	9		4	3
4	5	6	7	8	9	10		5	4
5	6	7	8	9	10	11		6	5
6	7	8	9	10	11	12		7	6
								8	5
								9	4
p(sum < 5) = 6/36								10	3
p(sum = 7) = 6/36								11	2
p(sum > 11) = 1/36								12	1

11. Roll 2 dice. Answers will differ.

12. Toss 2 coins.   Theoretical

    p(1 head) = 2/4
    p(at least 1 head) = 3/4
    p(0 heads) = 1/4

	H	H	HH
H	T	H	HT
	H	T	TH
T	T	T	TT

13. Answers will differ.

14.

				Number of heads
H	H	H	H	3
	H	H	H	2
	H	T	H	2
	H	T	T	1
	T	H	H	2
	T	H	T	1
	T	T	H	1
	T	T	T	0

p(1 head) = 3/8
p(2 or more) = 4/8
p(3 heads) = 1/8

15. Answers will differ.

Section 4.6

1. Not E is not getting no heads; getting at least 1 head.

   P(E) = 20/100
   P(not E) = 80/100

2. Theoretical probabilities

   p(E) = 1/4
   p(not E) = 3/4

3. Not A is not getting an ace.

4. Pick a card from a shuffled deck, record, return, and repeat.
   Find P(A) and subtract it from 1. or count number of non Aces and
   find P(not A) directly.

5. P(W) = 6/60 = 1/10
   P(not W) = 54/100 = 9/10
   Not W is not (not working) or is working.

6. Model: Coin
                  Head — Girl
                  Tail — Boy
   Trial: Toss coin 4 times (once for each child)
   Successful trial: Occurs if at least one head (girl) is obtained.
   Repeat
   P (at least one girl) = succ
   $\qquad\qquad\qquad\qquad$ trials

7.

First	Second	Third	Fourth		Outcomes			$\underline{f}$

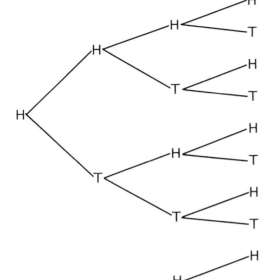

		Outcomes			$\underline{f}$
H	H	H	H		4
H	H	H	T		3
H	H	T	H		3
H	H	T	T		2
H	T	H	H		3
H	T	H	T		2
H	T	H	H		3
H	T	T	T		1
T	H	H	H		3
T	H	H	T		2
T	H	T	H		2
T	H	T	T		3
T	T	H	H		2
T	T	H	T		1
T	T	H	H		2
T	T	T	T		0

p(at least 1 girl) = 15/16

8. p(12) = 1/36
p(6) = 6/36

9. p(pass math) = .8   p(fail math) = .2
p(pass Eng) = .6   p(fail Eng) = .4
p(pass both) = .48   or   (.8) (.6)
p(fail both) = .08   or   (.2) (.4)

10. p(A) = .9
p(B) = .8   p(all) = (.9) (.8) (.7)
p(C) = .7   = .504

11. p(none) = (.1) (.2) (.3)
          = .006

12. Model: 2-digit RN
              01-15 get bid
              16-99 & 00 not get bid
    Trial: Read 4 RN (one for each contract)
    Succ. Trial: Occurs if all 4 RN are in 16-99 & 00 interval.
    Repeat
    Prob. (receiving no bids) = $\frac{\text{succ}}{\text{trials}}$

13. (a) Model: 1-digit RN, each represents a person
         Trial: Read 10 sets of RNs. Be sure that no person has herself
         as a friend.
         Stat. of Int.: Record the number of isolates.
         Repeat
         Mean value = _____

    b) Model: Same
        Trial: Same
        Succ. trial: Occurs if no one is an isolate.
        Repeat
        P (no isolates) = $\frac{\text{succ}}{\text{trials}}$

14. G is winning home game; not G is not winning home game and is
    complement of G
    p(not G) = 1 - .68 = .32
    p(not G, not G) = (.32) (.32) or .1024
        Experimentally
    Model: 2-digit RN
              01-68 win
              67-99 & 00 loose
    Trial: Read 2 2-digit RN, one for each home game.
    Succ. Trial: Occurs if both numbers are in 67 to 99 & 00 interval.
    Repeat
    P (losing 2 home games) = $\frac{\text{succ}}{\text{trials}}$

Chapter 5   Section 5.1

1.   <u>Sample</u>   <u>Population</u>

    (a) 40 high school seniors   senior class
    (b) a few pieces of rock   all rocks in the valley
    (c) a spoonful of soup   pot of soup
    (d) toe   body
    (e) 5 samples of mix   truckloads
    (f) blood sample   blood of entire body

2. (a) In (a) find mean number of those questioned who favor raising
         age. Convert to proportion and use to describe the total senior
         class.

In (f) find mean blood cell count for sample and use it to describe her entire body blood count.

(b) In (a) find variance of responses of the 40 seniors and use it as an estimate of entire senior class.

In (e) find variance of the 5 samples and use it to estimate the entire set of truckloads.

3. Answers will differ. Examples:

Who will win the Chicago mayoral election? Random sample of 1000 Chicago residents.

or Do you favor the final exam arrangement, i.e., 3 days of no classes? Sample of 50 from each class.

or Who will win the Super Bowl? Telephone sample of 100 from a community.

4. Watch paper for sample population articles.

5. Sample consists of students surveyed by National Assessment of Educational Progress today and 5 years ago.
Population is American students today and 5 years ago.

6. Sample is those surveyed by the Weekend magazine.
Population seems to be all Canadians.

7. Sample U.S. college and university students from 760 schools.
Population seems to be all U.S. college and university students.

8. Sample 130,000 respondents to the Family Weekly's survey.
Population implied is all Americans--more realistically it could be Family Weekly's readers.

9. In the first catch, the experiment is set up by the tagging.
In the second catch those caught with tags (sample) represent all tagged fish (population) in the lake.
Those not tagged (sample) represent those not tagged (population) in lake.
Assume 100 are tagged to set up experiment.
Suppose 50 are then caught of which 7 are tagged and 43 are not.
So 7/50 or .14 of population is tagged.
$$.14 \, P = 100$$
$$P = 714.28$$

Section 5.2

1 (a) P (16 or more heads) = (7 + 5 + 2)/100 or .14
P (18 or more heads) = 2/100 or .02
P (20 or more heads) = 0

(b) P (12 or fewer heads) = (18 + 14 + 9 + 7 + 2 + 1)/100 = .51
P (9 or fewer heads) = (7 + 2 + 1)/100 = .10
P (5 or fewer heads) = 0

2. Answers will differ

3. P (18 or more) = 2/100 or .02

    Therefore it seems unlikely that the community is truly split.

4. P (19 or more) = 0

    Therefore it seems unlikely that the teams were equally matched.

5. P (14 or more) = 6/100 or .06

    Therefore it seems unlikely that the voters are evenly split.

6. P (7 or less) = 13/100 or .13

    Since .13 is fairly large probability we do not have evidence that the community is evenly split.

7. Model: Coin   H → correct
                          T → incorrect

    Trial: Toss coin 12 times; once for each cup of tea.

    Outcome of trial: Record the number of heads (correct ans)

    Repeat 100 times

    P (8 or more correct) = 12/100 or .12

8. Model: Coin   H → man
                          T → woman

    Trial: Toss coin 12 times; once for each juror

    Outcome: Record number of heads (men)

    Repeat 100 times

    P (8 or more men) = 12/100 or .12
    P (9 or more men) = 4/100 or .04

Section 5.3

1. P (6 or fewer girls) = (3 + 1)/50 = .08
2. P (13 or more girls) = (2 + 1)/50 = .06
3. Answers will vary

4. Answers will vary

5. P (17 or more yes's) = (8 + 10 + 5 + 5 + 2 + 1)/100 = .31
6. Answers will vary

7. Answers will vary

8. Model: Bead box   1/2 Black
                            1/2 White
                    Black - yes - own
                    White - no - not own

Trial: Use 40 - paddle since sample size is 40.

Outcome: Record number of Black beads obtained in sample.

Repeat

P (30 or more owners) =

    Answers will vary.

9. Answers will vary.

10. Model: Bead Box   1/2 Brass
                            1/2 Copper
                    Brass - Man
                    Copper - Woman

Trial: Use 12 paddle since sample size is 12.

Outcome: Record number of copper beads (women)

Repeat

P (9 or more women) =

Section 5.4

1. P (8 or more) = (5 + 1)/100 = .06

Therefore unusual event - conclude he likely has ESP.

2. Answers will vary.

3. Model: Coin   H → correct
                   T → incorrect

Trial: Toss coin 12 times; once for each cup of tea

Outcome of trial: Record the number of heads (correct answers)

Repeat

P (8 or more correct) =

Decision:

4. Model: Coin   H - National League wins
                  T - American League wins

   Trial: Toss coin 20 times (once for each game)

   Outcome of trial: Record the number of heads (NL wins)

   Repeat

   P (19 or more NL wins) =

   Decision:

5. Model: Coin   H → favor
                      T → oppose

   Trial: Toss coin 30 times (once for each call)

   Outcome of trial: Record number of heads (favors)

   Repeat 100 times

   P (19 or more favor) = _____

   Decision:

6. Model: RN   1 digit   1-5 → woman
                                6-9 + 0 → man

   Trial: Read 12 RN (one for each juror)

   Outcome of trial: record number of digits in 6-9 + 0 interval (men)

   Repeat

   P (8 or more men) =

   Decision:

7. Model: RN   1 digit
                1-5 → female
                6-9 + 0 → male

   Trial: Read 24 RN one for each offspring.

   Outcome: record number of digits in 1-5 interval (females)

   Repeat

   P (15 or more females)

   Decision:

8. Model: RN   1 digit
               1-5 → like
               6-9, 0 → not like

    Trial: Read 10 RN one for each person

    Outcome: Record number of 1-5's (prefers)

    Repeat

    P (7 or more likes) =

    Decision:

9. Change (in prob 8)

    Trial: Read 25 RN...

    P (15 or more likes) =

10. Model: die

    Trial: Roll die 50 times

    Outcome: Record number of evens

    Repeat

    P (35 or more evens) =

    Decision:

11. Model: coin   H   No
                        T   Yes

    Trial: Toss coin 30 times, once for each person called

    Outcome: Record number of heads (noes)

    Repeat

    P (11 or less no's) =

    Decision:

12. Use #6 with change

    P (4 or less women) =

    Decision:

13. Use #7 with change

    P (9 or less males) =

    Decision:

Section 5.5

1. Model: p = .6
              RN   1 to 6 → make it
                        7 to 9 + 0 → not

   Trial: Read 12 1-digit RN (one for each shot)

   Outcome: Record number of baskets obtained (1 to 6's)

   Repeat 100 times

   P (8 or more) = $\frac{10 + 5 + 3 + 1}{100}$ = $\frac{19}{100}$

   Decision: Since 19% is <u>not</u> unusual, conclude model is OK.   No evidence shooting has improved.

2. Answers will vary.

3. Model: p = .8   RN   1-8 → cure
                                   9+0 → no cure

   Trial: Read 20 RN, one for each patient

   Outcome: Record the number of digits in 1-8 interval (cures)

   Repeat 100 times

   P (17 or more cures) = $\frac{10 + 5 + 3 + 1}{100}$ or $\frac{19}{100}$

   Decision: Since probability is large, (not unusual) conclude no evidence medication is more effective.

4. P (19 or more) = $\frac{3 + 1}{100}$ or .04

   Decision: Unlikely so conclude model of .8 is not accurate.

   New medication is better.

5. Model: p = .05   RN   01-05 → defective
                                 06-99, 00 → not defective

   Trial: Read 25 numbers (one for each valve)

   Outcome: Record the number in the 01 to 05 interval (defectives)

   Repeat

   P (3 or more) =

   Decision:

6. Model: p = .02
    RN   01-02 → defective
              03-99, 00 → not defective

    Trial: Read 100 RN (one for each transistor)

    Outcome: Record number in the 01 to 02 interval (defectives)

    Repeat

    P (9 or more def) =

    Decision:

7. Model: p = .30   RN   1-3 → running
                              4 - 9, 0 → not running

    Trial: Read 20 RN (one for each car manufactured 10 years ago)

    Outcome: Record number in 1-3 interval (cars still running)

    Repeat 100 times

    P (3 or less still running) = $\dfrac{1 + 6 + 7}{100}$ = .14

    Decision: Since probability is large, model is acceptable.

8. Model: p = .55   RN   01-55 → Supporters
                              56-99 + 00 → Not supporters

    Trial: Read 100 RN (one for each person polled)

    Outcome: Record (number of supporters) number in 01-55 interval

    Repeat

    P (45 or less supporters) =

    Decision:

9. Model: p = .3   RN   1-3 → Woman
                            4-9 + 0 → Man

    Trial: Read 12 RN, one for each juror

    Outcome: Record number in 1-3 interval (women)

    Repeat

    P (1 or less woman) =

    Decision:

Section 5.6

1. P (8 or more) $= \dfrac{5}{50}$ or .10

    Decision: Not unlikely, by our definition; so no evidence that new method is different from old.

2. Model: Form 1 group using all 17 weights. Write weights on cards.

    Trial: Select 9 for group I

    Outcome: Record number greater than median 109*

    Repeat

    P (8 or more having weights over 109)

    Decision:

    *To find median, arrange all weights in numerical order, select the 9th one (since there are 17).

3. A   8, 9, 12, 14, 14, 14, 17
    B   7, 8, 8, 8, 11, 12

        median - 11½
        5 above in group A

    Model: Assume maze run is unrelated to group assignment. Write errors on cards.

    Trial: Deal 7 cards for group A

    Outcome: Record number greater than 11½

    Repeat

    P (5 or more over 11½) =

    Decision:

4. Median is 10;   9 in farm group less than or equal to median

    Model: Assume no diff. Write scores on cards

    Trial: Deal 10 cards for farmers

    Outcome: Record number of farmers with scores of 10 or less

    P (9 or more below or equal to 10) =

    Decision:

Chapter 6   Section 6.1

1. Expected N = 150 (1/6) or 25
    Expected N = 300 (1/6) or 50
    Expected N = 600 (1/6) or 100

2. Answers will differ.

3.
Outcome	Freq.	Rel freq.
1	4	.13
2	7	.23
3	4	.13
4	6	.20
5	8	.26
6	1	.03
	30	

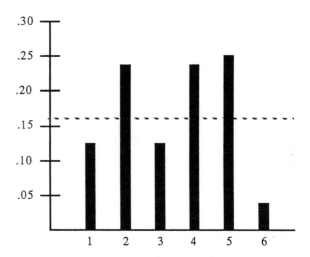

4.

digit	Freq.	Rel freq.
0	1	.02
1	6	.12
2	3	.06
3	2	.04
4	5	.10
5	7	.14
6	2	.04
7	10	.20
8	8	.16
9	0	0
	50	

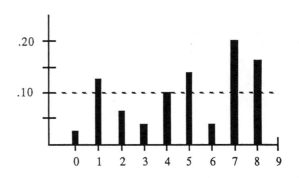

5. Octahedral die

Outcome	Obt
1	10
2	8
3	20
4	14
5	13
6	5
7	18
8	8
	96

Exp = 96/8
    = 12

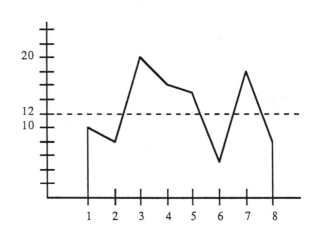

6. Expected = 20/4 = 5
   Largest number is 20
   Smallest number is 0

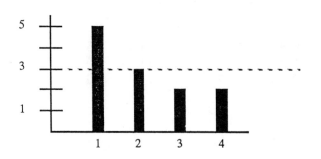

Section 6.2

1.
Outcome	Exp	Obt	Diff	|Diff|
1	15	20	-5	5
2	15	16	-1	1
3	15	11	4	4
4	15	12	3	3
5	15	16	-1	1
6	15	15	0	0
	90	90		

Total diff = 14

2. Answers will vary

(Example)

Outcome	Exp	Obt	Diff	|Diff|
1	15	11	4	4
2	15	17	-2	2
3	15	20	-5	5
4	15	17	-2	2
5	15	14	1	1
6	15	11	4	4
	90	90		

Total diff = 18

3. Probably yes--14 is small enough--Discuss "What is too big."

4. Same idea--yes

5. Answers will vary

Example:

Color	Exp	Obt	Diff
1	3	5	-2
2	3	3	0
3	3	2	1
4	3	2	1
		12	

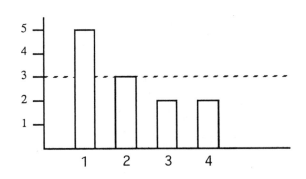

6. Total difference = 4

7. Answers will vary

(Example)

Color	Exp	Freq	Diff
1	5	6	-1
2	5	7	-2
3	5	3	2
4	5	4	1
		20	

Total diff is 6

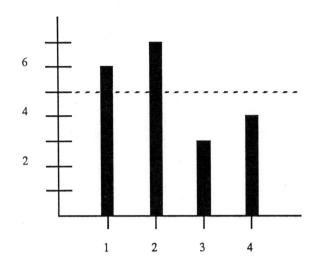

8.

Outcome	Exp	Obt	Diff
Fresh	10	13	-3
F. D.	10	11	-1
Frozen	10	8	2
Canned	10	8	2
		40	

9.

Int	Exp	Obt	Diff
1-1000	5.6	5	.6
1001 - 2000	5.6	0	5.6
2001 - 3000	5.6	3	2.6
3001 - 4000	5.6	1	4.6
4001 - 5000	5.6	7	-1.4
5001 - 6000	5.6	8	-2.4
6001 - 7000	5.6	11	-5.4
7001 - 8000	5.6	7	-1.4
8001 - 9000	5.6	8	-2.4

Total Diff = 26.4

10.

Hour	Exp	Obt	Diff
1	21	19	2
2	21	17	4
3	21	15	6
4	21	24	-3
5	21	20	1
6	21	26	-5
7	21	22	-1
8	21	25	-4

Total Diff = 26

Section 6.3

1. Total Diff = 14 (from 6.2.1)
    $D = 14/15$

2. Total Diff = 8 (from 6.2.8)
    $D = 8/10$

3. | Outcome | Exp | Obt | Diff |
    |---------|-----|-----|------|
    | 1 | 25 | 15 | 10 |
    | 2 | 25 | 32 | - 7 |
    | 3 | 25 | 31 | - 6 |
    | 4 | 25 | 9 | 16 |
    | 5 | 25 | 30 | - 5 |
    | 6 | 25 | 33 | - 8 |

    $D = 52/25$ or 2.08

4. $P (D \geq 1.20) = 4/30$
    $P (D \leq .80) = 15/30$

5. $P (D \geq 1.44) = 2/30$
    $P (D \leq 2.0 \cdot) = 30/30$

6. $P (D = 0) = 0$

7. $D = 2.08$ so
    $P (D \geq 2.08) = 0$

    Since 2.08 is a large difference, it is unlikely that die is fair.

8. $P (D \geq 1.60) = 8/50$
    $P (D \geq 1.87) = 2/50$

9. $P (D \geq 1.40) = 12/50$
    $P (D \leq 2.0) = 49/50$

10. | Color | Exp | Obt | Diff |
    |-------|-----|-----|------|
    | SB | 15 | 17 | - 2 |
    | PP | 15 | 31 | -16 |
    | DP | 15 | 7 | 8 |
    | BO | 15 | 10 | 5 |
    | BB | 15 | 9 | 6 |
    | AA | 15 | $\overline{16}$ | - 1 |
    | | | 90 | |

    $D = 38/15$ or $2.5\bar{3}$

    $P (D \geq 2.53) = 0$; it does not appear they are choosing at random; there is evidence that people do prefer one kind over the others.

11. Answers will vary

12. Answers will vary.

13. Answers will vary.

Section 6.4

1. $P(\chi_2^2 \geq 2.2) = 25/30$
    $P(\chi^2 \leq 1.6) = 5/30$

2. $P(\chi_2^2 \geq 5.0) = 17/30$
    $P(\chi^2 \leq 5.0) = 16/30$ This includes three 5.0's and thirteen less than 5.00

3. $P(\chi_2^2 \geq 7.8) = 4/30$
    $P(\chi^2 \leq 10.0) = 29/30$

4. | Outcome | Exp | Obt | Diff | Diff^2 |
    |---------|-----|-----|------|----------|
    | 1 | 10 | 8 | 2 | 4 |
    | 2 | 10 | 7 | 3 | 9 |
    | 3 | 10 | 13 | - 3 | 9 |
    | 4 | 10 | 11 | - 1 | 1 |
    | 5 | 10 | 15 | - 5 | 25 |
    | 6 | 10 | 6 | 4 | 16 |
    | | | 60 | | |

    $D = (18)/10$ or 1.8
    $\chi^2 = (64)/10$ or 6.4

5. $P(\chi^2 \geq 6.4) = 10/30$ or $.33$, so it appears die is fair.

6. $\chi^2 = (4 + 256 + 64 + 25 + 36 + 1)/15$
    $= (386)/15$ or 25.73

    $P(\chi^2 \geq 25.73) = 0$, so random selection seems unlikely; there appears to be a preference.

7. Traffic Tickets

Location	Exp	Obt	Diff	Diff^2
A	15	12	3	9
B	15	7	8	64
C	15	21	- 6	36
D	15	15	0	0
E	15	11	4	16
F	15	24	- 9	81
		90		

    $\chi^2 = 1/15\ (206)$ or 13.73

    $P(\chi^2 \geq 13.73) = 0$, so ticket distribution is not equally likely at all locations.

8. Answers will differ.

9. $D = (2+4+0+2)/10$ or $8/10$ or $.8$

10. 4-sided die

	Exp	Obt	Diff	Diff^2
1	10	12	- 2	4
2	10	7	3	9
3	10	14	- 4	16
4	10	7	3	9
		40		

$\chi^2 = 1/10 \ (38)$ or 3.8

11. $P(\chi^2 \geq 3) = .40$
It appears to be about 2/5 of the total area.

12. $P(\chi_2^2 > 2.0) = 31/50$
$P(\chi^2 \leq 3.0) = 30/50$

13. $P(\chi_2^2 > 3.0) = 21/50$
$P(\chi^2 \leq 6.2) = 48/50$

14. $P(\chi_2^2 > 5.0) = 6/50$
$P(\chi^2 \leq 0.6) = 7/50$

15. $P(\chi_2^2 > 8.0) = 1/50$
$P(\chi^2 \leq 3.6) = 36/50$

16. Orange Juice Preference

Kind	Exp	Obt	Diff	Diff^2
Fresh	10	13	-3	9
Freeze-dried	10	11	-1	1
Frozen	10	8	2	4
Canned	10	8	2	4
		40		

$\chi^2 = (18)/10$ or 1.8
$P(\chi_2^2 \geq 1.8) = 33/50$

No convincing evidence. These results occur frequently given assumption of "no preference."

Section 6.5

1. $P(\chi_2^2 \geq 13.5) = 5/50$ or .10
$P(\chi^2 \geq 18.0) = 1/50$ or .02

2. $P(\chi_2^2 \leq 5.1) = 20/50$ or .40
$P(\chi^2 \leq 3.0) = 5/50$ or .10

3. $P(\chi_2^2 \geq 6.0) = 38/50$ or .76
$P(\chi^2 \leq 4.8) = 8/50$ or .16

4. $P(\chi_2^2 \geq 15.2) = 3/50$ or .06
$P(\chi^2 \leq 4.4) = 7/50$ or .14

5. 8-sided Die   --   168 times

	Exp	Ob	Diff	Diff^2
1	21	29	- 8	64
2	21	22	- 1	1
3	21	18	3	9
4	21	19	2	4
5	21	20	1	1
6	21	23	- 2	4
7	21	12	9	81
8	21	25	- 4	16
		168		

$\chi^2 = (180)/21$ or 8.57

$P(\chi^2 \geq 8.6) = 16/50$ or .32

Not unlikely--so die seems fair (not loaded)

6. Favorite Number

	Exp	Obt	Diff	Diff^2
0	10	5	5	25
1	10	3	7	49
2	10	11	-1	1
3	10	10	0	0
4	10	19	-9	81
5	10	9	1	1
6	10	11	-1	1
7	10	15	-5	25
8	10	13	-3	9
9	10	4	6	36
		100		

$\chi^2 = (228)/10$ or 22.8

$P(\chi^2 \geq 22.8) = 0$, so it is unlikely that no preference exists. It seems that there are favorite numbers.

7. Tie Color

	Exp	Obt	Diff	Diff^2
Amber	10	7	3	9
Blue	10	9	1	1
Orange	10	14	-4	16
Maroon	10	10	0	0
		40		

$\chi^2 = 1/10 (26)$ or 2.6

$\underline{P}(\chi^2 \geq 2.6) = 21/50$ or .42, so colors appear to be preferred equally.

8.   Telephone digits

	Exp	Obt	Diff	Diff^2
0	10	3	7	49
1	10	8	2	4
2	10	15	-5	25
3	10	14	-4	16
4	10	10	0	0
5	10	7	3	9
6	10	8	2	4
7	10	9	1	1
8	10	11	-1	1
9	10	15	-5	25
		$\overline{100}$		

$\chi^2 = (134)/10$ or 13.4

$P(\chi^2 \geq 13.4) = 3/50$ or $.06$

Unlikely; so, reject theory that outcomes are equally likely.   This phone book page does not appear to be a good source of random numbers.

Section 6.6

1. $P(\chi^2_3 \geq 5.7) = 4/50$

$P(\chi^2_3 \geq 9.9) = 2/50$

2. $P(\chi^2_5 \geq 6.0) = 12/50$

$P(\chi^2_5 \geq 8.0) = 6/50$

3. $P(\chi^2_5 \geq 11.2) = 2/50$

$P(\chi^2_5 \geq 9.6) = 3/50$

4. $P(\chi^2_9 \geq 10.0) = 17/50$

$P(\chi^2_9 \geq 15.0) = 4/50$

5.   6 sided die

Outcome	Exp	Obt	Diff	Diff^2
1	15	17	-2	4
2	15	13	2	4
3	15	17	-2	4
4	15	10	5	25
5	15	16	-1	1
6	15	17	-2	4
		$\overline{90}$		

(a) $\chi^2 = (42)/15 = 2.8$

(b)   5 df (one less than number of outcomes)

(c) $P(\chi_5^2 \geq 2.8) = 41/50$

(d) It seems to be a fair die. Results are consistent with theory that outcomes are equally likely.

6. Key Problem -- 8 hours of shift, so df = 7

7. Telephone numbers for Random Digits; 9 df since 10 possible digits (outcomes)

8. 20 artists -- 19 df -- one less than number of outcomes.

Section 6.7

1. $P(\chi_5^2 \geq 4.4) = 25/50$ or .5 $p(\chi_5^2 \geq 4.4) \doteq .50$

2. $P(\chi_5^2 \geq 7.4) = 8/50$ or .16 $p(\chi_5^2 \geq 7.4) \doteq .20$

3. $P(\chi_5^2 \geq 9.2) = 3/50$ or .06 $p(\chi_5^2 \geq 9.2) \doteq .10$

4. $P(\chi_5^2 \geq 11.2) = 2/50$ or .04 $p(\chi_5^2 \geq 11.2) \doteq .05$

5. $P(\chi_3^2 \geq 4.6) = 6/50$ or .12 $p(\chi_3^2 \geq 4.6) \doteq .20$

6. $P(\chi_3^2 \geq 6.5) = 3/50$ or .06 $p(\chi_3^2 \geq 6.5) \doteq .10$

7. (a) $p(\chi_4^2 \geq 9.5) = .05$

    (b) $p(\chi_4^2 \geq 13.3) = .01$

8. (a) $p(\chi_7^2 \geq 12.0) = .10$

    (b) $p(\chi_7^2 \geq 14.1) = .05$

9. (a) $p(\chi_{10}^2 \geq 12.0) = .20$ (.32 by interpolation)

    (b) $p(\chi_{10}^2 \geq 20.0) = .05$ (.04 by interpolation)

10. (a) $p(\chi_{20}^2 \geq 18.0) = .50$ (.46 by interpolation)

    (b) $p(\chi_{20}^2 \geq 40.0) = .01$ (.0069 by interpolation)

11.

	Exp	Obt	Diff	Diff^2
1	16	26	-10	100
2	16	7	9	81
3	16	17	- 1	1
4	16	19	- 3	9
5	16	14	2	4
6	16	13	3	9
		96		

$\chi^2 = (204)/16 = 12.75$

$p(\chi_5^2 \geq 12.75) = .05$

Unlikely--so, conclude die is not fair.

12.

	Exp	Obt	Diff	Diff^2
0	38.0	0	38	1444
1	38.0	12	26	676
2	38.0	27	11	121
3	38.0	56	-18	324
4	38.0	37	1	1
5	38.0	40	- 2	4
6	38.0	58	-20	400
7	38.0	103	-65	4225
8	38.0	31	7	49
9	38.0	16	22	484

$\chi^2 = 7728/38$

$p \ (\chi_9^2 \geq 203.368) = 0$

Very unlikely. Conclude students do prefer some numbers.

13. Stock

	Exp	Obt	Diff	D^2
0	39.6	60	-20.4	416.16
1/8	39.6	30	9.6	92.6
2/8	39.6	29	10.6	112.36
3/8	39.6	27	12.6	158.76
4/8	39.6	47	- 7.4	54.76
5/8	39.6	49	- 9.4	88.36
6/8	39.6	37	2.6	6.76
7/8	39.6	38	1.6	2.56
		317		

$\chi_7^2 = 931.88/39.6$

$p \ (\chi_7^2 \geq 22.53) = .0001$

Reject theory that all are equally likely, so some fractions appear to be more common than others.

14. Sales slips

	Exp	Obt	Diff	Diff^2
0	17.4	11	6.4	40.96
1	17.4	10	7.4	54.76
2	17.4	10	7.4	54.76
3	17.4	34	-16.6	275.56
4	17.4	7	10.4	108.16
5	17.4	25	- 7.6	57.76
6	17.4	4	13.4	179.56
7	17.4	18	- .6	.36
8	17.4	6	11.4	129.96
9	17.4	49	-31.6	998.56
		174		

$\chi_9^2 = 1900.4/17.4$ or 109.21

$p \ (\chi_9^2 > 109.21) = .0001$

So it is unlikely that final digits are equally likely. Some digits occur more than others.

Chapter 7   Section 7.1

1. (a) time spent watching TV (in hours) and quality of school work (grades, written evaluations)

    (b) amount of expansion and increase in temperature

    (c) vaccinated (yes/no) and get polio (yes/no)

    (d) amount of air (in pounds) and the mileage rate (miles per gallon)

2. Time spent watching TV (in hours per week) and aggressive behavior (fights, hitting, other activities?)

3. <u>Time</u> devoted to active sports and <u>age</u>. As age increases, time decreases.

4. Time (months) following gas shortage:
        and vehicular accident deaths;
        and chronic lung deaths;
        and cardiovascular disease deaths

5. (a) approximately   650,000 in 1967
         approximately 1,100,000 in 1982

    (b) Year and number of stolen motor vehicles

    (c) More motor vehicles are stolen each year

6. (a) Income bracket and percentage favoring cuts in federal aid for college students

    (b) The higher the income, the higher the percentage of those favoring cuts

7. Answers will vary.

                            Section 7.2

1. $S = 3R$ $Y = 1/2X$ $X = 2W + 2$

2. $M = N + 1$ $Y = X - 3$ $W = 2X + 1/2$

N	M		X	Y		X	W
0	1		10	7		0	1/2
1	2		6	3		1	2 1/2
3	4		5	2		1.25	3
7	8		3	0		2	4 1/2
10	11		1	-2		3	6 1/2

3. $Y = 3.3X + 21.9$

    (a) X = 5   Y = 38.4
    (b) X = 2.1   Y = 28.83
    (c) X = 10   Y = 54.9

4.

Adult dose	Clark's Rule $C = 75/100A$		Child's dose
1 t	75/150 (1)	or	1/2 t
2 t	75/150 (2)	or	1 t
3 t	75/150 (3)	or	1 1/2 t

5.   (a)   C = 50/150 A or 1/3 A   (b)   C = 100/150 A or 2/3 A

A	C		A	C
1 t	1/3		1 t	2/3
2 t	2/3		2 t	4/3
3 t	3/3 or 1		3 t	6/3 or 2

6. $t = 1/4\ w + 2.5$

w	rule	t
4	1 + 2.5	3.5
8	2 + 2.5	4.5
16	4 + 2.5	6.5
18	4.5 + 2.5	7.0
20	5 + 2.5	7.5

7. $v = 10\ t + 50$

t	rule	v
0	0 + 50	50
1	10 + 50	60
5	50 + 50	100
10	100 + 50	150
25	250 + 50	300

8. $s = 16\ t^2$

    (a) $1600 = 16t^2$

          $100 = t^2$
           $10 = t$ 10 seconds

    (b) $s = 16(5)^2$
          $s = 16.25$
          $s = 400$ 400 feet

9. $N = 100 - 2\ A$

    (a) N = 100 - 40
          = 60 pushups for 20 years

(b) N = 100 - 90
        = 10 pushups for 45 years

Section 7.3

1.   Y = X + 2

X	Y
-2	0
-1	1
1	3
2	4
5	7

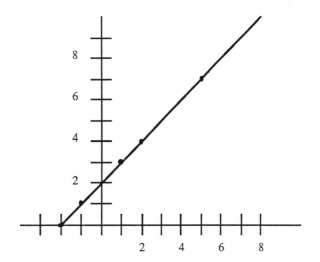

2.   C = 5/9 (F - 32)

F	C
212	100
32	0
100	37.7
0	- 17.7
- 18	- 27.7
68	20

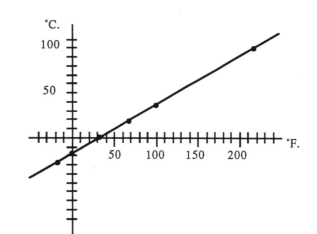

3.

	Fuel gauge	Gallons Needed
(a)	3/4	5
(b)	1/2	10
(c)	1/4	15
(d)	1/8	17.5

4.

	Fuel gauge	Miles
(a)	1/2	100
(b)	3/8	75
(c)	1/4	50
(d)	1/8	25

5.

H	W = 3H − 90	W
43	3(43) − 90	39
50	3(50) − 90	60
55	3(55) − 90	75
60	3(60) − 90	90

6.

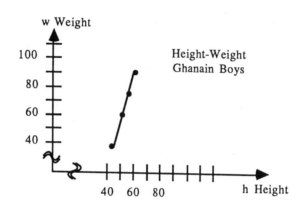

Height-Weight
Ghanain Boys

7.   V = 10T + 30

T		V
0	10(0) + 30	30
5	10(5) + 30	80
10	10(10) + 30	130
15	10(15) + 30	180
20	10(20) + 30	230

(meters)

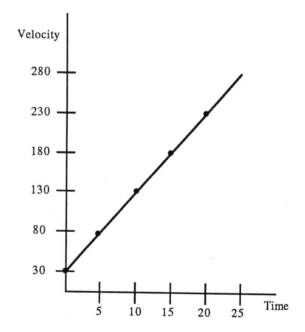

8.

P	R
30	9
40	12
50	15
60	18
70	21
80	24
90	27

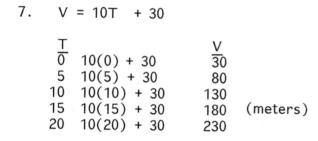

R = P - (P/10).7   OR

P = R/3.$\bar{3}$ OR

R = .3 P

Verbal descriptions also can be interesting.

Section 7.4

1. (a) 3   (b) 2   (c) 5   (d) 1/2
    (e) 1/4   (f) 1   (g) 1   (h) 2
    (i) -3   (j) -4   (k) -1/2

2. (a) 2   (b) 3   (c) -3   (d) 6
    (e) -1   (f) 1   (g) 0   (h) 0
    (i) 2   (j) -3   (k) 0

3.

	Y-form	slope	Y-int
(a)	Y = 2X + 6	2	6
(b)	Y = 3X + 4	3	4
(c)	Y = -3X - 9	-3	-9
(d)	Y = -1/2X + 2	-1/2	2
(e)	Y = 6X + 9	6	9
(f)	Y = 1/2X	1/2	0
(g)	Y = X + 5	1	5
(h)	Y = 2X + 7	2	7
(i)	Y = -2/5X + 2	-2/5	2
(j)	Y = -1/2X + 12	-1/2	12
(k)	Y = 1/2X + 2	1/2	2

4. (a) Y = 3X + 2   (b) Y = 5X - 3

X	Y		X	Y
-1	-1		-1	-8
0	2		0	-3
1	5		1	2
2	8		2	7
3	11		3	12
4	14		4	17
5	17		5	22

(c)   Y = X

X	Y
-1	-1
0	0
1	1
2	2
3	3
4	4
5	5

(d)   Y = -1/2X

X	Y
-1	1/2
0	0
1	-1/2
2	-1
3	-3/2
4	-2
5	-5/2

5.

a)
y=3x+2

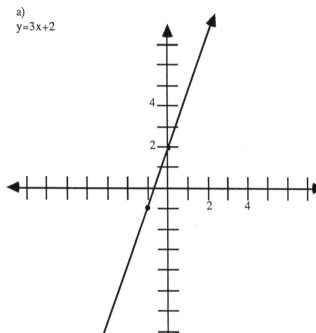

b)
y=5x-3

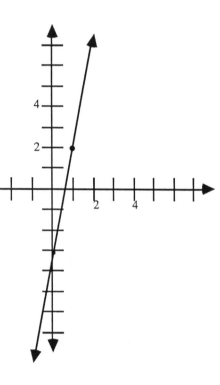

c)
y=x

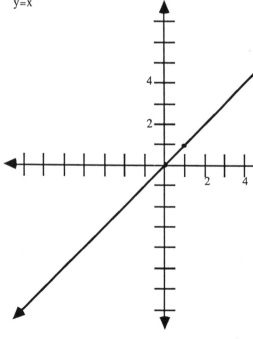

d)
y=-1/2 x

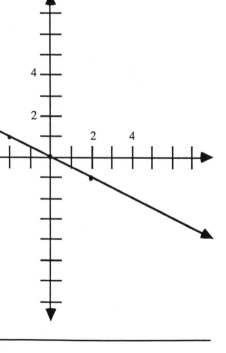

6.

	slope	Y-int
(a)	3	2
(b)	5	-3
(c)	1	0
(d)	-1/2	0

7. (a)   Y = 2 (X + 3)
       OR   Y = 2X + 6

X	Y
-2	2
-1	4
0	6
1	8
2	10
3	12
4	14
5	16

(b)   Y = -1/2 (X - 4)
     OR   Y = -1/2X + 2

X	Y
-2	3
-1	2 1/2
0	2
1	1 1/2
2	1
3	1/2
4	0
5	-1/2

(c)   Y - X = 5
     Y = X + 5

X	Y
-2	3
-1	4
0	5
1	6
2	7
3	8
4	9
5	10

(d)   X = 2Y
     Y = 1/2 X

X	Y
-2	-1
-1	-1/2
0	0
1	1/2
2	1
3	3/2
4	2
5	5/2

8.

a)
y=2x+6

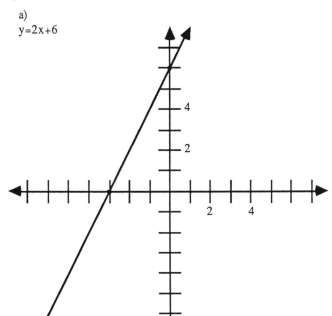

b)
y=-1/2 x+2

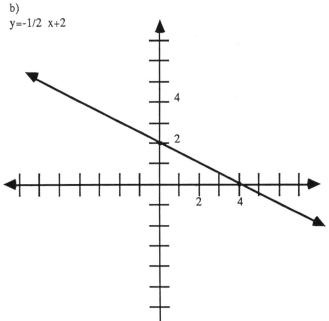

c)
y=x+5

d)
y=1/2 x

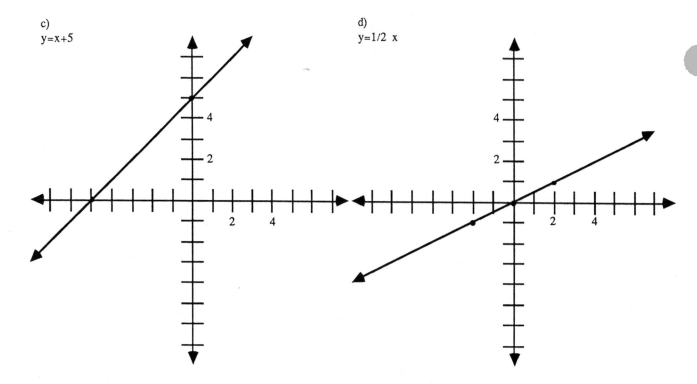

9. (a) m = 2; C = 6
    (b) m = -1/2; C = 2
    (c) m = 1; C = 5
    (d) m = 1/2; C = 0

10. (a) Y = 2X + 1
     (b) Y = -2X + 3
     (c) Y = 1/4X + 3
     (d) Y = 3X
     (e) Y = X + 1
     (f) Y = X
     (g) Y = 2

11. (a) m = 1   C = 2   Y = 1X + 2 = X + 2
     (b) m = 1/3   C = 0   Y = 1/3X + 0 = 1/3X
     (c) m = -3/2   C = 5½   Y = -3/2X + 5½

Section 7.5

1.

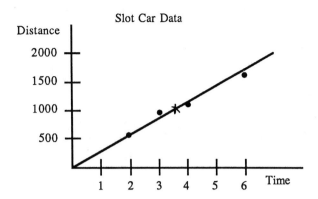

$\bar{X}$ = 3.75

$\bar{Y}$ = 975

2.   Y' = 260X + 0

OR   Y' = 250X + 0

(Answers will vary)

3.

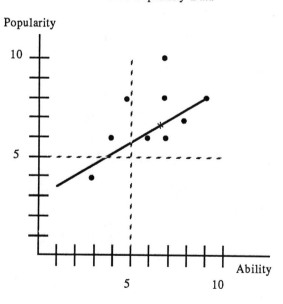

$\bar{X}$ = 6.4

$\bar{Y}$ = 6.9

Y' = .75X + 2
Answers will
vary

4.

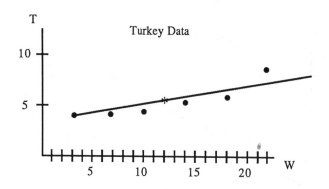

$\bar{W}$ = 12.6

$\bar{T}$ = 5.5

   T' = .4W   Answers will vary

   T is time, W is weight, answer is one of many. Is problem
   with variables or formula?

5.

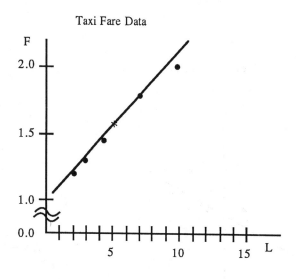

$\bar{F}$ = 1.53

$\bar{D}$ = 5.3

F = .10D + 1.1

Answers will vary

6.   Mice Data

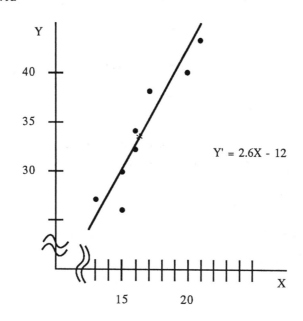

$Y' = 2.6X - 12$

(15,30)

$$\bar{X} = \frac{133}{8} \text{ or } 16.625$$

$$\bar{Y} = \frac{270}{8} \text{ or } 33.75$$

$$m = \frac{3.75}{1.625} \text{ or } 2.3 \text{ using } (15,30) \text{ \& } (\bar{X}, \bar{Y})$$

$Y' = 2.3X + C \qquad\qquad C = -4.5$

$Y' = 2.3X - 4.5$

7.   High School/College Math Data

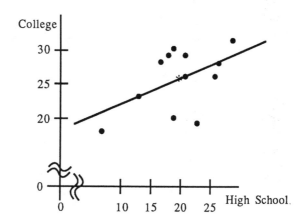

$\bar{X}$ = 19.9   m = 2/7 or .3 using $(\bar{X}, \bar{Y})$ & (13,23)

$\bar{Y}$ = 25.5   Y' = 2/7X + 19

C = 19   Answers will differ

Section 7.6

1. Slot Car Data   All answers will differ.   Examples
   $\bar{X}$ = 3.75   (time)   are given.

   $\bar{Y}$ = 975   (distance)

   Eq. Y' = 260X
        Y' = 200X + 225
        Y' = 300X - 150

2. Athlete's Popularity Data
   $\bar{X}$ = 6.4

   $\bar{Y}$ = 6.9

   Eq.
   Y' = .57 X + 3.7
   Y' = 2X - 5.9
   Y' = 3X - 12.3
   Y' = X + .5

3. Turkey Data
   $\bar{W}$ = 12.6

   $\bar{F}$ = 5.4   Y' = .3X + 1.7

4. Slot Car Data
   Y' = 260X

X	Y	Y'	Y-Y'
2	520	520	0
3	770	780	-10
4	1050	1040	10
6	1560	1560	0

mean error = 20/4 <u>or</u> 5

Y' = 200X + 225

X	Y	Y'	Y'-Y'
2	520	625	-105
3	770	825	- 55
4	1050	1025	25
6	1560	1425	135

mean error (320)/4 <u>or</u> 80

$Y' = 300X - 150$

X	Y	Y'	Y-Y'
2	520	450	70
3	770	750	20
4	1050	1050	0
6	1560	1650	-90

mean error = $(180)/4 = 45$

5. Athlete's Popularity

Abil	Pop	Eq $Y' = .57X + 3.7$	
X	Y	Y'	Y-Y'
8	7	8.26	-1.26
4	5	5.98	- .98
7	8	7.69	.31
7	6	7.69	-1.69
3	4	5.41	-1.41
5	8	6.55	1.45
9	8	8.83	- .83
7	10	7.69	2.31
6	6	7.12	-1.12
8	7	8.26	-1.26

mean error = $(12.62)/10$ or 1.262

6. Turkey Data $T' = .3W + 1.7$

W	T	T'	T-T'
5	3.5	3.2	-.3
7	4.0	3.8	.2
10	4.5	4.7	.2
14	5.5	5.9	.4
18	6.75	7.1	.35
22	8.5	8.3	-.2

mean error = $(1.65)/6$
= $.275$

7. Birmingham boys
       $Y' = 2X - 40.2$

X	Y	Y'	Y-Y'
43	42	45.8	-3.8
46	46	51.8	-5.8
48	51	55.8	-4.8
50	57	59.8	-2.8
52	62	63.8	-1.8
54	68	67.8	.2
55	73	69.8	3.2
58	82	75.8	6.2
59	88	77.8	10.2

mean error = $(38.8)/9$ or 4.3
Best line is $Y' = 3.08X - 95.9$
since its error is 1.75

8. Cricket Data   Y' = 3.2X + 27

X	Y	Y'	Y-Y'
20	89	91.0	-2
16	72	78.2	-6.2
20	93	91.0	2.
18	84	84.6	- .6
17	81	81.4	- .4
16	75	78.2	-3.2
15	70	75.0	-5.0
17	82	81.4	.6
15	69	75.0	-6.0
16	83	78.2	4.8
15	80	75.0	5.0
17	83	81.4	1.6
16	81	78.2	2.8
17	84	81.4	2.6
14	76	71.8	4.2

Mean error = (47)/15
= 3.13

9. Mice Data
$\bar{X}$ = 16.625

$\bar{Y}$ = 33.75

Eq	Error
Y' = 2X + .5	1.5
Y' = 2.1X − 1.2	1.4
Y' = 2.2X − 2.8	1.6

10. High School/College Math Data
$\bar{X}$ = 19.91$\bar{6}$

$\bar{Y}$ = 25.5

Eq	Error
Y' = .4X + 17.5	2.91
Y' = X + 5.6	4.58
Y' = .3X + 19.5	3.0

Section 7.7

1.

X	Y	Y' = 4X + 12	Y'	Y - Y'
14	76	4(14) + 12	68	8
15	80	4(15) + 12	72	8
15	69	4(15) + 12	72	-3
15	70	4(15) + 12	72	-2
16	72	4(16) + 12	76	-4

16	75	4(16) + 12	76	-1
16	81	4(16) + 12	76	5
16	83	4(16) + 12	76	7
17	81	4(17) + 12	80	1
17	82	4(17) + 12	80	2
17	83	4(17) + 12	80	3
17	84	4(17) + 12	80	4
18	84	4(18) + 12	84	0
20	89	4(20) + 12	92	-3
20	93	4(20) + 12	92	1

2. Wallpaper data

30	9
40	12
50	15
60	18
70	21
80	24
90	27

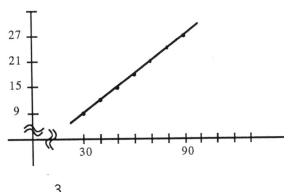

$$Y' = \frac{3}{10} X$$

Using median points (40,12) and (80,24),

$$m = \frac{80-40}{24-12} \text{ or } \frac{40}{12} \text{ or } \frac{10}{3}$$

3.

diam	cir
3	10
4.5	18
5	16
6.8	21
10	32.3
10.8	32.5
13	40

Using median points
(4.5, 16) and (10.8, 32.5)

$$m = \frac{32.5-16}{10.8-4.5} = \frac{16.5}{6.3}$$

$m = 2.6$ so $16 = 2.6(4.5) + C$
                    $4.3 = C$

$Y' = 2.6X + 4.3$

4.

X	Y	Y' = 3X - 92	error
43	42	37	5
46	46	46	0
48	51	52	-1
50	57	58	-1
52	62	64	-2
54	68	70	-2
55	73	73	0
58	82	82	0
59	88	85	3

$$m = \frac{82-46}{58-46} = 3$$

$$ME = 14/9 \text{ or } 1.\bar{5}$$

$46 = 3 (46) + C$
$-92 = C$
$Y' = 3X - 92$

This rule is better;
The mean error of 1.5
is smaller than mean error
obtained with rule $Y' = 3.08 - 95.9$

5. High School/College Math Data
    Arranged in order of High School Exam

X	Y	Y' = .4X + 17.8
7	18	20.6
13	23	23.0
17	27	24.6
18	29	25.0
19	20	25.4
19	30	25.4
21	26	26.2
21	29	26.2
23	19	27.0
26	26	28.2
27	28	28.6
28	31	29.0

$$m = \frac{28-23}{27-13}$$

$$= 5/14 \text{ or } .357$$

$23 = .4(13) + C$
$17.8 = C$

so equation is $Y' = .4X + 17.8$

Chapter 8   Section 8.1

1. Mice data see 7.5.6 for graph
    Mean data pt (16.625, 33.75)

2. Mice data
    ME = Sum Y - Y'/8
        = 12/8 or 1.5

3. Weight loss data
    $Y' = 1.5X + C$ mean data pt (8.3, 19)

    $19 = 1.5 (8.3) + C$
    $19 = 12.5 + C$
    $6.5 = C$

    so $Y' = 1.5X + 6.5$

4. Weight loss

    $$ME = \frac{46}{9} \text{ or } 5.1$$

5. High school/college math data
   See 7.5.7 for graph using mean data point (19.1, 25.5)
   Y' = .3X + 19.5   is equation if m = .3
   or   Y' = .5X + 15.5   is equation if m = .5
   Other answers possible.

6. High school/college math data
   Y' = .4X + 17.7

X	Y	Y'	Y-Y'
13	23	22.9	.1
27	23	28.5	- .5
18	29	24.9	4.1
17	27	24.5	2.5
21	29	26.1	2.9
16	26	24.1	1.9
28	31	28.9	2.1
19	20	25.3	-5.3
23	19	26.9	7.9
7	18	20.5	-2.5
21	26	26.1	- .1
19	30	25.3	4.7

$$ME = \frac{34.6}{12} = 2.88$$

7. Cricket data
   Y' = 4X + 12

X	Y	Y'	Y-Y'
20	89	92	-3
16	72	76	-4
20	93	92	1
18	84	84	0
17	81	80	1
16	75	76	-1
15	70	72	-2
17	82	80	2
15	69	72	-3
16	83	76	7
15	80	72	8
17	83	80	3
16	81	72	9
17	84	80	4
14	76	68	8

$$ME = \frac{56}{15} \text{ or } 3.73$$

Section 8.2

1. Mice data
   Y' = X + 17.13

   $$ME = \frac{25}{8} \text{ or } 3.125$$

2. Mice data
   Y' = 2X + .5
   ME = 1.5

   so this equation is better - smaller error.

3. Cricket data
   Y' = 3X + 30.3
   ME = 46.67/15 = 3.1

4. Weight loss data
   $$Y' = 1.9\ X + 3.16$$

   ME = $\frac{1}{9}$ (44.93)/9 or 4.99

5. Spelling - reading data
   $$Y' = 2X - 3.8$$

X	Y	Y'
12	20	20.2
10	12	16.2
10	18	16.2
8	10	12.2
7	12	10.2
6	14	8.2
6	6	8.2
5	7	6.2
4	3	4.2
2	1	.2

6. Reading/spelling data
   Y' = 2.3X - 5.8
   ME = (24)/10
      = 2.4

7. Mice data
   best slope m = 2; mean data point is (16.625, 33.75);
   33.75 = 2(16.625) + C
   .5 = C
   Eq is Y' = 2X + .5

8. Mice   Y' = 2X + .5
   a) 15 cm   Y' = 2(15) + .5
                 Y' = 30.5
   b) 18 cm   Y' = 2(18) + .5
                 Y' = 36.5
   c) 20 cm   Y' = 2(20) + .5
                 Y' = 40.5

9. Cricket data
   best slope m = 2.8; mean data point is (16.6, 80.1);

   80.1 = 2.8(16.6) + C
   80.1 = 46.48 + C
   33.6 = C
   Eq is Y' = 2.8X + 33.6

10. Cricket data
     $Y' = 2.8X + 33.6$

 (a) if $X = 16$ $Y' = 2.8(16) + 33.6$
                      $Y' = 44.8 + 33.6$
                      $Y' = 78.4$

 (b) if $X = 20$ $Y' = 2.8(20) + 33.6$
                      $Y' = 56 + 33.6$
                      $Y' = 89.6$

 (c) if $X = 24$ $Y' = 2.8(24) + 33.6$
                      $Y' = 67.2$
                      $Y' = 100.8$

11. Math Interest/ability data

     Using bottom and top 3 pts

     * medians (23, 19) and (33, 22)

     $m = 3/10$ or $.3$

     $19 = .3 (23) + C$
     $19 = 6.9 + C$
     $12.1 = C$

     so $Y' = .3X + 12.1$

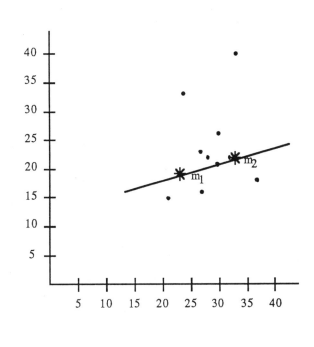

X	Y	Y'	Y-Y'
27	23	20.2	2.8
33	40	22.0	18.0
32	22	21.7	0.3
30	21	21.1	- .1
27	16	20.2	-4.2
21	15	18.4	-3.4
37	18	23.2	-5.2
23	24	19.0	5.0
30	26	21.1	4.9
28	22	20.5	1.5
24	33	19.3	13.7

     mean error = 59.1/11 or 5.37

Section 8.3

1. Mice data
    $Y' = 1.5X + 8.8$

    $MSE = \dfrac{55.9688}{8}$ or 7.00

2. Mice data
    Y' = 1.9X + 2.16

    MSE = $\frac{37.9988}{8}$ or 4.75

3. (b) is better; MSE is smaller.

4. Cricket data
    Y' = 4X + 13.7

    MSE = $\frac{226.89}{15}$ or 15.126

5. Spelling/reading data
    Y' = X + 3.3

    MSE = $\frac{122.1}{10}$ = 12.21

6. Spelling/reading data
    Y' = 1.5X - .2

$(Y-Y')^2$
4.84
7.84
10.24
3.24
2.89
27.04
7.84
.09
7.84
3.24

    MSE = (75.10)/10 or 7.51

7. a is better since MSE is smaller

8. Spelling/reading data
    Slope of best fitting line is m = 1.8. Mean data point is (7, 10.3) so

    10.3 = 1.8(7) + C
    -2.3 = C
        Y' = 1.8X -2.3

9. Weight loss data
    Y' = 1.5X + 6.5

    MSE = $\frac{305.50}{9}$ or 33.94

10. Weight loss data
    Slope of best fitting line is m = 1.4. Mean data point is (8.3, 19.0), so

    $$19.0 = 1.4(8.3) + C$$
    $$19.0 = 11.62 + C$$
    $$7.4 = C$$
    $$Y' = 1.4X + 7.4$$

11. Cricket data
    Slope is 3.2 for mean square best fitting line; slope is 2 when using mean error; error variance is 13.4265

12. Mice data
    m is 2.1   Mean data point (16.625, 33.75)

    $$33.75 = 2.1(16.625) + C$$
    $$33.75 = 34.91 + C$$

    $$-1.16 = C$$
    $$Y' = 2.1X - 1.16$$

13. Mice data

	X	Y'
$Y' = 2.1X - 1.16$	18	36.64
	22	45.04
	26	53.44
$Y' = 2.2X - 2.83$	18	36.77
	22	45.57
	26	54.37
$Y' = 2.15X - 1.99$	18	36.71
	22	45.31
	26	53.91

Section 8.4

1. Math anxiety data
   $$Y' = -.6X + C \qquad (41.65, 20.55)$$

   $$20.55 = -.6(41.65) + C$$
   $$45.54 = C$$
   $$Y' = -.6X + 45.54$$

2. Math anxiety data
   $$Y' = -.7X + 54.6$$

X	Y	Y'	Y-Y'
42	20	24.36	- 4.36
15	37	43.80	- 6.80
34	40	30.12	9.88
53	14	16.44	- 2.44
36	30	28.68	1.32
23	5	38.04	-33.04
40	9	25.80	-16.80
34	35	30.12	4.88
50	13	18.60	- 5.60
62	7	9.96	- 2.96
49	21	19.32	1.68
46	18	21.48	- 3.48
20	33	40.20	- 7.20
60	9	11.40	- 2.40
35	32	11.40	2.60
30	31	33.00	- 2.00
44	24	22.92	1.08
59	7	12.12	- 5.12
63	12	9.24	2.76
38	14	27.24	-13.24

$$ME = 129.64/20$$
$$= 6.482$$

3. Science Interest/exam data

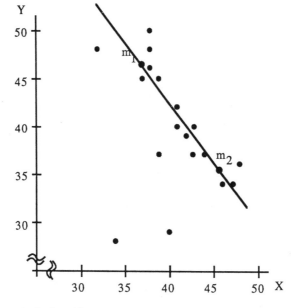

medians (37, 47) and (46.36) using 7, 6, 7 in groups

$$m = \frac{47 - 36}{37-46} = \frac{11}{-9} \text{ or } -1.2$$

$$47 = -1.2 \ (37) + C$$

$$47 = -44.4 + C$$

$$91.4 = C \quad \text{so} \quad \text{Eq } Y' = -1.2X + 91.4$$

4. Science Interest/exam data
    Y' = -X +81   (pts in X order)

X	Y	Y'	Y-Y'	$(Y-Y')^2$
32	48	49	-1	1
33	47	48	-1	1
34	33	47	-14	196
37	45	44	1	1
38	50	43	7	49
38	48	43	5	25
38	46	43	3	9
39	37	42	-5	25
39	45	42	3	9
40	34	41	-7	49
41	40	40	0	0
41	42	40	2	4
42	39	39	0	0
43	37	38	-1	1
43	40	38	2	4
44	37	37	0	0
46	34	35	-1	1
47	34	34	0	0
47	34	34	0	0
48	36	33	3	9

$ME = \dfrac{384}{20}$ or 19.2

5. Answers will differ: $\bar{X}$ = 40.5; $\bar{Y}$ = 40.3.   Theoretical
    "best" m is -.77, so eq is Y' = -.77X + 71 and MSE is 18.
    (for median fit, MSE is 28)

6. Push ups

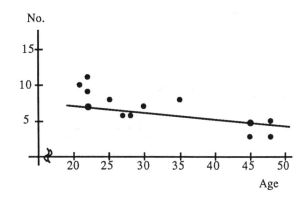

    medians using 5, 2, 5 in the groups are

    (22,9)   (38,5); $m = \dfrac{4}{-16}$ = -.25

    9 = -.25(22) + C   Y' = -.25X + 14.5
    14.5 = C

7. $Y' = - X + 40$

X	Y	Y'	Y-Y'	$(Y-Y')^2$
21	10	19	- 9	81
25	8	15	- 7	48
22	11	18	- 7	49
28	6	12	- 6	36
30	7	10	- 3	9
38	15	2	13	169
22	9	18	- 9	81
27	6	13	- 7	49
44	4	-4	8	64
48	3	-8	11	121
35	8	5	3	9
48	5	-8	13	169

ME = 96/12 or 8
MSE = 886/12 or 73.8

8.   Best slope is -.2;   mean data pt (32.3, 7.6)

7.6 = -.2(32.3) + C
7.6 = -6.46 + C
14.06 = C

$Y' = -.2X + 14.1$

9.   Infant mortality data

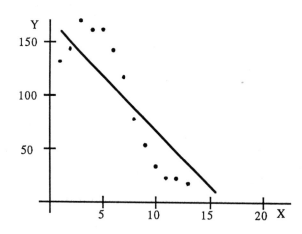

10. Infant mortality data
     Y' = -14X + 194

X	Y	Y'	Y-Y'
1	131	180	49
2	143	166	23
3	170	152	18
4	161	138	23
5	163	124	39
6	41	110	31
7	116	96	20
8	78	82	4
9	54	68	14
10	34	54	20
11	23	40	17
12	22	26	4
13	17	12	5

$ME = \frac{267}{13}$ or 20.53

for X = 14   Y = -14(14) + 194
                      = -2

for X = 15   Y = -14(15) + 194
                      = -16

Not good for predicting future!

11. Track data using 5, 2, 5 arrangement of points gives medians
     (3, 290) and (10, 276)

$m = \frac{14}{-7}$ or -2

290 = -2(3) + C
296 = C   so Y' = -2X + 296

14 $\underline{^{th}}$ decade   Y' = -2(13) + 296 or 270

15 $\underline{^{th}}$ decade   Y' = -2(14) + 296 or 268

Track data graph

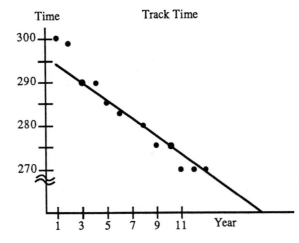

Section 8.5

1. Cricket data
    $\bar{X}$ = 16.6
    $\bar{Y}$ = 80.13
    Covar = 8.92; VAR(X) = 2.77

2. Cricket data
    m = 3.2 gives error 13.4265

    $m = \dfrac{8.92}{2.77} = 3.2$ (not bad)

3. Mice data
    $\bar{X}$ = 16.625
    $\bar{Y}$ = 33.75
    Covar = 13.406
    Var(X) = 6.23

4. Mice data

    $m = \dfrac{13.406}{6.23} = 2.15$

    - very close!

5. Math anxiety data
    $\bar{X}$ = 41.65
    $\bar{Y}$ = 20.55
    Covar = -96.41
    Var(X) = 182.83

6. Math anxiety data

    $m = \dfrac{-96.41}{182.83}$ or -.527

    and from table, m =-.55. Very close.

7. Push-up data
    $\bar{X}$ = 32.33   Covar = -14.56
    $\bar{Y}$ = 7.66
    var (X) = 92.89

8. $m = \dfrac{-14.56}{92.89} = -.16$

    and from table, m = -.2. Very close.

9. Push-up data
    Y' = -.16X + 12.83
    (a) X = 26   b) X = 3.9   c) X = 50
         Y' = (-.16)26 + 12.83   Y' = -.16(39) + 12.83   Y' = -.16(50) + 12.83
         Y' = 8.67   Y' = 6.59   Y' = 4.83
    Assumptions: 1) Group is male, 2) Original group was representative

10. Radiation data
$\bar{X}$ = 4.99
$\bar{Y}$ = 159.8
Covar = 833/8 = 104.2
var(X) = 87.4/8 or 10.9

11. Radiation Data

$m = \dfrac{104.2}{10.9} = 9.6$

Y' = mX + C
159.8 = 9.6(5) + C
159.8-48 = C
111.8 = C   Y' = 9.6X + 111.8

12. Radiation data
Using eq from 11
(a) X = 1.0
     Y' = 9.6 + 111.8
     Y' = 121.4
(b) X = 5.0
     Y' = 9.6(5) + 111.8
     Y' = 159.8
(c) X = 10
     Y' = 9.6(10) = 111.8
     Y' = 207.8

Section 8.6

1. (a) strong neg.   (b) weak pos.
   (c) strong pos.   (d) weak neg.
   These are possible answers. Good justification can be given for
   other answers. Encourage discussion.

2. (a) strong pos.
   (b) weak pos
   (c) weak pos
   (d) weak pos
   (e) weak pos
   (f) strong neg
   (g) strong pos
   (h) weak pos

3. Spelling/reading data
   $\bar{X}$ = 7.0   Covar = 15.2

   $\bar{Y}$ = 10.3
                          Var(X) = 8.4; SDx = 2.90
                          Var(Y) = 34.21; SDy = 5.85

              $r = \dfrac{15.2}{(2.9)(5.85)} = .90$

4. Push-up data
   Covar = -14.56
   SDx = 3.17
   SDy = 9.63

   $$r = \frac{-14.56}{(3.17)9.64} = -.476$$

5. Mice data
   Covar = 13.406
   Sx = 2.50
   Sy = 5.76

   $$r = \frac{13.406}{(2.50)(5.76)} = .93$$

6. Cricket data
   Covar = 8.92
   SDx = 1.66
   SDy = 6.49

   $$r = \frac{8.92}{(1.66)(6.49)} = .827$$

7. Radiation data
   Covar = 104.2
   Sx = 3.30
   Sy = 33.99

   $$r = \frac{104.2}{(3.30)(33.99)} = .929$$

8. Weight loss/slenderization data

   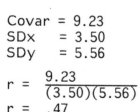

   Covar = 9.23
   SDx = 3.50
   SDy = 5.56

   $$r = \frac{9.23}{(3.50)(5.56)}$$
   $$r = .47$$

9. Push-up data
   Error variance = 7.94

   $$r^2 = 1 - \frac{(7.94)}{10.05}$$
   $$r^2 = 1 - .79$$
   $$r^2 = .21$$
   $$r = -.46$$

   Correlation is negative because slope is negative.

10. Mice data

$$r = m \frac{(S_x)}{(S_y)} \qquad \text{using } m = 2.15$$

$$= 2.15 \frac{(2.50)}{5.76}$$

$$r = .93$$

11. Cricket data
     $m = 3.2$; Error var = 13.43; $(SDy)^2 = (6.49)^2$

$$r^2 = 1 - \frac{13.43}{42.12}$$

$$r^2 = 1 - .319$$
$$r^2 = .68$$
$$r = .82$$

Section 8.7

1. Fouls/points data
    $\bar{X} = 9.2$
    $\bar{Y} = 22.5$
    $Var(X) = 92.9 \qquad SDx = 9.6$
    $Var(Y) = 599.5 \qquad SDy = 24.48$
    $Covar = 220.82$
    $r = .94$

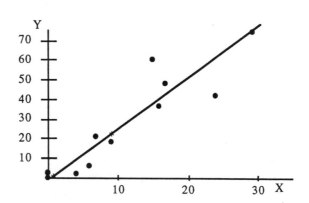

(b)   m = 2.5
      22.5 = 2.5 (9.2) + C
      -.5 = C

      eq   Y' = 2.5X - .5

(c)   r = $\dfrac{220.8}{(9.6)(24.5)}$

      = .94

(d)   If points were caused by fouls, coach would suggest more fouls. More valid is the reasoning which states <u>both</u> fouls and points are related to some 3rd factor, e.g., time played.

2. weight and calorie intake
    less calories cause weight loss
    In this case, causal relationship seems reasonable.

3. Collect from students

4. a)   Population (human) increased with time,
    b)   Extinction of mammals and birds increased with time.

    Conclusion: Human population increased and mammal and bird population decreased, over time.

    Changes in land use could have caused both.

Chapter 9   Section 9.1

1.   Old score   Slide factor   New score
        3   +5   8
        6   +5   11
        7   +5   12
        6   +5   11
        8   +5   13
       12   +5   17

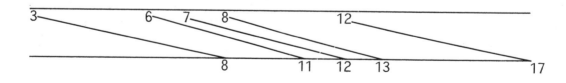

2.   Old mean 42/6 or 7; new mean 12
     Old range 9; new range 9

3.

Old price	Slide factor	New price
48	+5	53
52	+5	57
49	+5	54
58	+5	63
52	+5	57
61	+5	66
59	+5	64
55	+5	60

Range
61-48 = 13

Range
66-53 = 13

4.

Old price	Slide factor	New price
15.50	-1.65	13.85
16.25	-1.65	14.60
14.95	-1.65	13.30
15.80	-1.65	14.15
16.50	-1.65	14.85
15.80	-1.65	14.15

Range   16.50-14.95
1.55

14.85-13.30
1.55

5.

Old Score	Stretch factor	New score
6	x3	18
7	x3	21
9	x3	27
10	x3	30
6	x3	18
7	x3	21

6. mean = old X3   or $\overline{X}$ = (135)/6
       = 3 (7.5)   = 22.5
       = 22.5

7.

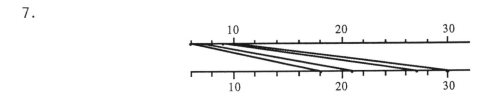

8.

Old	Shrink Factor		new
24	× 1/3 or	3	8
18	× 1/3 or	3	6
15	× 1/3 or	3	5

9. Mean
    $\overline{old}$ = 1/3 (57)   new = 1/3 (8 + 6 + 5) = 6.$\bar{3}$

          = 19

    new = 1/3 (19)

          = 6.$\bar{3}$

10.

    Range is 9   and   Range is 3

11. | Old price | Shrink Factor | Sale price |
     |-----------|---------------|------------|
     | 6.50 | × 1/2 | 3.25 |
     | 6.25 | × 1/2 | 3.13 |
     | 7.00 | × 1/2 | 3.50 |
     | 5.95 | × 1/2 | 2.98 |
     | 5.50 | × 1/3 | 2.75 |

12. $\overline{X}$ = 1/5 (31.20) $\overline{X}$ = 1/5 (15.61)
         = 6.24   = 3.12

13. Range = 1.50   and   Range = .75

Section 9.2

1. | Quiz score | dev | $(dev)^2$ |
    |------------|-----|-----------|
    | 8 | 1 | 1 |
    | 5 | -2 | 4 |
    | 7 | 0 | 0 |
    | 5 | -2 | 4 |
    | 8 | 1 | 1 |
    | 9 | 2 | 4 |
    | 42 | | 14 |

        $\overline{X}$ = 1/6 (42)   Var = 1/6 (14)

            = 7   = 2.$\bar{3}$

                                    SD = $\sqrt{2.\bar{3}}$ or 1.53

    Range 9-5=4

b   New score   (old + 10)
        18
        15   mean = 17
        17   range = 4
        15   SD = 1.53
        18
        19
       102

New score: (5 × old)

40	mean = 5 (7) = 35
25	range = 5 (4) = 20
35	SD = 5 (1.53) = 7.65
25	
40	
45	

3. New score: (5 × old) + 10

50	mean = 5 (7) + 10 = 45
35	range = 5 (4) = 20
45	SD = 5 (1.53) = 7.65
35	
50	
55	

4. If transformation, (old + 10) × 5 is used, mean is (7 + 10) × 5 or 85. Transformation in problem 3 gives mean of 45. Therefore, order of transformation affects results.

5. (a) $\dfrac{\text{Old score}-5}{3}$

3	b) mean = (7-5)= 2
0	range = 4
2	SD = 1.53
0	
3	
4	

6. (a) Old score ÷ 2

4	(b) mean = 7/2 = 3.5
2.5	range = 4/2 = 2
3.5	SD = 1.53/2 = .77
2.5	
4.	
4.5	

7. $\dfrac{(\text{Old score} - 5)}{2}$

1.5	
0	mean = (7-5)/2 = 1
1	
0	SD = (1.53)/2 = .77
1.5	
2	

8. $\bar{X} = 10$
    SD = 2

    new $\bar{X}$ = 3 (10) + 5 = 35
    new SD = 3 (2) = 6

9. $\overline{X} = 50$
   SD = 10

   new $\overline{X} = 2\,(50) + 10 = 110$
   new SD = 2 (10) = 20

10.

Score	New score
6	16
5	15
8	18
8	18
7	17

old mean = 34/5 or 6.8

new mean 16.8

11.

Old	New		
8	18	1	1
5	15	-2	4
7	17	0	0
5	15	-2	4
8	18	1	1
9	19	2	4

   Old $\overline{X} = 7$ Var = (14) 1/6 = $2.\overline{3}$

   New $\overline{X} = 17$ SD = 1.53   new SD same as old SD

12. Add 5: new mean - old mean = slide
    divide by 1.53 & mult by 5 = stretch

    $\dfrac{5}{1.53}$ or 3.268 is the stretch factor.

13. Stretch x 3

14. Answer if one transformation is to give $\overline{X} = 12$ & SD = 5

	x	3.27	-	10.9
		26.2		15.3
8		26.2		15.3
5		16.0		5.1
7		22.9		12.0
5		16.0		5.1
8		26.2		15.3
9		29.4		19.1
		137.7		71.9

   Stretch by x 5/1.53 or 3.27

   new mean = 22.9 or 137.7/6

   After slide of -10.9 mean is 12 (or 71.9/6)

Section 9.3

1.

Old	Dev	$(Dev)^2$
5	-1	1
7	+1	1
6	0	0
5	-1	1
7	1	1

$\bar{X} = 1/5\ (30)$ $var = 1/5\ (4)$
    $= 6$ $= .8$
                        $SD = \sqrt{.8}$
                            $= .89$

Old	Slide -6	Shrink ÷ .89	=	z score
5	-1	-1/.89	=	-1.12
7	1	1/.89	=	1.12
6	0	0		0
5	-1	-1/.89	=	-1.12
7	1	1/.89	=	1.12

2. Change each value, X, to corresponding z score

$z = \dfrac{X - 18.1}{4.2}$

3. $z = \dfrac{X - 20.3}{5.3}$

4. Find transformed score T;

$T = z\ (20) + 50$

or $T = \left(\dfrac{X - 18.1}{4.2}\right)(20) + 50$

5. $T = z\ (50) + 500$
    or
    $T = \dfrac{(X - 18.1)}{4.2}(50) + 500$

6. $\bar{X} = 45.3$
    $SD = 4.8$

    Polly   Ron

    $z = \dfrac{52 - 45.3}{4.8}$ $z = \dfrac{40 - 45.3}{4.8}$

    $z = 1.400$ $z = -1.104$

7. $Z_I = \dfrac{40 - 34}{5.3}$ $Z_{II} = \dfrac{44 - 48.3}{6.8}$

   $= 1.132$ $= -.632$

               Better on test I

8. $T_I = 1.132 \times 100 + 200$

      $= 113.2 + 200$

      $= 313.2$

   $T_{II} = -.632 \,(100) + 200$

      $= -63.2 + 200$

      $= 136.8$

               Better on test I

9.

Old	Dev	$(Dev)^2$	z	T*
5	- .3	.09	- .21	48
7	1.7	2.89	1.20	62
3	-2.3	5.29	-1.62	34
4	-1.3	1.69	- .92	41
5	- .3	.09	- .21	48
5	- .3	.09	- .21	48
6	.7	.49	.49	55
4	-1.3	1.69	- .92	41
8	2.7	7.29	1.90	69
6	.7	.49	.49	55

$\overline{X} = 5.3$ $Var = \dfrac{20.1}{10}$ $z = \dfrac{X - 5.3}{1.42}$ $T = 10\,z + 50$

               $= 2.01$

         $SD = 2.01$

               $= 1.42$

* Rounded

10.

Score	Dev	(Dev)^2	z	T
32	-12.8	163.84	-1.99	70.15
45	.2	.04	.03	100.45
43	- 1.8	3.24	- .28	95.80
48	3.2	10.24	.50	107.50
51	6.2	38.44	.97	114.55
50	5.2	27.04	.81	112.15
43	- 1.8	3.24	- .28	95.80
44	- .8	.64	- .12	98.20
37	- 7.8	60.84	-1.21	81.85
55	10.2	104.04	1.59	123.85

$\overline{X} = 44.8$

$\text{Var } X = \dfrac{411.6}{10} \quad \text{or} \quad 41.6$

$SD = 6.42$

$z = \dfrac{X-44.8}{6.42}$

$T = 15z + 100$

Section 9.4

1.

Outcome	f	rel. freq.
1	23	.19
2	18	.15
3	17	.14
4	25	.21
5	21	.18
6	16	.13

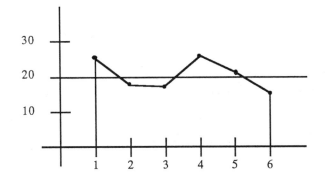
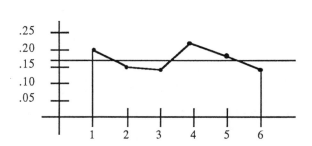

pass through .17 approximately

T = 1.4 (10) + 100   T = -1.104 (10) + 100
  = 14 + 100   = -11. + 100
  = 114   = 89

2.   Example data

	f	rel freq
Heads	34	.5$\bar{6}$
Tails	26	.43

Answers may differ,

but pass through .5

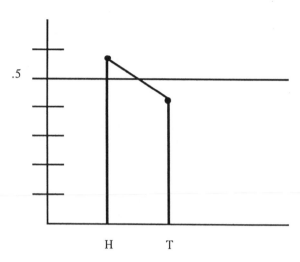

3.

Digit	freq.	rel freq
1	77	.077
2	93	.093
3	106	.106
4	123	.123
5	94	.094
6	88	.088
7	117	.117
8	104	.104
9	92	.092
0	106	.106
	1000	

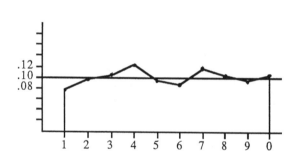

passes through .10

P (1) = .077   p (1) = .10
P (5) = .094   p (6) = .10
P (even) = .514   p (0) = .10
                      p (even) = .50

4.   Student data; Answers will differ.

5.

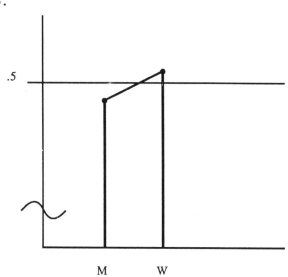

Total 3,967,008,000

$$P\ (M) = \frac{1979956000}{3967005000}$$

or .49911

$$P\ (W) = \frac{1987049000}{3967008000}$$

or .50089

p (W) = .5

6.

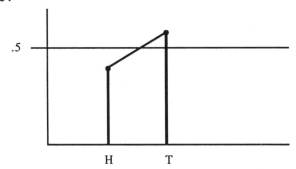

(a) P (H) = .457
(b) P (T) = .543

(c) p (H) = .5
(d) p (T) = .5

7.   Sample answer

Outcome	f	rel freq	Outcome	f	rel freq
(0,1)	7	.12	(1,1)	3	.05
(0,2)	8	.13	(1,2)	5	.08
(0,3)	2	.03	(1,3)	4	.01
(0,4)	5	.08	(1,4)	5	.08
(0,5)	7	.12	(1,5)	4	.07
(0,6)	2	.03	(1,6)	8	.13

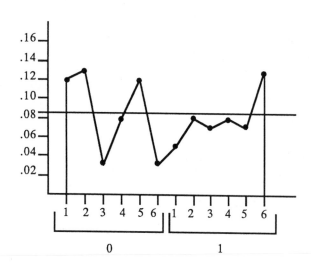

(a) P (0,5) = .12
     P (1,6) = .13

(b) p (0,5) = 1/12 or .08$\bar{3}$
     p (1,6) = 1/12 or .08$\bar{3}$

8. Sample answer

Outcome	freq	rel freq
Clubs	12	.30
Diam	9	.225
Hearts	11	.275
Spades	8	.20
	40	

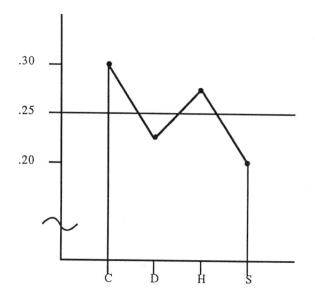

(a) P (H) = .275   (b) P (C) = .30   (c) P (Red) = 20/40 or .5
(d) p (H) $\doteq$ .25   (e) p (C) = .25   (f) p (Red) = .5

9.

outcome	freq	rel freq
top	109	.109
bottom	653	.653
side	238	.238
	1000	

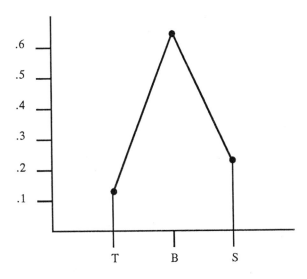

P (top) = .109

P (bottom) = .653

P (side) = .238

Horizontal line seems unlikely!

10.
Number of heads	freq	rel freq
0	10	.10
1	29	.29
2	41	.41
3	20	.20

P (0 heads) = .10
P (1 heads) = .29
P (3 heads) = .20

Horizontal line not good--model for equally likely isn't appropriate

11. Stock closings for 317 stocks

Fractions	freq	rel freq
0	60	.189
1/8	30	.095
1/4	29	.091
3/8	27	.085
1/2	47	.148
5/8	49	.155
3/4	37	.117
7/8	38	.120

Expected number is 39.625

12. Stock losing - no zero fraction- for 257 stocks.

Eights	Exp	Freq	E-0	$(E-0)^2$
1	37	30	7	49
2	37	29	8	64
3	37	27	10	100
4	37	47	-10	100
5	37	49	-12	144
6	37	37	0	0
7	37	38	-1	1

Exp = 257/7 = 36.7 or 37

$\chi^2 = 1/37 \ (458)$ or 12.4

$p \ (\chi^2_6 > 12.4) = .05$ Reject idea of uniform probability model

13.

Digit	Exp	f	E-0	$(E - 0)^2$
0	1000	1026	26	676
1	1000	1107	107	11449
2	1000	997	-3	9
3	1000	966	-34	1156
4	1000	1095	75	5625
5	1000	933	-67	4489
6	1000	1107	107	11449
7	1000	972	-28	784
8	1000	964	-36	1296
9	1000	853	-147	21609

Exp = 1000

$\chi^2 = (58542) \ /1000$

$\chi^2 = 58.542$

$p(\chi^2_9 > 58.542)$ is very small!

so we doubt that each number is equally likely; accept Carlson's assertion

Section 9.5

1.   Chest measurements for 1516 soldiers

	f
28	2
29	4
30	17
31	55
32	102
33	180
34	242
35	310
36	251
37	181
38	103
39	42
40	19
41	6
42	2
	1516

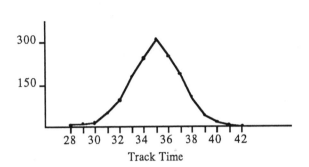

data appear normally distributed

2.   Height/cab scouts

```
              Leaf
Stem
4,8,5,5,3,5,7,0,0,4,6,4,9,9,0
5,3,2,0,1,3,1,5,0,3,0,3,0,0,8,1
6,2
```

3.   Mean = (1467)/30
          = 48.9

Var = (766.7)/30
          = 25.56

SD $\doteq$ 5.06

4.   Washers
```
Stem        Leaf
2.9         6,3,6,8,6
3.0         9,6,8,4,0,8,9,7,3,5,6,2,0,2,0,9,7,9,6,6.
3.1         7,8,3,3,8,0,2,9,4,7,2,1,7,6,4,2,2,2,3
3.2         0,0,0,3,5,0
```

Interval	freq	Rel. Freq.
2.90 - 2.99	5	.10
3.00 - 3.09	20	.40
3.10 - 3.19	19	.38
3.20 - 3.29	6	.12

rel. freq. poly
freq. poly

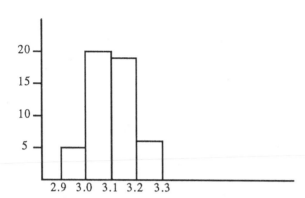

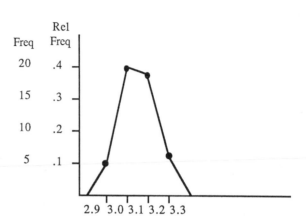

5.   Pennies

Stem x100	leaf	freq	rel freq
300	1	1	.025
301		0	0
302	4	1	.025
303	7493	4	.100
304	122	3	.075
305	95	2	.05
306	6631	4	.100
307	303	3	.075
308	17	2	.05
309	29	2	.05
310	2	1	.025
311	221	3	.075
312	805575	6	.15
313		0	0
314		0	0
315	74	2	.05
316	440	3	.075
317	164	3	.075
		40	

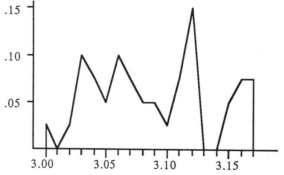

6.   Washers

P(2.99 < W < 3.20) = .40 + .38
                  = .78

P(W < 3.00) = .10

7.   Pennies

P(W > 3.10) = 18/40 = .45

8.   Weights for male recruits   (Recorded by going down each column)

stem	leaf	freq	Rel freq
10	6,5,4	3	.06
11	0,7,3,3,7,4,9,9,5	9	.18
12	0,6,1,3,8,7,4	7	.14
13	5,7,6,1,8,1,5,9,9,8	10	.20
14	0,1,7,6,3,7,8,8,0,6,4,0	12	.24
15	8,7,7,4	4	.08
16	9,9,1,3,6	5	.10

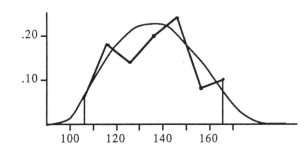

probably normal - but hard to tell from so few cases.

9. $\bar{X}$ = 135.3   Recruit's weight
     SD = 17.3
     Interval = 135.3 $\pm$ 17.3
     Interval is 118 to 152.6
          How many actually?
               2 + 7 + 10 + 12 + 0 = 31
          (110's 120's 130's 140's 150's)
          (31 of 50 or 62%)

10.   Pennies' weight
      $\bar{X}$ = 3.09
      SD = .05
      Interval 3.09 $\pm$ .05
      so   3.04 t̄o 3.14
      Counting 3 + 2 + 4 + 3 + 2 + 2 + 1 + 3 + 6 = 26
      Theoretically .68(40) or 27.2

11.   50 mice - data appear normal

stem	leaf	freq
10	7,5	2
11	6,4,2	3
12	2,4,8,8,6,0,7,3,4,8	10
13	5,5,4,5,4,1,4,0,8,3,6,6,2,1,6	15
14	3,5,3,6,2,1,2,0,2	9
15	3,4,5,4,9	5
16	0,0,0	3
17	0,2	2

Data appear normal.

12.   Sum in rolling 2 6-sided dice.

      Answers will vary; data seem normally distributed.

Section 9.6

1.   (a)   p(z < 1.96) = .9750
     (b)   p(z < -1.96) = .0250
     (c)   p(z < 1.0) = .8413
     (d)   p(z < -1.0) = .1587
     (e)   p(z < +.5) = .6915
     (f)   p(z < -.5) = .3085
     (g)   p(z < 0) = .5000

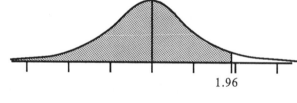

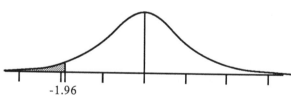

2.   (a)   p(z > 1.96) = 1-.9750 = .025
     (b)   p(z > -1.96) = 1-.025 = .9750
     (c)   p(z > 1.0) = 1-.8413 = .1587
     (d)   p(z > -1.0) = 1-.1587 = .8413
     (e)   p(z > .5) = 1-.6915 = .3085
     (f)   p(z > 0) = 1-.5 = .5

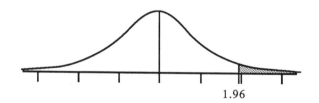

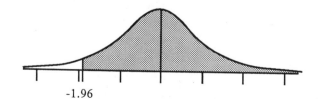

3.   (a) p(z<.68) = .7517
     (b) p(z>.68) = 1-.7517 = .2483
     (c) p(z<-.68) = .2483
     (d) p(z>-.68) = 1-.2483 = .7517

4.   (a) p(z < ?) = .95
                1.645
     (b) p(z < ?) = .90
                1.28
     (c) p(z < ?) = .98
                2.05
     (d) p(z < ?) = .66
                .41
     (e) p(z < ?) = .50
                0

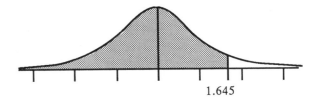

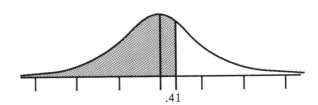

5.   (a) p(z < ?) = .05
                -1.64
     (b) p(z < ?) = .25
                -.67
     (c) p(z < ?) = .01
                -2.32
     (d) p(z < ?) = .10
                -1.2
     (e) p(z < ?0) = .5

     These are not to scale

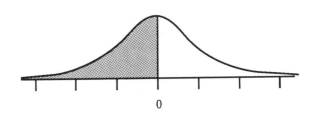

6.   (a) p(z > ?) = .95
                1-.95 = .05
                    -1.64

     (b) p(z > ?) = .90
                1-.90 = .10
                    -1.28

     (c) p(z > ?) = .99
                1-.99 = .01
                    -2.33

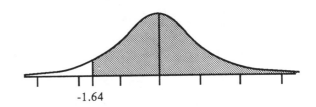

(d) p(z > ?) = .05
          1-.05 = .95
                1.64

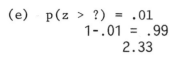

(e) p(z > ?) = .01
          1-.01 = .99
                2.33

(f) p(z > ?) = .10
          1-.10 = .90
                1.28

7. (a) p(z < ?) = .68   pos
              .47
    (b) p(z < ?) = .16   neg
              -.99
    (c) p(z < ?) = .80   pos
              .84
    (d) p(z < ?) = .20   neg
              -.84
    (e) p(z > ?) = .20   pos
          1-.20 = .80
                .84
    (f) p(z > ?) = .15   pos
          1-.15 = .85
                1.04
    (g) p(z > ?) = .68   neg
          1-.68 = .32
                -.47
    (h) p(z > ?) = .98   neg
          1-.98 = .02
                -2.05
    (i) p(z > ?) = .5   zero
          1-.5
                0

8. (a) pos p(z > ?) = .40
              1-.40 = .60
                    .25

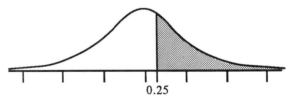

    (b) pos p(z < ?) = .88
                    1.17

    (c) neg p(z > ?) = .93
              1-.93 = .07
                  -1.47

    (d) neg p(z < ?) = .25
                  -.67

9. (a) $p(z < 2.38) = .9913$

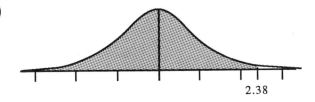

(b) $p(z > -1.65) = 1-.0495$
$= .9505$

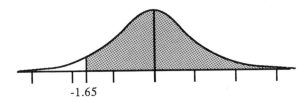

(c) $p(z < ?) = .005$
-2.57

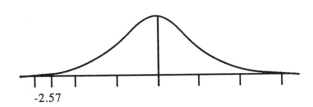

(d) $p(z > ?) = .975$
$1-.975 = .025$
-1.96

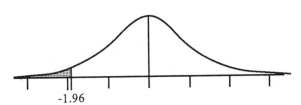

10. $\bar{X} = 35$
SD = 2

About 2/3 or 68% between
33 & 37 or 1031

By counting 180 + 242 + 310 + 251 + 181
or 1164

Section 9.7

1. $\bar{X} = 40$ $z = \dfrac{45-40}{6}$
SD = 6
X = 45 $= .83$

$p(z > .83) =$
$1-.7967$
$.2033$
Approx 20%

2. $\bar{X} = 118.67$ $z = \dfrac{130-118.67}{16.9}$
SD = 16.9
X = 130 $z = .67$

$p(z > .67) =$
$1-.7486$
$.2514$
Approx 25% (Actually 30)

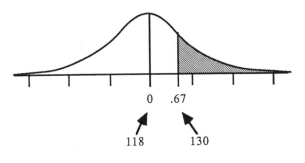

3. $\overline{X}$ = 52
    SD = 6

    p(z > ?) = .15   p(z > ?) = .15
          ? = 1.04   -1.04

    T = 1.04(6) + 52   T = (-1.04)4 + 52
      = 6.24 + 52   = -6.24 + 52
      = 58.24   = 45.76

    Lowest A is 58
    Highest F is 46

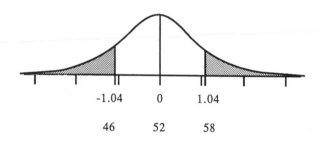

```
        -1.04      0      1.04

         46       52       58
```

4. $\overline{X}$ = 3.11
    SD = .043

    $z = \dfrac{3.08 - 3.22}{.043}$ $z = \dfrac{3.10 - 3.11}{.043}$

           = -.70   = .-23

    p(3.08 < penny < 3.10) =

    p(-.70 < z < -.23) = .4090 - .2420

                       = .1670

    and there are 17 in that interval.

    $z = \dfrac{3.06 - 3.11}{.043}$ = -1.16

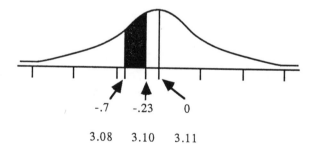

```
         -.7    -.23    0

        3.08   3.10   3.11
```

    p(penny < 3.06) =
    p(z < -1.16) = .123
    and there are 13.

    $z = \dfrac{3.14 - 3.11}{.043}$ = .70

    p(penny > 3.14) =

    p(z > .70) = 1 - .7580

               = .2420

    and there are 22.

5. $\overline{X}$ = 41 $z = \dfrac{40 - 41}{.25}$
     SD = .25
     X = 40   z = -4

     p(z < -4) = .000032

     .000032 (1,000,000,000) =
     32,000 boxes

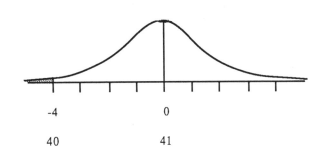

Section 9.8

1.   P(H < 500) = .36 + .28
                  = .64
     P(H > 1500) = .06

2.   Deaths from horse kicks

K	f	rel f
0	109	.545
1	65	.325
2	22	.110
3	3	.015
4	1	.005
	200	

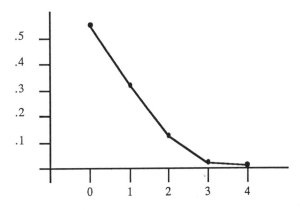

   (a) p(K = 0) = .545

   (b) p(K > 1) = .11 + .015 + .005
                 = .13

3.

Stem	Leaf	f	Rel freq
19	0,9	2	.06
20	0,1	2	.0$\overline{6}$
21	5,8	2	.0$\overline{6}$
22	5,8,8,	4	.1$\overline{3}$
23	0,1,2,3,0,5,8,7,7,2	10	.3$\overline{3}$
24	2,0,0,5,0,2,3	7	.2$\overline{3}$
25	3,7,4	3	.10

Data do not seem normally distributed.

a)   P(W < 200) = .0$\overline{6}$

b)   P(200<W<220) = 4/30 or .1$\overline{3}$

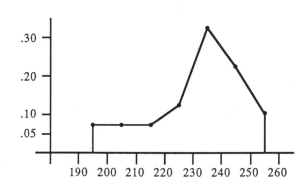

4.

Time	Tally	freq	Rel freq
7:50	11	2	.07
7:51	1111	4	.15
7:52	111	3	.11
7:53	111	3	.11
7:54	11	2	.07
7:55	1111	4	.15
7:56	1	1	.04
7:57	111	3	.11
7:58	1	1	.04
7:59	1111	4	.15

$$\overline{27}$$

Arrival time

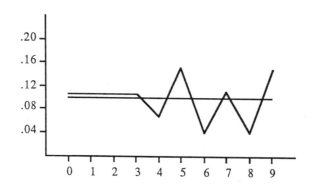

smooth
curve
p = 1/10

7:5

(a) P(T > 7:55) = 9/27 or .33

(b) P(T < 7:53) = 9/27 or .33

(c) p(T > 7:55) = .4

(d) p(T < 7:53) = .4

5.   (a) P(R = 0) = 50/200 or .25

(b) P(R < 2) = $\dfrac{50 + 24}{200}$ = .37

(c) P(R = 12) = 55/200 = .275

Chapter 10   Section 10.1

1.   Measure - answers will vary.

2.   Measurement of human hair

47	////	5
48	////	5
49	//// //	7
50	//	2
51	////	5
52	////	4
53	//	2

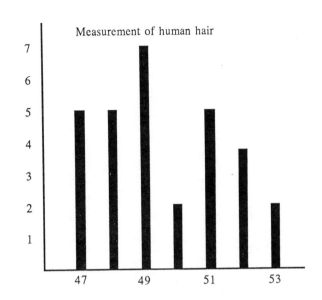

Measurement of human hair

mean = 1/30 (1487)
     = 49.6

Var. = 3.512
SD = 1.874

3.   Error in gas pumps

Error	Tally	f
2	///	3
1	////	4
0	////	4
-1	//// //	7
-2	//// //	7
-3	//// ////	9
-4	//// //// /	11
-5	//	2
-6	//	2
-7	/	1

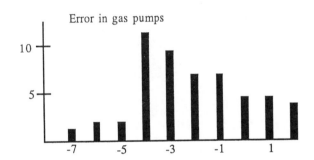

Error in gas pumps

$P(\text{error of more than } 5) = \frac{2+1}{50}$ or .06

   Seems normally dist.

Theoretical

$\bar{X} = -2.22$
$SD = 2.157$

so $z = \dfrac{-2.22 - (-5)}{2.157} = 1.28$

and $p(z > 1.28)$ or .10

4. Cement

Stem	Leaf
35	89
36	76,26
37	71,77,75
38	10,42,25,89,88,71,48
39	48,22,14,07
40	81,84,30,72,18,05,46,17,84,56
41	54,23,35,72,80,26,34,35,20,41,28,81,30
42	28,41,51
43	00,34,39
44	66,09,47
45	24

$\bar{X} = 4057.68$ SD $= 210.01$

P(Strength > 4358) = 4/50 or .08   Percent tests > 4358 = 8%

Theoretical

$$z = \frac{4358 - 4058}{210}$$

$z = 1.43$

$p\ (z > 1.43) =$

$1 - .9236 =$

$.076$

Section 10.2

1. Range 179. - 165.1 = 13.9

$\bar{X} = 175.5$
SD $= 4.364$

Mean dev = (.3 + 3.5 + 5.5 + 10.4 + 4 + .3 + 3.5 + .2 + 10 + .3)/10
= 38/10 or 3.8

2. Chalkboard measurements

$\bar{X}$ = (1637)/7
= 233.86

SD = 9.67

Range 249-223 = 26

There is much variation in the measurements.

3. Measurement of human hair

Method A	Method B
$\bar{X} = 73.3$	$\bar{X} = 74.4$
SD = 5.98	SD = 2.06

Method B has less error in measuring

4. Scale

A	B
$\bar{X} = 76.4$	$\bar{X} = 75.0$
SD $\doteq$ 1.74	SD = 3.71

Scale A appears to have less error.

5. First has less error--less spread--less variation.

Section 10.3

1. New pennies - weights

Weight	freq
28.56	1
29.25	1
29.37	1
29.43	5
29.62	1
29.81	1

$\bar{W} = 29.276$ and is good estimate of true weight.
SE = .416

2. $\bar{W} = 29.57$
SE = .610

3. Radiation

Stem	Leaf
47	25,87
48	18,87,86,62,43,62
49	81,50,81,00,25,25,93,93
50	93,00,06,81,37,25
51	18,81,68

    $\overline{X}$ = 49.58

    SE = 1:16

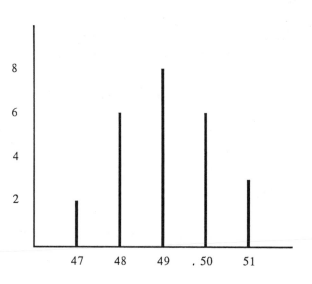

4. Radiation

Stem	Leaf
48	84,32,20
49	88,08,84,16, 0,56,60,56,45,76,96,44,92,72,84,84,24,32
50	08,20,08,20

    $\overline{X}$ = 49.56

    SE = .583

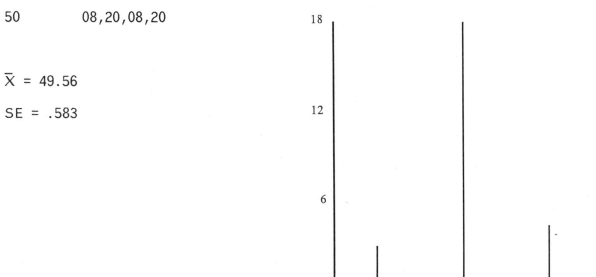

    There is less variation when the number in the sample is large.

5. Value of T from the Netherlands

    $\overline{T}$ = 131.51   good estimate of time

    SD = 1.50

Section 10.4

1. Thermometer error +15   78.7 to 81.1

Stem	Leaf
78	7,9
79	7,5,0,2
80	9,6,4
81	1

$\overline{X} = 79.8$ Correct $\overline{X} = 79.8 - .5$ $\overline{X} = 79.8 - 5 = 74.8$

                                        $= 79.3$

SD = .84

Note: In the first printing of the first edition the error was misstated as +5°F instead of the correct +.5°F

2. Another thermometer

Stem	Leaf
79	7
80	7,2,7
81	7,9,3,0,2,1

$\overline{X} = 80.95$

SD = .63

The second is more precise--less variation.

It seems biased--too high--if it is the same greenhouse as prob. 1.

3. Weight of precipitate

Scale A		Scale B
	5 46	
	47	
4,0	48	6,0,5,0
5,0,5,2	49	6,6,8
5,4,6	50	5,2
9,5	51	1,2
5,0	52	3,0,2
	53	
	54	1
4	55	

$\overline{X}$ = 50.326 $\overline{X}$ = 50.313

S.D = 2.088   S.D = 1.66

B is more precise--less variation
True weight approx 50.3

4.   Insect

Length   freq

28	1
35	1
36	0
37	2
38	4
39	4
40	4
41	1
42	3

$\overline{X}$ = 38.6
SD = 1.786
Est. length 38.6
Could be more precise
Be more careful measuring

Section 10.5

1.   Chalkboard

Stem	Leaf
236	6
237	8
238	5,8,6,5,6
239	
240	4,4,0,7,5,0,2
241	6,6,1,0,3,1

$\overline{X}$ = 239.87
SE = 1.36

2.   Sewing thread

Stem	Leaf
48	84,84,52
49	48,80,52,16,28,68,48,72,68,80,84,48,96,08
50	28,12,48

$\overline{X}$ = 49.552 and is good estimate of true strength.

SE = .484

3.   Cartographer

$\overline{X}$ = 39.2928 and is good estimate of area.

SE = .542

4.   Gravity

$\bar{X}$ = 64.4375 and is good estimate of gravity.

SE = .504

5. $\bar{X}_{class\ I}$ = 1.105 $\bar{X}_{class\ II}$ = 1.00375
     SD = .00866   SD = .025

Class I has the smaller standard error.

Class I also has more bias.

Since true mean is 1, Class II is more accurate.

Section 10.6

1.   Y' = .07X + 1.8

     X = 200   Y' = .07(200) + 1.8
                               = 14 + 1.8
                            Y' = 15.8

     X = 350   Y' = 07(350) + 1.8
                               = 24.5 + 1.8
                            Y' = 26.3

     X = 425   Y' = .07(425) + 1.8
                               = 29.75 + 1.8
                            Y' = 31.55

     X = 500   Y' = .07(500) + 1.8
                               = 35 + 1.8
                            Y' = 36.8

2.   Answers will vary

3.   y = .07X + 1.8

     10 = .07X + 1.8 for Y = 10;   cm = 10 millimeters

     8.2 = .07x

     117 = X

     so 117 pages

     Answers will differ for second equation.

4.   History book

Number of pages	Number of Sheets	Total Thickness (X)	
400	200	16.9	.085
60	30	3.3	.110
188	94	11.0	.117
120	60	2.2	.037
356	178	16.4	.092
352	176	14.1	.080
110	55	7.1	.129
210	105	9.5	.090
392	196	15.7	.080
262	131	11.4	.087
352	176	10.2	.060
238	119	6.9	.060
126	63	5.3	.080
406	203	14.1	.069
708	354	26.2	.074
140	70	7.9	.112
308	154	11.6	.075
470	235	18.8	.080
172	86	9.8	.114
176	88	7.8	.089

$\bar{X} = 138.65$ $\bar{Y} = 11.315$

$Var(X) = 578.93$ $Var(Y) = 31.04$

$SD(X) = 76.08$ $SD(Y) = 5.57$

                 Covar = 400.52

$m = .069$ and Y-int = -2.55

so equation is $Y' = 0.69 X - 2.55$

Chapter 11   Section 11.1

1.   (a) Temp (parameter) in Los Angeles (population) is estimated
          as 73 °F (statistic) at the Airport (sample).

      (b) The percent opposed (parameter) from a large college (population)
          is estimated to be 63% (statistic) based on 64 freshmen (sample).

      (c) The pollen count (parameter) in Champaign-Urbana (population)
          is estimated to be 228/cu yd (statistic) based on one cubic
          yard of air (sample).

(d) The amount of moisture (parameter) in a truck load of corn (population) is estimated to be 35% (statistic) found in 250 grams (sample).

2. $\bar{X} = (66)/20 = 3.3$ Range is 5-3 or 2

$\bar{X}$ could be used to estimate the mean preference of the entire population - all those at the shopping center, or in the community.

3. The parameter could be the percent of college students who have liberal views. Based on the random sample, the estimate is 5/25 or 20%.

4. Samples of 10 trees are used to determine tree ring width (statistic). These are used to estimate ring width (parameter) for all trees (population).

Samples should be randomly selected from each group to insure that the population is represented.

5. Sample 188,000 students (freshmen) who entered college in fall 1982. Population could be <u>all</u> students who attended college in fall 1982.

Example. In sample 43.8% preferred living in a dorm. This statistic could estimate that 43.8% of <u>all</u> college students prefer living in a dorm.

6. Answers will vary.
Find articles.

7. .15 (total) = 112.82 so total is $\frac{112.82}{.15}$ or $752.13

8. .20 (total) = 92.50 so total = $\frac{92.50}{.20}$ or $462.50

Section 11.2

1. $\mu = 50$
$\sigma = 10$

(a) N = 4

$P(48 < \bar{X} < 52) = (9 + 9 + 5 + 3)/100$ or .25

(b) N = 16

P(48 < $\bar{X}$ < 52) = (14 + 14 + 16 + 13 + 2)/100 or .59

(c) N = 36

P(48 < $\bar{X}$ < 52.0) = (20 + 25 + 19 + 10 + 1)/100 or .75

2.   μ = 45

σ = 12

N = 16

P($\bar{X}$ > 47) = (14 + 4 + 6 + 4 + 1 + 1)/100 or .30

P($\bar{X}$ < 40) = (2 + 4)/100 or .06

3.   μ = 45

σ = 12

N = 25

P(43 $\leq$ $\bar{X}$ $\leq$ 47.0) = (21 + 14 + 15 + 11 + 1)/100

= .62

Add frequencies for 43 to 46 inclusive, plus one 47).

4.   μ = 45

σ = 12

N = 100

P(43 $\leq$ $\bar{X}$ < 47.0) = (85)/100
= .85

Add frequencies for 43 to 46 inclusive

Section 11.3

1.   Army recruits   N = 10

(a) $\bar{X}$ = 128/10 or 12.8

X	X$-\bar{\text{X}}$	$(\text{X}-\bar{\text{X}})^2$
15	2.2	4.84
10	-2.8	.4
12	- .8	.64
14	1.2	1.44
14	1.2	1.44
16	3.2	10.24
12	-1.8	.64
11	-1.8	3.24
11	-1.8	3.24
13	.2	.04
		33.90

(b) Var = 33.9/10   Var = 33.9/9

Biased   Unbiased

Var = 3.39   Var = 3.73

(c) SD = 1.83   SD = 1.93

2. gas pumps   N = 20

Error	freq
5	1
4	1
3	3
2	1
1	2
0	4
-1	2
-2	5
-6	1

(a) $\bar{\text{X}}$ = .2

(b) Unbiased   Biased

Var = 6.91   Var = 6.56

(c) SD = 2.62   SD = 2.56

3. Cola preference   N = 20

Rating	freq
5	1
4	7
3	9
2	3
1	0

(a) $\bar{X}$ = 3.3

(b) Biased   Unbiased

     Var = .62   Var = .64

(c) SD = .79   SD = .80

Section 11.4

1. Sample mean is close to population mean--so unbiased estimate.

2. Theoretical

    (a) N = 4   SE = 10/2 or 5
    (b) N = 16   SE = 10/4 or 2.5
    (c) N = 36   SE = 10/6 or 1.7

3. Estimated

    (a) N = 4   SE = 5.3 close

    (b) N = 16   SE = 2.5 exact!

    (c) N = 36   SE = 1.7 exact! (within rounding)

4. 2/3 of population is within one standard deviation so interval is
    63.5 $\pm$ 12/6 or 61.5 to 65.5

5. 63.5 + 12/5
    63.5 $\pm$ 2.4
    Interval 61.1 to 65.9

6. 63.5 + 12/2
    63.5 $\pm$ 6
    Interval 57.5 to 69.5

7. 63.5 + 12/10
    63.5 $\pm$ 1.2
    Interval 62.3 to 64.7

8. For 95%   Z = $\pm$ 1.96
    Score = Z(SE) + mean
    (a) N = 36
        $\pm$ 1.96 (12/6) + 63.5
        $\pm$ 3.92 + 63.5
        59.58 to 67.42

    (b) N = 25
        $\pm$ 1.96 (12/5) + 63.5
        $\pm$ 4.704 + 63.5
        58.796 to 68.204

(c) N = 4
     $\pm$ 1.96 (12/2) + 63.5
     $\pm$ 11.76 + 63.5
     51.74 to 75.26

(d) N = 100
     $\pm$ 1.96 (12/10) + 63.5
     $\pm$ 2.352 + 63.5
     61.148 to 65.852

Section 11.5

1. Bong Show
    $\bar{X}$ = 31   N = 100
    SD = 4.7   CI 99% (CI is Confidence Interval)
    Find z for 99% CI   z = $\pm$ 2.54
    T = z(SD) + mean
    T = $\pm$ 2.54 (.43) + 31
    T = $\pm$ 1.09 + 31
    so interval is 29.91 to 32.09

2. Corn moisture
    $\bar{X}$ = 38.2   n = 36
                                   CI = 90%
    S.D = 2.3   z = $\pm$ 1.65
    T = $\pm$ 1.65 (2.3/6) + 38.2
    T = $\pm$ .6325 + 38.2
    so interval is 37.57 to 38.83
    95% CI; z = $\pm$ 1.96
    Interval 37.45 to 38.95

3. Long distance calls
    $\bar{X}$ = .89   n = 67
                               99% CI
    SD = .15   z = $\pm$ 2.58
    T = $\pm$ 2.58 (.15/$\sqrt{67}$) + .89
    T = $\pm$ .047 + .89
    So interval is .843 to .937

4. length of micro-organism
    $\bar{X}$ = 27.5   N = 64
                          90% CI
    SD = 3.2   z = $\pm$ 1.64
    T = $\pm$ 1.64 (3.2/8) + 27.5
    T = $\pm$ .656 + 27.5
    so interval is 26.844 to 28.156
    b)   95% CI   z = $\pm$ 1.96
         T = $\pm$ 1.96 (3.2/8) + 27.5
         T = $\pm$ .784 + 27.5
         so interval is 26.716 to 28.284

    c)   99% CI   z = $\pm$ 2.58
         T = $\pm$ 2.58 (3.2/8) + 27.5
         T = $\pm$ 1.032 + 27.5
         so interval is 26.468 to 28.532

5. Increasing sample size decreases size of interval

6. Montreal
   point estimates
       favor .40
       oppose .37
       undec .23
   Not possible to give Confidence Interval; Level of Confidence is not given.

7. Key   Prob   Deer
   The goodness of the estimate depends on the representativeness of the sample.

Chapter 12   Section 12.1

1. Batteries
   $P(\text{mean} \leq 14.5) = (15 + 20)/100$ or $.35$
   A large probability; do not reject claim

2. Light bulbs
   $P(\text{mean} \leq 47.5) = 3/100$
                    $= .03$
   unlikely; so reject claim.

3. Iron ore
   $P(\text{mean} \geq 14) = 3/100$ or $.03$
   It is reasonable to doubt the claim.

4. Gasoline pumps
   $P(\bar{X} \leq 229) = 3/100$ or $.03$
   So results do cause one to doubt the claim.

5. Gasoline pumps
   $P(\bar{X} \leq 230.3) = 18/100$ or $.18$
   No evidence to doubt accuracy of pumps.

6. School district
   $p(\text{mean} \leq 83) = 3/100$ or $.03$
   It seems group is below the national mean.

Section 12.2

1. Batteries
   Since $p(\bar{X} \leq 13.5) = .04$
   Do not reject claim if $.01$ defined as unusual.

2. Batteries
   If $\mu = 14$

   $$z = \frac{13.5 - 14.}{.83} \qquad = \frac{-.5}{.83} \qquad = -.59$$

p ($z \leq -.59$) = .2776
Accept company claim concerning the mean.

3.   Iron ore (12.1.3)

$$z = \frac{14 - 12}{6.1/\sqrt{40}} = 2.07$$

p ($z \geq 2.07$) = .0192 or
about .02 which is close to .03; same decision

4.   Gasoline pumps (12.1.4)

$$z = \frac{229 - 231}{2.1/\sqrt{36}}$$

$$= \frac{-2}{.35} \quad \text{or} \quad -5.7$$

p ($z < -5.7$) is very small (not on chart) so decision is the same.

5.   School district (12.1.6)

$$z = \frac{83 - 85}{7.3/\sqrt{50}}$$

$$= \frac{-2}{1.03} \quad \text{or} \quad -1.94$$

p ($z \leq -1.94$) = .0262
Very different from data from sample; so decision is different.

6.   Groceries

$$z = \frac{86 - 80}{9/\sqrt{64}}$$

$$= \frac{6}{1.125} \quad \text{or} \quad 5.33$$

p ($z \geq 5.33$) is very small so conclude claim is doubtful.

7.   Groceries

$$z = \frac{86 - 80}{9/\sqrt{36}}$$

$$= \frac{6}{1.5} \quad \text{or} \quad 4$$

p ($z \geq 4$) is still small so conclude claim is doubtful.

8.   Golden Rectangle

$\bar{X}$ = 66.05, SD = 9.02; N = 20

$z = \dfrac{66.05 - 61.8}{9.02/\sqrt{20}}$ or   2.107

p (z > 2.107) = .0174   so artwork does vary significantly.

9.   Nite - Nite Bulb
$\bar{X}$ = 48.3
SD = 4.19
N = 36

so $z = \dfrac{48.3 - 50}{4.19/6} = \dfrac{-1.7}{.6983} = -2.43$

p (z $\leq$ -2.43) = .0075
So doubtful that bulb life is 50 hours.

Section 12.3

1.   Since p ($\bar{X}$ $\leq$ 13.5) = .04, would accept the claim if "unusual" is defined as .$\overline{01}$.
There is no chance of a Type I error when claim is accepted.

2.   Increasing sample size decreases the standard error.
Increasing the sample size decreases the chance of a Type I error.
Increasing the sample size increases the chance of a Type II error.

3.   Groceries

Type I error would occur if claim that average expenditure for groceries is $80.00 is rejected when it really is true.

Type II error would occur if claim of $80 average expenditure was accepted when, in fact, it was not true.

4.   Air sickness: Claim - new way is better.

Type I error would result in saying new way is not better when, in fact, it is. (Reject true)

Type II error would result in saying that new way is better when, in fact, it is not. (Accept false)

5.   Answers will vary.

Section 12.4

1. (a) P (t > 1.8) = .04   (b) P (t > 2.3) = .02
    (c) P (t > 1.4) = .13   (d) P (t < -1.8) = .03
    (e) P (t < -2.1) = 0   (f) P (t < -1.4) = .05

    (Note: > , < does not include =)

2. Theoretical 9 df

    (a) p (t > 1.8) = .05   (b) p (t > 2.3) = .025
    (c) p (t > 1.4) = .10   (d) p (t < -1.8) = .05
    (e) p (t < -2.3) = .025   (f) p (t < -1.4) = .10

3. (a) df = 11; p (t > 1.80) = .05
    (b) df = 6;   p (t > -1.44) = .10
    (c) df = 21; p (t > 1.32) = .10
    (d) df = 24; p (t < -2.06) = .025

4. (a) df = 11; p (t > 2.0) = .075
    (b) df = 16; p (t < -2.5) = .013
    (c) df = 23; p (t > 2.6) = .008
    (d) df = 9;   p (t < -1.9) = .048

    (a) 1.8   .05 $\frac{.2}{.4} = \frac{X}{.025}$
        2.0   ?
        2.2   .025   .013 = X

        .05 - .013 = .037

    (b) 2.12   .025 $\frac{.38}{.46} = \frac{X}{.015}$
        2.50   ?
        2.58   .010   .012 = X

        .025 - .012 = .013

    (c) 2.50   .010 $\frac{.10}{.31} = \frac{X}{.005}$
        2.60   ?
        2.81   .005   .002 = X

    .01 - .002 = .008

    (d) 1.83   .050 $\frac{.07}{.43} = \frac{X}{.025}$
        1.90   ?
        2.26   .025   .004 = X

        .050 - .004 = .046

Section 12.5

1.   95% CI   t = 2.13

   U = 2.13 (5.88) + 140.50
     = 12.52 + 140.50
     = 153.02

   L = 2.13 (5.88) + 140.50
     = 12.52 + 140.50
     = 127.98

   So CI is from 127.8 to 153.02

   99% CI   t = 2.95

   U = 2.95 (5.88) + 140.50
     = 157.85

   L = -2.95 (5.88) + 140.50
     = 123.15

   CI is from 123.15 to 157.85

2.   IQ $\bar{X}$ = 115   N = 9 so df = 8
          SD = 11.2   t = 2.31 for 95% CI

   CI   = ± 2.31 (11.2/3) + 115
        = ± 8.62 + 115

   CI is from 106.38 to 123.62

3.   Popularity of entertainers

   $\bar{X}$ = 4.1   n = 12
   SD = .2   t = 3.11 for 99%

   CI = 99%

   C1 = ± 3.11 (.2/$\sqrt{12}$) + 4.1
      = ± .18 + 4.1

        3.92 to 4.28

4.   Gold in a vein

   CI 90%

   $\bar{X}$ = 12.3   N = 10 so df = 9
   SD = 2.5   t = 1.83

   C1 = ±1.83 (2.5/$\sqrt{10}$) + 12.3

CI = ±1.447 + 12.3

so 10.85% to 13.75%

5.   Discoveries   CI 90%

$\bar{X}$ = 35.42   N = 12
SD = 6.92   t = 1.80
SD (unbiased) = 7.22

CI = ±1.80 (7.22/$\sqrt{12}$) + 35.42
   = ±3.75 + 35.42

so 31.67 to 39.17

Section 12.6

1.   Ninth-graders' weight

$\bar{X}$ = 118
SD = 5 $t = \dfrac{118-114}{5/\sqrt{12}}$
μ = 114
N = 12
df = 11 $t = 2.77$

$p\ (t \geq 2.77) = .01$

Doubtful that total class has mean weight of 114 pounds--probably
weighs more.

2.   Manganese deposit

$\bar{X}$ = 81.3 $t = \dfrac{81.3 - 77}{3.2/\sqrt{16}}$
SD = 3.2
μ = 77
N = 16 $t = 5.375$

$p\ (t \geq 5.375)$ is very small

So: conclude claim of 77 is not true.   Sample differs significantly from
the population.

3.   Crow Indians

from data

N = 10 $t = \dfrac{61.05 - 61.8}{14.29/\sqrt{10}}$
$\bar{X}$ = 61.05
SD_{n-1} = 14.29

μ = 61.8 $t = -.160$

SD (unbiased) = 14.29   p (t $\leq$ -.160) is large

near .50 (but not in Table)

So appears Crow Indians did use golden ratio.

4.   Transylvania Effect

$\bar{X}$ = 13.3 $t = \dfrac{13.3 - 11.2}{5.50/\sqrt{12}}$
SD = 5.26

N = 12

SD (unbiased) = 5.50

μ = 11.2   t = 1.32

p (t $\geq$ 1.32) = .10   (a little more)

Since value is more than .10, claim that admissions were 11.2 on the average would not be rejected--do not have sufficient evidence of more admissions during full moon.

Chapter 13   Section 13.1

1.

Pref	Ex	Ob	E - 0	$(E - 0)^2$
LMH	5	10	-5	25
LHM	5	3	2	4
MLH	5	3	2	4
MHL	5	8	-3	9
HLM	5	1	4	16
HML	5	5	0	0
		30		

(a)   (30)/6 = 5 $\chi^2_2 = (58)/5$
                                     $\chi^2 = 11.6$

(b)   Six Steps
   1.   Model - die; 6 equally likely outcomes
   2.   Trial - roll die 30 times; once for each person
   3.   Outcome - compute the χ^2
   4.   Repeat -
   5.   P $(\chi^2_5 \geq 11.6)$ = .05
   6.   Decision: Since prob is small, model is <u>not</u> appropriate.
        It is unlikely that each crust is equally <u>well</u> liked.

(c)

		Exp	Obt	E - 0
LMH	.23	6.9	10	-3.1
LHM	.18	5.4	3	2.4
MLH	.18	5.4	3	2.4
MHL	.15	4.5	8	-3.5
HLM	.15	4.5	1	3.5
HML	.11	3.3	5	-1.7

$$\chi^2 = \frac{9.61}{6.9} + \frac{5.76}{5.4} + \frac{5.76}{5.4} + \frac{12.25}{4.5} + \frac{12.25}{4.5} + \frac{2.89}{3.3}$$

$$= 1.393 + 1.067 + 1.067 + 2.72 + 2.72 + .876$$

$$= 9.843$$

Steps 1.-4. as in b

5   $P(\chi^2_5 \geq 9.843) = .08$

6   Dec - Since prob is still small, model is not appropriate

2.   Mendel's experiment

		Exp	Obt	E - 0
Round & yellow	9/16	313	315	-2
Wrinkled & yellow	3/16	104	101	3
Round & green	3/16	104	108	-4
Wrinkled & green	1/16	35	32	3

$$\chi^2 = \frac{4}{313} + \frac{9}{104} + \frac{16}{104} + \frac{9}{35}$$

$$= .012 + .087 + .154 + .257$$

$$= .51$$

$p(\chi^2_3 \geq .51) \cong .90$

Since prob is large, no evidence model is inappropriate--cast no doubt upon his theory.

3.   Flower experiment

Flower	Exp	Obs	E - 0
AB	180	164	16
Ab	60	78	-18
aB	60	65	- 5
ab	20	13	7

$$\chi^2 = \frac{256}{180} + \frac{324}{60} + \frac{25}{60} + \frac{49}{20}$$

$$\chi^2 = 1.422 + 5.4 + .417 + 2.45$$

$$\chi^2 = 9.689$$

$p(\chi^2_3 \geq 9.689) \cong .02$

Since prob is small, data do not support the theory

4.   Candidates

	Exp	Obt	E - O
Alpha	60% or 391.8	503	-111.2
Beta	30% or 195.9	115	80.9
Gamma	10% or 65.3	35	30.3
		653	

$$\chi^2 = \frac{12365.44}{391.8} + \frac{6544.81}{195.9} + \frac{918.09}{30.3}$$

$$\chi^2 = 31.56 + 33.4 + 14.060$$

$$\chi^2 = 79.02$$

$$p\,(\chi^2_{\,2} \geq 79.02) = \text{very small}$$

Model not appropriate.   Poll not accurate

5.   City population

		Exp	Obs	E - O
White	30%	15	20	-5
Black	55%	27.5	20	7.5
Latino	15%	7.5	10	-2.5
			50	

$$\chi^2 = \frac{25}{15} + \frac{56.25}{27.5} + \frac{6.25}{7.5}$$

$$\chi^2 = 1.667 + 2.045 + .833$$

$$\chi^2 = 4.545$$

$$p\,(\chi^2_{\,2} \geq 4.545) \cong .10$$

Since p = .10, it is difficult to make a decision

6.   Typing errors

Number of errors	Prop	Exp	Obt	O - E
0	.59	98.53	103	-4.47
1	.31	51.77	45	6.77
2	.08	13.36	16	-2.64
3 or more	.02	3.34	3	.34
			167	

$$\chi^2 = \frac{19.98}{98.53} + \frac{45.82}{51.77} + \frac{6.97}{13.36} + \frac{.12}{3.34}$$

$$= .20 + .88 + .52 + 1.06$$

$$= 1.64$$

$$p\,(\chi^2_{\,4} \geq 1.64) = .50, \text{ so model seems appropriate}$$

7. Rain storms
    Number

heavy	Prob	Exp	Obt	E-O	$(E-O)^2$
0	.301	99.33	102	-2.67	7.13
1	.361	119.13	114	5.13	26.32
2	.216	71.28	74	-2.72	7.40
3	.086	28.38	28	.38	.14
4 or more	.036	11.88	12	-.12	.01

$$\chi^2 = .07 + .22 + .10 + .005 + 0$$

$$\chi^2 = .395$$

$$p\,(\chi^2_4 \geq .395) = .99$$

Model predicts well

8. Pebbles

	Exp	Obs	E-O
10	9.1	6	3.1
9	24.7	25	- .3
8	30.0	31	-1.0
7	21.7	28	-6.3
6	10.3	9	1.3
5	3.3	0	3.3
4 or less	.9	1	- .1

$$\chi^2 = \frac{9.61}{9.1} + \frac{.09}{24.7} + \frac{1}{30} + \frac{39.69}{21.7} + \frac{1.69}{10.3} + \frac{10.89}{3.3} + \frac{.01}{.9}$$

$$\chi^2 = 1.056 + .004 + .033 + 1.829 + .164 + 3.3 + .01$$

$$\chi^2 = 6.396$$

$$p\,(\chi^2_9 \geq 6.396) > .50$$

Since prob is large, model is appropriate and pebbles are probably distributed occording to that model.

Section 13.2

1.		Favorable		Neutral		Unf.		Total
	Cautious	80	62.3	10	9	10	28.7	100
	Middle	58	62.3	8	9	34	28.7	100
	Confident	49	62.3	9	9	42	28.7	100
	Total	187		27		86		300

$$\chi^2 = \frac{(17.7)^2}{62.3} + \frac{(-4.3)^2}{62.3} + \frac{(-13.3)^2}{62.3} + \frac{1^2}{9} + \frac{(-1)^2}{9} + \frac{0}{9}$$

$$+ \frac{(-18.7)^2}{28.7} + \frac{(5.3)^2}{28.7} + \frac{(13.3)^2}{28.7}$$

$$= \frac{508.67}{62.3} + \frac{2}{9} + \frac{554.67}{28.7}$$

$$= 8.16 + .22 + 19.33$$
$$= 27.71$$

$p\ (\chi^2_4 > 27.71) =$ is very small,
so conclude that personality type and opinion about small cars are not independent

2.

	Men	Women	Total
A	235 / 261.7	119 / 92.3	354
B	533 / 539.6	197 / 190.4	730
C	287 / 299.3	118 / 105.6	405
D	149 / 167.1	77 / 58.9	226
E	81 / 82.0	30 / 29.0	111
F	403 / 408.0	149 / 144	552
G	511 / 441.3	86 / 155.7	597
Total	2199	776	2975

Note: $261.7 \doteq 2199\,(354)/2975$

$$\chi^2 = \frac{(-26.7)^2}{261.7} + \frac{(26.7)^2}{92.3} \quad .081 + .229 + .505 + 1.456 + 1.961$$

$$+ 5.562 + .012 + .012 + .061 + .061 + 11.001 + 31.20$$

$$\chi^2 = 65.526$$

$p\ (\chi^2_6 > 65.526)$ is very small so doubtful that number of women selected was independent of the judge.

3. Amoebas

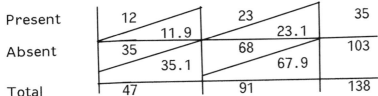

Present	12 / 11.9	23 / 23.1	35
Absent	35 / 35.1	68 / 67.9	103
Total	47	91	138

$$\chi^2 = \frac{.01}{11.9} + \frac{.01}{23.1} + \frac{.01}{35.1} + \frac{.01}{67.9}$$

$$= .0008 + .0004 + .0003 + .0001$$

$$\chi^2 = \text{very small}$$

$p(\chi^2_1 > 0)$ is very large, so conclude independence does exist

4. Fish

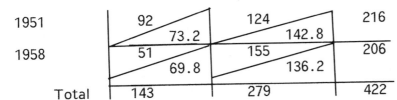

1951	92 / 73.2	124 / 142.8	216
1958	51 / 69.8	155 / 136.2	206
Total	143	279	422

$$\chi^2 = \frac{(18.8)^2}{73.2} + 2.475 + 5.064 + 2.600$$

$$\chi^2 = 14.967$$

$p(\chi^2_1 > 14.967)$ is very small so conclude that difference does exist. (Hypothesis of independence - no difference is not supported by data).

5. Cold Remedy

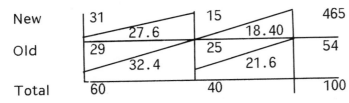

New	31 / 27.6	15 / 18.40	465
Old	29 / 32.4	25 / 21.6	54
Total	60	40	100

$$\chi^2 = .419 + .628 + .357 + .535$$

$$\chi^2 = 1.939$$

$$p(\chi^2_1 > 1.939) \cong .17$$

So conclude better results could be due to chance. No evidence to suggest changing to new treatment.

Section 13.3

1. Pascal's triangle

Row 5:	1	5	10	10	5	1		
6:	1	6	15	20	15	6	1	
7:	1	7	21	35	35	21	7	1

2.

Row 8:	1	8	28	56	70	56	28	8	1		
9:	1	9	36	84	126	126	84	36	9	1	
10:	1	10	45	120	210	252	210	120	45	10	1

3. 4 coins - theoretical
    (a) p (0 heads) = 1/16
    (b) p (1 head) = 4/16
    (c) p (2 heads) = 6/16
    (d) p (3 heads) = 4/16
    (e) p (4 heads) = 1/16

4. Answers will vary

5. (a) 6 coins $2^6 = 64$
        p (0 heads) = 1/64
        p (1 head) = 6/64
        p (2 heads) = 15/64
        p (3 heads) = 20/64
        p (4 heads) = 15/64
        p (5 heads) = 6/64
        p (6 heads) = 1/64

    (b) 10 coins $2^{10} = 1024$
        p (0 H) = 1/1024
        p (1 H) = 10/1024
        p (2 H) = 45/1024
        p (3 H) = 120/1024
        p (4 H) = 210/1024
        p (5 H) = 252/1024
        p (6 H) = 210/1024
        p (7 H) = 120/1024
        p (8 H) = 45/1024
        p (9 H) = 10/1024
        p (10 H) = 1/1024

    (c) 5 coins $2^5 = 32$
        p (0 H) = 1/32
        p (1 H) = 5/32
        p (2 H) = 10/32
        p (3 H) = 10/32
        p (4 H) = 5/32
        p (5 H) = 1/32

6. Toss 5 coins; answers will vary.

Section 13.4

1. Ninth graders (Small sample)
    $\bar{X} = 100$
    $S = 5$ $t = \dfrac{100-114}{5/\sqrt{9}}$ or -2.4
    $N = 9$
    $\mu = 114$
                $p\,(t < -2.4 \text{ or } t > 2.4) = .025 + .025$
                                            $= .05$

    So conclude sample does differ significantly from assumed mean.

2. Savings and loan (large sample)
    $\bar{X} = 145$
    $S = 25$ $z = \dfrac{145-150}{25/\sqrt{49}}$ or -1.4
    $N = 49$
    $\mu = 150$

                $p\,(z < -1.4 \text{ or } z > 1.4) = .0808 + .0808$
                                            $= .1616$

    So do not have evidence to doubt association's claim.

3. Manganese (small sample)
    $\bar{X} = 89.1$
    $S = 3.2$ $t = \dfrac{89.1-85}{3.2/\sqrt{16}} = 5.125$
    $N = 16$
    $\mu = 85$
                $p\,(t > 5.125)$ is very small

    So conclude that claim is not true.

4. School district (large sample)
    $\bar{X} = 83$
    $S = 7.3$ $z = \dfrac{83-85}{7.3/\sqrt{50}}$ or -1.94
    $N = 50$
    $\mu = 85$
                $p\,(z < -1.94) = .0262$

    So conclude achievement is below the national mean.

5. Supermarket (large sample)

    $\bar{X} = 105.96$ $(SD_{n-1} = 15.16)$

    $S = 14.85$ $z = \dfrac{105.96-95}{15.16/\sqrt{25}} = 3.61$
    $N = 25$
    $\mu = 95$
                $p\,(z > 3.61 \text{ or } z < -3.61)$ is very small, so reject claim.

6. Scholastic average of fraternity men
    $\bar{X} = 3.7$
    $S = .25$
    $$z = \frac{3.7 - 3.6}{.25/\sqrt{100}} = 4$$
    $N = 100$
    $\mu = 3.6$
    $p\ (z > 4)$ is very small so conclude that fraternity men have a higher average.

7. Teaching statistics
    $\bar{X} = 64$
    $S = 6.6$
    $$t = \frac{64 - 58}{6.6/\sqrt{4}} = 3.636$$
    $N = 16$
    $\mu = 58$

    $p\ (t > 3.636) \cong .01$

    So conclude teaching method is better.

8. $\bar{X} = 9.2$
    $S = 1.12$
    $$z = \frac{9.2-8.5}{1.12/\sqrt{49}} = 4.375$$
    $N = 49$
    $\mu = 8.5$

    $p\ (z > 4.375$ or $z < -4.375)$ is very small.

    So conclude sample is different.

9. $\bar{X} = 4.3$
    $S = 1.2$
    $$t = \frac{4.3-3.2}{1.2/\sqrt{9}} = 2.75$$
    $N = 9$
    $df = 8$
    $\mu = 3.2$

    $p\ (t > 2.75) = .01$

    Doubtful the number of letters has remained the same. Probably has increased.

Section 13.5

1. Equal freq. Test - Phone #

digit	E	O	E-O	$(E-O)^2$
0	40	46	-6	36
1	40	37	3	9
2	40	44	-4	16
3	40	35	5	25
4	40	36	4	16
5	40	48	-8	64
6	40	47	-7	49
7	40	30	10	100
8	40	35	5	25
9	40	42	-2	4

$\chi^2 = 8.6$

$p\ (\chi^2_9 > 8.6) \cong .50$

Hypothesis that digits are equally distributed seems reasonable.
Phone numbers appear to be a good source of random digits.

2. Occurrence of digits following 1.

Rows 1-5	7	0	9	8	7					
6-10	0	7	6	1	9	2	4	5		
11-15	7	6	8	1	4	8				
16-20	1	8	8	6	5	9	2	5		
21-25	3	1	2	0	9	4	5	4	9	5

Total 37

Digit	E	O	E-O	$(E-O)^2$
0	3.7	3	.7	.49
1	3.7	4	-.3	.09
2	3.7	3	.7	.49
3	3.7	1	2.7	7.29
4	3.7	4	-.3	.09
5	3.7	5	-1.3	1.69
6	3.7	3	.7	.49
7	3.7	4	-.3	.09
8	3.7	5	-1.3	1.69
9	3.7	5	-1.3	1.69

$\chi^2 = \dfrac{1}{3.7}\ (14.1)$ or 3.81

$p\ (\chi^2_9 > 3.81) \cong .92$ (between .95 and .90)

so conclude independence of 1 and following digits

3.

(a)

Digit	$\overline{E}$ 50	$\overline{O}$ 36	E-O
1	50	36	14
2	50	46	4
3	50	68	-18
4	50	47	3
5	50	50	0
6	50	53	- 3

$\chi^2 = 11.08$

$p\ (\chi^2_5 > 11.08) \doteq .05$

Die likely not fair.

(b) Answer will depend on the pattern checked - following 1 or 2 or . . .

4. Mid squares

digit	$\overline{E}$ 40	$\overline{O}$ 47	E-O
0	40	47	- 7
1	40	35	5
2	40	44	- 4
3	40	47	- 7
4	40	33	7
5	40	48	- 8
6	40	44	- 4
7	40	31	9
8	40	45	- 5
9	40	26	14

$\chi^2 = (570)/40$ or 14.25

$p\ (\chi^2_9 \geq 14.25) \cong .10$

so mid squares method is borderline!

5. digit preference
Answers will vary

6. Random digits from page of book.
Answers will vary
If selecting side without coin all numbers would be either even or odd.

7. Letters of alphabet → 01 to 26
Answers will vary

An equal frequency test would show that there are more occurrences of some letters.

Chapter 14

Answers are obtained using computer.   Solutions are omitted.

Chapter Tests

Test

Chapter 1   Name _____

1. Name 4 areas in which statistics is used. Give an example of one of these areas.

2. The following numbers represent the final grades on a statistics test. Classify these data using a stem and leaf plot. (Please work down each column to help in checking.)

88	54	91	70	93	62	89	61	81	67
72	87	80	76	83	58	75	86	78	92
80	56	75	60	73	69	97	77	65	81
92	71	63	71	64	79	88	62	51	73
85	67	95	50	75	71	72	90	78	69

_____

_____

_____

_____

_____

3. In a survey of 50 families, it was found that they had the following number of cars. Draw a cumulative frequency graph.

Number of cars		c.f.
0	2	2
1	7	9
2	27	36
3	11	47
4	2	49
5	1	50

What is the total number of cars that these families have?

4.   A group of 25 students rated their math teacher on a scale of 1 (low) to 5 (high).   The results were

Score	frequency	prop	cum freq	cum prop
1	1			
2	4			
3	11			
4	7			
5	2			

Complete the chart above and find the following.

The proportion of students rating the teacher '4' is _____

The proportion of students rating the teacher '3' or less' is _____

The number of students rating the teacher '5' is _____

The number of students rating the teacher '2 or less' is _____

The proportion of students rating the teacher 'more than 3' is _____

Draw a frequency polygon and a histogram using proportions for the data given above.

5.

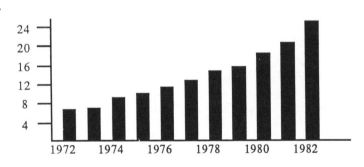

The graph at the left indicates the average wage cost/hour in the construction industry.

   a.   What is indicated on the horizontal axis?

   b.   What is indicated on the vertical axis?

   c.   What was the increase in hourly cost from 1974 to 1981?

   d.   What type of graph is this?

   e.   What major idea is being portrayed by the graph?

Test

Chapter 2 Sections 1 to 4   Name _____

1.   I tossed three coins 25 times with the following results:

No. of tails   freq.

        0   4
        1   9
        2   10
        3   2

Find the following: Mean_____ Median_____ Mode_____

3.   The following hourly wages were paid to the employees in a store.
     $3.60, 5.52, 3.18, 4.60, 3.18, 7.28, 3.18, 5.18, 5.62, 4.40

For these ten employees, find

Mean _____   Median _____   Mode _____

If you were an employee in the store, which average would you
report?
Why?

If you were the owner of the store, which average would you report?
Why?

3.   In 1980, the mean expenditures per pupil in a school district was
     $3992 and the district enrollment was 4796 students. What was the
     total expenditure for the district?

4. The following stem-and-leaf plot represents the speed in miles per hour of 32 selected animals. (The cheetah is the fastest -- 70 mph and the chicken is the slowest -- 9 mph.)

    Find the range _____   the median _____

    Q_1 _____ Q_3 _____

    Stem

0	9
1	1 2 5 8
2	0 5 7
3	0 0 0 0 0 2 2 5 5 5 5 9
4	0 0 0 2 3 5 5 7
5	0 0 0
6	1
7	0

5. The grades in the morning section of a college statistics test are:

    83   90   88   76   75   98   88   79   81

    92   89   79   87   63   90   78   70   77

    The grades in the afternoon section of the same course are:

    60   95   85   79   65   86   45   52

    76   85   70   92   76   55   80

    Draw a stem and leaf diagram and a box and whisker plot for these data. What two things can be said about these data?

Test

Chapter 2 Sections 5-7   Name _____

1. The high temperatures for last week were:

        56, 71, 63, 78, 66, 63, 72

    The range of these temperatures is _____

    The median of these temperatures is _____

    The mode of these temperatures is _____

    The mean of these temperatures is _____

2. I tossed 3 coins 50 times with the following results:

Number of tails	frequency
0	8
1	17
2	19
3	6

    The mean is _____.   The median range is _____.
    The mode is _____.   The   range   is _____.

3. The following ages were obtained in a random sample of 10 people
    riding the American Eagle at Great America. Find the deviation age
    for each and then find the mean deviation.

    Age

    38   _____

    12   _____

    64   _____

    32   _____

    10   _____

     4   _____

    28   _____

    68   _____

    11   _____

    17   _____

4.   A new sleeping pill is being tested in a laboratory. The amount of sleep gained (in hours) by 10 persons who tried the drug in an experiment was as follows: (a negative number means a sleep loss)

Person	Sleep gained	Deviation
A	2.0	.5
B	3.5	2.0
C	.5	-1.0
D	0.0	-1.5
E	-1.0	-2.5
F	2.0	.5
G	3.0	1.5
H	2.5	1.0
I	0.0	-1.5
J	2.5	1.0

Find the variance and the standard deviation for these data.

5.   Find the range, mean deviation, variance and standard deviation for the following. The numbers represent the yards gained by a football team in the last 5 weeks.

156,   289,   84,   302   214

Do you think the team is consistent?   Why?

Test

Chapter 3 Sections 1 - 3   Name _____

1.   The Key problem for Chapter 3 is:

About how many packages of bubble gum, on the average, would we expect to buy to obtain a complete set of 6 different flags? Assume that on each purchase of a stick of gum, the chances of obtaining each of the 6 flags are equal.

Model: Die each side corresponds to one of the 6 flags.
         Each roll of the die corresponds to the purchase of a stick of gum and therefore one flag.

Trial   Roll the die, record the result, continue until all six sides (flags) have occurred.

State of Int.   Record the number of rolls necessary to obtain all six numbers (flags)

Repeat 5 times

Mean Value =

Perform your 5 trials. Record your results on the form below

Trial	Outcomes 1	2	3	4	5	6
1						
2						
3						
4						
5						

2.   Three coins were tossed 4 times. This was repeated 10 times. The results are given below.

THT	HHT	HHT	THH		TTT	TTT	HHT	THH
THT	HTT	TTT	TTH		THH	HHT	TTT	THH
TTH	TTT	HTH	THH		HTT	HTH	TTT	HHH
HHT	THH	HTT	HHH		HHT	HHT	THH	TTH
THH	HTH	HHT	HTH		HHT	HHH	TTT	THH

In this experiment, what is a trial? _____

How many trials were there? _____

The statistic of interest is the number of times that 2 tails and 1 head was obtained.

Complete the frequency distribution and find the mean number of times that two tails and one head occurred.

2 tails and 1 head	frequency
0	_____
1	_____
2	_____
3	_____
4	_____

3. Two coins were tossed six times. The number of times 2 tails occurred was recorded. This was repeated 300 times. The results are shown below. Find the mean number of times that 2 tails appeared.

2 tails	frequency
0	5
1	30
2	64
3	93
4	75
5	27
6	6

4. Describe a model, a trial and the statistic of interest for the following.

A. What is the expected number of girls in a 5 child family?

Model

Trial

St of int

B. An excellent softball player has a .400 batting average. How many times in a row would you expect her to bat <u>without</u> getting a hit?

Model

Trial

St of int

C. In a multiple choice test with 3 responses for each question, what is the expected number of correct answers obtained by guessing if there are 25 questions on the test?

Model

Trial

St of int

D. A market research company claims that .75 of persons called agree to answer survey questions. Under this assumption, how many people in a row could be expected to respond to the researcher's questions?

Model

Trial

St of int

Test

Chapter 3 Sections 4-6   Name _____

1. A two dimensional walk of 10 steps was taken. This was repeated 5
    times. Find the terminal point, the distance from the origin for each
    walk and the mean distance for the 5 walks.

    HH → N
    HT → S
    TH → W
    TT → E

Steps	Point	Distance
HT HH TT HT TT HH TH TH HT HH	_____	_____
HT TT TH HH HT TH TH TT TT TH	_____	_____
HH HH TH TH HT TT TT TT HT TT	_____	_____
HH HH TH HT TT HT TH HH TH HH	_____	_____
TH TH HH HH HT TT HH TH TT HH	_____	_____

    The mean distance is _____

2. To find the approximate temperature at the point (4,2) on the steel
    plate (see page 72) 250 random walks were taken. The results were:

temp	3°	15°	30°	40°
no. of walks	25	88	6	131

    Find the approximate temperature.

3.   Describe a model, a trial and the statistic of interest for the following:

In a multiple choice test with 3 responses for each question, what is the expected number of correct answers obtained by guessing if there are 50 questions?

Model

Trial

St. of Int.

The teacher who keeps her classroom locked and the loose keys in her purse now has only four keys. She still pulls out a key and tries it. If the key does not fit, she returns it to her purse and tries again. On the average, how many tries will she have to make before she succeeds in opening the door?

Model

Trial

St. of Int.

4.   The following number of steps were taken before reaching a barrier at 5 or -5 in a one dimensional random walk. Make 5 statistical statements concerning these data.

25,   9, 19, 27, 49, 23, 33, 15, 15,   8,

14, 14,   6, 11,   7, 21 37,   9, 11, 21

21,   5, 17, 15, 35, 10,   5, 21,   9,   5

15, 31, 13,   7,   9, 31, 13,   7, 62, 14

5.   Perform 10 trials for the following problem.

   What is the expected number of people necessary to obtain a 'shared' birth month?

   Model   12 outcomes (a coin and a die as indicated below)

   Trial   Toss coin and die; record result. Continue to toss until one result (month) is repeated.

   St. of int.   Record the number of tosses necessary to obtain a repeated result (duplicate birth month)

   Repeat 20 times

   Mean value =

Trial \ month	1 1h	2 2h	3 3h	4 4h	5 5h	6 6h	7 1t	8 2t	9 3t	10 4t	11 5t	12 6t	TOTAL
1													
2													
3													
4													
5													
6													
7													
8													
9													
10													

Test

Chapter 4   Name _____

1. Find the estimated probabilities for the following. (The capital P
    represents an estimated probability). Give answer in decimal form.

    Airline records show that 6640 people actually showed up for flights
    when 7000 reservations had been made.

    P(showing up for a flight) = _____
    P(not showing up for a flight) = _____

    A baseball player had 137 hits in 465 times at bat.

    P(getting a hit) = _____

    In picking from a deck of cards, I obtained a king 11 times and
    non-king 89 times.

    P(picking a king) = _____

    In rolling 2 dice 20 times, I obtained a sum of 8 three times.

    P(sum of 8) = _____

2. Find the theoretical probabilities for the following. (The small p
    represents the theoretical probability). Give answer in fraction form.

    Two dice are rolled

    p(sum of 4) = _____
    P(sum of 10 or more) = _____

    A card is drawn from a well shuffled deck

    p(club) = _____

    p(four of diamonds) = _____

    p(jack) = _____

    Four coins are tossed. Use a tree diagram to illustrate the outcomes.

    p(0 heads) = _____

    p(1 head) = _____

    p(2 heads) = _____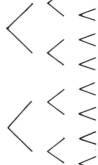

    p(3 heads) = _____

    p(4 heads) = _____

Write the 5 step procedure for the following. Do not perform the trials.

3. The probability of being left-handed is .10 (10%). In a class of 23 students, what is the probability of having 4 or more left-handed students?

4. A restaurant has found that 15 percent of those making reservations do not show up. If that restaurant has 25 tables and has taken 28 reservations, find the probability that everyone who shows up will be accommodated.

5. Perform 15 trials for the following. Use your random number sheet.

    The probability of rain in Chicago is .7 and the probability of rain in San Juan is .4; find the probability of rain in both cities.

    Model   1 digit R N

                1 to 7 rain in Chi; 8,9,0 no rain in Chi
                1 to 4 rain in San Juan; 5 to 9 and 0 no rain in San Juan

    Trial   Read two one-digit random numbers (one for each city)

    Succ. Trial occurs if first digit is in 1 to 7 interval and second digit
                is in 1 to 4 interval.

    Repeat 15 times

Prob (rain in both cities) = $\overline{15}$

Trial	Rain in Chi	Rain in S J	Success
	1 to 7	1 to 4	
1	_____	_____	_____
2	_____	_____	_____
3	_____	_____	_____
4	_____	_____	_____
5	_____	_____	_____
6	_____	_____	_____
7	_____	_____	_____
8	_____	_____	_____
9	_____	_____	_____
10	_____	_____	_____
11	_____	_____	_____
12	_____	_____	_____
13	_____	_____	_____
14	_____	_____	_____
15	_____	_____	_____

What is P(rain in Chi)?   _____
What is P(rain in S J)?   _____

What is P(rain in Chi) $\cdot$ P(rain in S J)? = _____
What is p(rain in Chi) $\cdot$ p(rain in S J)? = _____

Test

Chapter 5   Name _____

1.   For each of the following, identify the sample and the population.

      (a) 5000 people responded to a <u>Tribune</u> survey concerning the effect of
           the economy on Chicago area residents.

      (b) A national survey of 2100 families rated Dallas as the top TV show.

      (c) When cooking fudge, I dropped a small amount into cold water to see
           if it had cooked long enough.

      (d) A poll of 60 New Trier seniors was taken to find out how many
           graduation ceremonies would be preferred. (1200 seniors attend
           New Trier.)

      (e) To determine the "life" of a set of 10,000 batteries, the researcher
           used 5 until they burned out.

      <u>Sample</u>   <u>Population</u>

(a)_____   _____

(b)_____   _____

(c)_____   _____

(d)_____   _____

(e)_____   _____

2.   Why is sampling used? Give two reasons.

Write the six steps for the following

3.   CBS News carried a report on March 21, 1979 concerning research
      done in Japan on predicting earthquakes. It had been noticed that
      out of 20 occasions, the whiskers of catfish were observed to wriggle
      on 17 occasions just before earthquakes took place. Suppose that
      catfish whiskers wriggling has no relation to earthquakes' happening.
      What is the probability that the wriggles would take place 17 out of
      20 times by chance? Do 100 trials.

4.   A producer of television sets believes that the transistors they are getting from a supplier are not as reliable as they used to be.   In the batch of 100 that they just received, they find 9 defectives.   Is this conclusive evidence that the manufacturer's claim is not correct? The claim is 5% defective.

5.   A girl's batting average is .260 before attending a training camp. Following her attendance, she obtained 11 hits in her next 30 times at bat.   Can you conclude that her hitting has improved?

6.   I am interested in how many girls are in a class of 30.   Use your printout for sample size 30 and p = .50 to find

   P(exactly 15 girls) = _____

   P(20 or more girls) = _____

   P(less than 12 girls) = _____

   P(13 to 18 girls inclusive) = _____

   If a class of 30 included 25 girls, would you believe that the population from which the class was drawn was evenly divided between boys and girls?   Explain.

7.   In general, 80% of certain seeds germinate when planted correctly. You have carefully planted 20 seeds. Use your printout for sample size 20 and p = .80 to find

P(exactly 16 germinate) = _____

P(19 or more germinate) = _____

P(10 or less germinate) = _____

P(13 to 19 inclusive germinate) = _____

If only 12 of your seeds germinated, would you be justified in claiming that your seeds were inferior? Explain.

SIZE OF EACH SAMPLE = 30
50% MARKED
NUMBER OF SAMPLES = 100

        FREQUENCY
0
1
2
3
4
5
6
7
8   ^1
9   ^1
10   ^^^^4
11   ^^^^^5
12   ^^^^^^^^^^^11
13   ^^^^^^^7
14   ^^^^^^^^8
15   ^^^^^^^^^^^^^^^15
16   ^^^^^^^^^^^^^^^^^^^19
17   ^^^^^^^^^^^12
18   ^^^^^^^^8
19   ^^^^^5
20 3
21   ^1
22
23
24
25
26
27
28
29
30

SIZE OF EACH SAMPLE = 20
80% MARKED
NUMBER OF SAMPLES = 100

        FREQUENCY
0
1
2
3
4
5
6
7
8
9
10
11
12   ^^2
13   ^1
14   ^^^^^^^^^^^^^^^^16
15   ^^^^^^^^^^^^^^^^^17
16   ^^^^^^^^^^^^^^^^^^^^^^^^^^^27
17   ^^^^^^^^^^^^^^^^^17
18   ^^^^^^^^^^^^^^^15
19   ^^^^^5
20

Test

Chapter 6   Name _____

1.   Toss your die 30 times and record the outcomes.   Then find $\underline{D}$ and χ^2

OUTCOME	EXPECTED	OBTAINED
1		
2		
3		
4		
5		
6		

2.   Draw a relative frequency polygon for the chi squares shown below. These values were obtained from 50 trials of 120 rolls of a six sided die.

Interval	Freq	Prop
0 - .9	1	
1 - 1.9	3	-
2 - 2.9	4	-
3 - 3.9	8	-
4 - 4.9	9	-
5 - 5.9	10	-
6 - 6.9	7	-
7 - 7.9	3	-
8 - 8.9	2	-
9 - 9.9	1	-
10 -10.9	1	-
11 -11.9	1	

Shade the area of the graph which represents the probability of obtaining your χ^2 from problem 1.

3. Use Appendix A on page 426 to complete the following.

    (a) $p(\chi_3^2 \geq 6) =$ _____

    (b) $p(\chi_{20}^2 \geq 20) =$ _____

    (c) $p(\chi_9^2 \geq$ ____$) = .05$

    (d) $p(\chi_5^2 \geq$ ____$) = .01$

    (e) The mean value of χ^2 with n degrees of freedom is _____.

4. Five boxes of different brands of canned salmon were examined for high quality specifications. The number of cans which failed to meet specifications are indicated below. Is there a significant difference among these brands? Explain using chi square.

Brand	Expected	Obtained
A		5
B		14
C		6
D		3
E		7

5. According to Mendelian Inheritance theory, offspring of a certain crossing should be colored red, black or white. The chart below gives the theoretical proportions and the number actually obtained. Do these data substantiate the theory? Use chi-square to answer.

	Expected	Obtained
Red	9/16	69
Black	3/16	37
White	4/16	38

Form an interval table for the chi-squares listed below.   These data are the result of 60 trials of 90 rolls of a 6-sided die.

Chi-square	freq.
.4	2
1.46	1
1.6	1
1.86	5
2.13	1
2.26	1
2.4	1
2.53	1
2.66	1
2.8	1
2.93	2
3.33	1
3.46	3
3.6	1
3.73	1
3.86	2
4	2
4.4	1
4.53	1
4.8	1
5.2	1
5.33	2
5.46	1
5.6	2
5.73	1
6.13	1
6.26	1
6.53	1
6.66	1
7.46	2
8	1
8.53	1
8.66	1
11.46	2
12.93	1
14	1

Mean chi-square = 4.76

Test

Chapter 7   Name _____

1.   What two variables are of interest in the following questions?

      Is the age of a car related to its trade-in value?

      _____   _____

      Is crime related to the rate of inflation?

      _____   _____

      Does the amount of snow in the North affect tourism in the South?

      _____   _____

      Is the amount of alcohol drunk by a pregnant woman related to the
      size of the baby at birth?

      _____   _____

      Does life insurance cost more as one gets older?

      _____   _____

2.   Find the following

      The equation of a line with slope .85 and Y intercept -5.2

      _____

      The slope of the line containing the points (5,8) and (2,10)

      _____

      The point (18, 43) is on the line $Y = 2X + C$.   Find C

      _____

      The equation of the line shown at the right

      _____

3. Graph the following
    on the same axis

    $Y = \frac{1}{3}X - 6$

    $Y = -2X + 1$

4. Graph the following points.
    Find the mean data point.

X	Y
7	8
10	9
2	5
4	4
2	3
10	7

    Mean data point

    _____

5. Complete the following equation and find the mean error for the given
    equation.

    $Y' = .1x + 1.10$

X	Y	Y'	Y - Y'
2	1.2	_____	_____
3	1.3	_____	_____
4.5	1.45	_____	_____
7	1.80	_____	_____
10	2.00	_____	_____
15	3.00	_____	_____
20	4.75	_____	_____

6.   The following table shows the indices with which 10 students graduated from high school and the annual salary which they earned 10 years after graduation.

Index	Salary
2.3	24,000
1.5	12,000
1.6	18,000
2.8	21,000
1.1	18,000
1.2	11,000
1.0	9,000
1.9	15,000
2.4	19,000
1.6	12,000

Sketch the graph of the points given above.

Find a rule that gives the salary in terms of the index (the prediction eq)
Show your work so I can see how you found the slope and y intercept.
Extra Credit. Find the mean error for your line.

Test

Chapter 8   Name _____

1. The following questions refer to
    the article at the right.

    What variables are reported to
    be related?

    What causal relationship
    is implied?

    What do you think about this information?

2. The following statistics were computed for a set of data.

    $\bar{X}$ = 68.6 $\bar{Y}$ = 156.8

    var(X) = 12.1   var(Y) = 570.8   covar(X,Y) = 75.9

    Find the equation of the least squares best fitting line.
    (Hint: find the slope of the line using the formula; then find the Y
    intercept using the mean data point.)

    Find the correlation between X and Y.

3. Would you expect strong or weak positive, strong or weak negative,
    or no correlation between the following pairs of data?

    (a) The weights and lengths of newborn babies. _____

    (b) Weight of a car and miles per gallon of gas. _____

    (c) Hat size of adults and their I.Q. scores.   _____

    (d) Ages of husbands and their wives.   _____

    (e) Speed of travel and travel time.   _____

4. Describe the correlation presented in the following graphs.

The following data are the height and weight for 7 college men. Complete the table and find the information requested.

ht X	wt Y	X - X̄	Y - Ȳ	(X - X̄)(Y - Ȳ)	(X - X̄)²	(Y - Ȳ)²
72	185					
68	163					
66	142					
70	162					
69	152					
64	127					
74	182					

X̄ = _____

Ȳ = _____

var(X) = _____

var(Y) = _____

covar (X,Y) = _____

6. The following data give mass transit fares and the mean number of annual riders.

Fare in cents X	Rider (thousands) Y	Y'	Y - Y'	$(Y - Y')^2$
45	200			
50	180			
60	150			
75	120			
90	115			
100	110			
125	90			

$\bar{X}$ = 77.9 $\bar{Y}$ = 137.9

(a) Graph the data

(b) For the equations Y' = -1.3X + C, find C.

(c) Complete the chart above and find the mean square error.

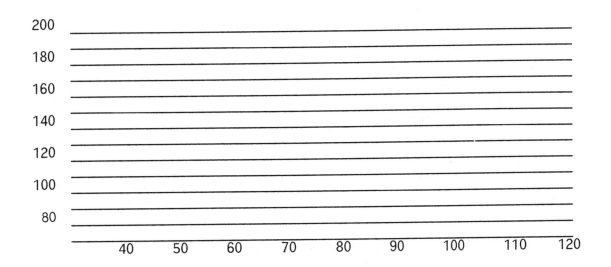

Test

Chapter 9 Sections 1-5   Name _____

1.   Transform the following scores as indicated. Use original scores for each transformation. Then find the new mean and the new standard deviation.

SCORE	Slide -14	Shrink ÷ 5
52	_____	_____
58	_____	_____
63	_____	_____
74	_____	_____
82	_____	_____
MEAN 65.8	_____	_____
SD 10.9	_____	_____

2.   Suppose you receive a score of 107 on both Test I and Test II. Find your z-score for each.

	mean	SD	z-score
Test I	98	7.2	_____
Test II	125	21.4	_____

3.   Find the transformed score for each of the following z-scores

z	new mean	new SD	Transformed score
-.57	400	80	_____
1.18	100	15	_____

4.   Transform the following quiz scores so that they have a mean of 50 and a standard deviation of 10.

Score   Transformed   score

    5
    6
    11
    13
    15

5. A coin was tossed 1,000 times; 457 heads and 543 tails resulted.   Use
    a chi-square test to decide if the coin is fair.

6. Three hundred cards were drawn at random from a bridge deck.
    Draw a relative frequency polygon.   Sketch in an appropriate smooth
    curve.

    Clubs   84   -
    Diamonds 72   -
    Hearts   75   -
    Spades   69   -

    _____

              C   D   H   S

7. The following table gives the weights of 50 Girl Scouts at a summer
    camp.   Draw a frequency polygon and sketch in a smooth curve which
    seems appropriate for the data.

Interval	Frequency
70 - 79	4
80 - 89	7
90 - 99	9
100 - 109	13
110 - 119	8
120 - 129	6
130 - 139	3

    _____

    Find the following probabilities (w represents weight)

    $P(w < 90)$ = _____

    $P(w \geq 120)$ = _____

    $P(90 \leq w < 120)$ = _____

8. The following numbers represent final scores on a statistics test. Classify the data using the stem and leaf method

88	54	91	70	93	62	89	61	81	67
72	87	80	76	83	58	75	86	78	92
80	56	75	60	73	69	97	77	65	81
92	71	63	71	64	79	88	62	51	73
85	67	95	50	75	71	72	90	78	69

Stem	Leaf	Interval	Freq.
____	_____	_____	____
____	_____	_____	____
____	_____	_____	____
____	_____	_____	____
____	_____	_____	____

The mean of these data is 78.8 and the standard deviation is 11.9 Assume the data are normally distributed and find an interval around the mean in which about 68% of the scores are found.

How <u>many</u> grades are actually in this interval?

What percent of the grades are actually in this interval?

Test

Chapter 9 Sections 6-8   Name _____

Complete the followng and illustrate information on the graph.

1.   p(z < 1.28) = _____

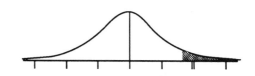

2.   p(z < -2.13) = _____

3.   p(z > 1.75) = _____

4.   p(z > -1.05) = _____

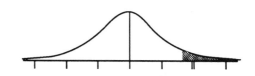

5.   p(z < _____) = .30

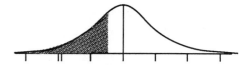

6.   p(z < _____) = .85

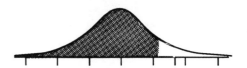

7.   p(z > _____) = .10

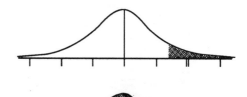

8.   p(z > _____) = .75

9. Assume that the heights of women are normally distributed with a mean of 66" (5'6") and a standard deviation of 4".

    (a) What percentage of women would you expect to be under 60" (5')?

    (b) What is the lowest height that would place a woman in the tallest 10% of the group?

10. The following stem and leaf diagram gives the final statistics grades for a class of 19 students. Draw a relative frequency polygon and answer the questions.

Stem	Leaf
9	8 5 5 4 2 1 0
8	8 8 5 4 3 0
7	9 5 2
6	8 0
5	3

    $P(71 < G < 87) =$ _____

    $P(G \geq 88) =$ _____

    $P(G \leq 65) =$ _____

    The median is _____

    Is the distribution normal? _____

    What observations can you make about this class?

<u>Test</u>

Chapter 10   Name _____

1. In an experiment measuring the percent shrinkage in drying, 40 clay
    test specimens produced the following results:

19.3	20.5	17.9	17.3
15.8	16.9	17.1	19.5
20.7	18.5	17.1	19.1
18.4	18.7	19.4	16.8
14.9	12.3	18.8	17.5
17.3	19.5	17.4	16.3
21.3	23.4	18.5	19.0
16.1	18.8	17.5	18.2
18.6	18.3	16.5	17.4
20.5	16.9	17.5	18.2

    (a) Organize these data using a stem and leaf table.

    (b) Draw a histogram of these data.

Stem	Leaf
12	_____
13	_____
14	_____
15	_____
16	_____
17	_____
18	_____
19	_____
20	_____
21	_____
22	_____
23	_____

2. Three groups of students measured a chalkboard known to be 6
    meters long. They obtained these results:

Group I	Group II	Group III
6.03	6.05	6.09
6.05	5.97	6.07
5.89	6.04	6.05
5.93	6.08	6.10
6.10	5.92	6.08

(a) What are the mean and standard deviation of each group?

(b) Which group seems to have the smallest error?

(c) Which group seems the most biased?

(d) What recommendations would you make for improving the results?

3. Find the least squares regression equation for estimating the 1980 median price for a house in the New Trier district. (New Trier West serves students from the suburbs listed below.) The median price for 1970 is given in thousands and is represented by X. The median price for 1980, also given in thousands, is represented by Y.

	X	Y
Glenview	41.9	111.9
Kenilworth	50.0	200.0
Northfield	48.4	117.9
Wilmette	46.5	121.8
Winnetka	50.0	172.0

Test

Chapter 11   Name _____

1. Identify the sample, the population, the statistic and the parameter in each of the following.

   The owner of a small store wishes to estimate the proportion of those who enter her store who actually buy something. She carefully observes 20 randomly selected people who enter the store and finds that 13 of them make a purchase.

   A group of 100 Central High students was asked "Approximately how many hours per week do you study?" The responses ranged from 0 to 23 and the mean was 8.4

2. Use the stem-and-leaf plots from Tables 11.12 a,b,c; page 321 & 322 the numbers represent the unbiased variances from 100 samples. Find the following.

   For n = 4, P(90 $\leq$ var $\leq$ 110) = _____   P(80 $\leq$ var $\leq$ 120) = _____

   For n = 16, P(90 $\leq$ var $\leq$ 110) = _____   P(80 $\leq$ var $\leq$ 120) = _____

   For n = 36, P(90 $\leq$ var $\leq$ 110) = _____   P(80 $\leq$ var $\leq$ 120) = _____

   What conclusions can you draw from your answers?

3. Give the meaning of the following:

    Statistical bias

    The sample mean is unbiased

    The sample variance is biased

    The Central Limit Theorem

4. A random sample of 49 adults is tested for pulse rates. The result-
    ing mean is 75.8 beats per minute. Assume standard deviation of the
    population is 10 and find the 95% Confidence Interval for the means of
    all such samples.

    Sketch a graph of this information.

5. Find the mean, the biased and unbiased standard deviation of the
    data below. Show your work neatly. You may check using the
    calculator BUT I MUST see your work.

    72.89   62.37   76.32   52.49   75.33

Test

Chapter 12   Name _____

1.   A school district is interested in whether student achievement in
     mathematics is significantly higher than the nationwide mean of 75.   A
     random sample of 50 students takes the test and gets a mean of 77
     and a standard deviation of 7.3.

     To answer the question experimentally 100 random samples of size 50
     were taken from a population with mean 75 and s.d. 7.3.   What
     answer do these data suggest?

     72   2
     73   7
     74   28
     75   36
     76   21
     77   4
     78   1
     79   1

     To answer the question by theoretical means, find the z score and
     use the normal curve chart.   What conclusion do you draw based on
     this information?

     Sketch a graph illustrating your theoretical results.

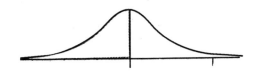

2.   Write the six steps and perform 10 trials for the following problem.

In a large set of applicants for similar jobs, there are 60 men and 40 women applying. If 20 jobs are to be filled and 16 are given to men, would you say that there is evidence of discrimination in the selection process?

Model

Trial

Outcome

Repeat

Probability

Decision

3.   (a) Define:

Type I Error

Type II Error

(b) Complete.   Use t table

df = 15 $p(t < -1.34) =$

df = 24 $p(t > 2.49) =$

df = 4 $p(t < -2.78) =$

df = 8 $p(t > 1.86) =$

4. A survey of 9 automobile drivers indicated that the mean number of miles driven per day was 32.7 with a standard deviation of 6.8 miles. Find a 99% Confidence Interval for the mean distance travelled in a day. Also find a 90% Confidence Interval.

5. A random sample of 16 college freshmen indicated that they studied the following number of hours per week:

40	5	27	21
28	20	35	30
33	19	38	58
61	32	37	0

Do a statistical test to determine if these freshmen differ significantly from the national mean of 32 hours per week.

Test

Chapter 13   Name _____

1. A survey of 32 four-children families was conducted. The expected and observed number of sons is given in the following chart. Use chi square to determine if the observed is consistent with the expected.

Number of sons	expected	observed
0	1/16	4
1	4/16	8
2	6/16	9
3	4/16	9
4	1/16	2

2. A certain drug is claimed to be more effective in curing headaches. In an experiment with 150 people, half were given the drug, and half were given sugar pills. The patients' reactions to the treatment are recorded in the following table. Test the hypothesis that the drug and the sugar pills yield similar reactions.

	Helped	Harmed	No reaction
Drug	50	8	17
Sugar Pill	41	10	24

3. Use Pascal's Triangle, for six tosses of a fair coin, to find the following:

    p(0 Heads) =

    p(2 Heads) =

    p(5 Heads) =

4. A random sample of 100 college students indicated that the average number of classes missed per week was 4.2 with a standard deviation of .85. Is this significantly different from the University's statement that students missed 3.5 classes per week?

5. Take-home question. Use a local phone book as a source of random digits. Select 400 digits.

    (a) Describe how you selected the digits.

    (b) Perform two tests of your choice to determine if the digits are in fact random.

Test

Name

Chapter 1

1. Name 4 areas in which statistics is used. Give an example of one of these areas.

Business, Sports, Medicine, Economics, Teaching, Research, Weather, Politics

2. The following numbers represent the final grades on a statistics test. Classify these data using a stem and leaf plot. (Please work down each column to help in checking.)

88	54	91	70	93	62	89	61	81	67
72	87	80	76	83	58	75	86	78	92
80	56	75	60	73	69	97	77	65	81
92	71	63	71	64	79	88	62	51	73
85	67	95	50	75	71	72	90	78	69

5   4 6 0 8 1   (5)

6   7 3 0 4 2 9 / 2 5 7 9   (11)

7   2 / 5 0 6 / 3 5 7 / 5 2 7 8 8 3   (16)

8   8 0 5 7 0 3 9 8 6 1 1   (11)

9   2 1 5 3 7 0 2   (17)

3. In a survey of 50 families, it was found that they had the following number of cars. Draw a cumulative frequency graph.

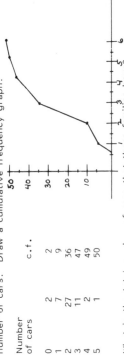

Number of cars	c.f.
0	2	2
1	7	9
2	27	36
3	11	47
4	2	49
5	1	50

What is the total number of cars that these families have?

$0 + 7 + 54 + 33 + 8 + 5 = 107$

a. What is indicated on the horizontal axis?
   years from 1972 to 1982

b. What is indicated on the vertical axis?
   hourly employment costs

c. What was the increase in hourly cost from 1974 to 1981?
   20 - 9 = 11 dollars per hour

d. What type of graph is this?
   histogram

e. What major idea is being portrayed by the graph?
   Costs are going up

Name _____

Test
_____

Chapter 2 Sections 1 to 4

1. I tossed three coins 25 times with the following results:

No. of tails	freq.
0	4
1	9
2	10
3	2

Find the following: Mean _1.4_   Median _1_   Mode _2_

Mean = 1/25 (0 + 9 + 20 + 6) or 35/25

3. The following hourly wages were paid to the employees in a store.
$3.60, 5.52, 3.18, 4.60, 3.18, 7.28, 3.18, 5.18, 5.62, 4.40

For these ten employees, find

Mean _4.57_   Median _4.50_   Mode _3.18_

If you were an employee in the store, which average would you report? Why?   *Answers will vary*

If you were the owner of the store, which average would you report? Why?   *Answers will vary*

3. In 1980, the mean expenditures per pupil in a school district was $3992 and the district enrollment was 4796 students. What was the total expenditure for the district?

T = $3992 (4796)
T = $19,145,632

4. A group of 25 students rated their math teacher on a scale of 1 (low) to 5 (high). The results were

Score	frequency	prop	cum freq	cum prop
1	1	.04	1	.04
2	4	.16	5	.20
3	11	.44	16	.64
4	7	.28	23	.92
5	2	.08	25	1.00

Complete the chart above and find the following.

The proportion of students rating the teacher '4' is _.28_

The proportion of students rating the teacher '3' or less' is _.64_

The number of students rating the teacher '5' is _2_

The number of students rating the teacher '2 or less' is _5_

The proportion of students rating the teacher 'more than 3' is _.36_

Draw a frequency polygon and a histogram using proportions for the data given above.

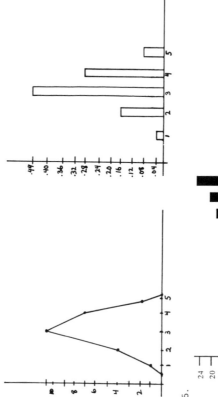

The graph at the left indicates the average wage cost/hour in the construction industry.

5.

Test

Chapter 2 Sections 5-7   Name _____

1. The high temperatures for last week were:

   56, 71, 63, 78, 66, 63, 72

   The range of these temperatures is __22__

   The median of these temperatures is __66__

   The mode of these temperatures is __63__

   The mean of these temperatures is __67__

2. I tossed 3 coins 50 times with the following results:

Number of tails	frequency
0	8
1	17
2	19
3	6

   The mean is __1.46__ .   The median range is __1.5__ .

   The mode is __2__ .   The range is __3__ .

3. The following ages were obtained in a random sample of 10 people riding the American Eagle at Great America. Find the deviation age for each and then find the mean deviation.

Age	
38	9.6
12	-16.4
64	35.6
32	3.6
10	-18.4
4	-24.4
28	-.4
68	39.6
11	-17.4
17	-11.4

   mean 28.4

   mean deviation = $\dfrac{176.8}{10}$

   σ 17.68

4. The following stem-and-leaf plot represents the speed in miles per hour of 32 selected animals. (The cheetah is the fastest -- 70 mph and the chicken is the slowest -- 9 mph.)

   Find the range __61__   the median __35__

   Q$_1$ __28½__   Q$_3$ __44__

Stem	
0	9
1	258
2	057
3	0000025559
4	0002357
5	000
6	1
7	0

5. The grades in the morning section of a college statistics test are:

   83 90 88 76 75 98 88 79 81
   92 89 79 87 63 90 78 70 77

   median 88

   The grades in the afternoon section of the same course are:

   60 95 85 79 65 86 45 52
   76 85 70 92 76 55 80

   median 76

   Draw a stem and leaf diagram and a box and whisker plot for these data. What two things can be said about these data?

	Stem	
	4	5
	5	25
	3 · · 6	05
0567899	7	0669
137889	8	0556
0028	9	25

   median of morning is higher than median of afternoon

   spread of morning is less than spread of afternoon

Test

Name _____

Chapter 3 Sections 1 - 3

1. The Key problem for Chapter 3 is:

About how many packages of bubble gum, on the average, would we expect to buy to obtain a complete set of 6 different flags? Assume that on each purchase of a stick of gum, the chances of obtaining each of the 6 flags are equal.

Model: Die each side corresponds to one of the 6 flags.
Each roll of the die corresponds to the purchase of a stick of gum and therefore one flag.

Trial Roll the die, record the result, continue until all six sides (flags) have occurred.

State of Int. Record the number of rolls necessary to obtain all six numbers (flags)

Repeat 5 times

Mean Value = *Answers will differ*

Perform your 5 trials. Record your results on the form below

Trial	Outcomes 1	2	3	4	5	6
1						
2						
3						
4						
5						

2. Three coins were tossed 4 times. This was repeated 10 times. The results are given below.

THT	HHT	HHT	THH /	TTT	THH 0
THT	TTT	HTH	TTH 3	HHT	TTH 0
TTH	HTT	THH	HHT /	TTT	HHH /
HHT	THH	HTT	HHH /	THH	TTH /
THH	HTH	HHT	HTH 0	HHH	TTH 0

4. A new sleeping pill is being tested in a laboratory. The amount of sleep gained (in hours) by 10 persons who tried the drug in an experiment was as follows: (a negative number means a sleep loss)

Person	Sleep gained	Deviation	
A	2.0	.5	.25
B	3.5	2.0	4.00
C	.5	-1.0	1.00
D	0.0	-1.5	2.25
E	-1.0	-2.5	6.25
F	2.0	.5	.25
G	3.0	1.5	2.25
H	2.5	1.0	1.00
I	0.0	-1.5	2.25
J	2.5	1.0	1.00

Find the variance and the standard deviation for these data.

$$\text{Variance} = {}^{20.5}/_{10} \text{ or } 2.05$$
$$SD = \sqrt{2.05} \text{ or } 1.43$$

5. Find the range, mean deviation, variance and standard deviation for the following. The numbers represent the yards gained by a football team in the last 5 weeks.

156, 289, 84, 302, 214   Range = 218

Mean dev = $\frac{356}{5}$

84	-125	15625
156	-53	2809
214	5	25
289	80	6400
302	93	8649
		33508

or 71.2

Variance = 33508 / 5

or 6 701.6

SD = 81.86

Mean = $\frac{1045}{5}$ or 209

Do you think the team is consistent?   Why?

Answers will vary

No. Range, mean deviation, etc are all large.

In this experiment, what is a trial? *tossing 3 coins 4 times*

How many trials were there? *10*

The statistic of interest is the number of times that 2 tails and 1 head was obtained.

Complete the frequency distribution and find the mean number of times that two tails and one head occurred.

2 tails and 1 head	frequency
0	*4*
1	*5* *mean = 8/10*
2	*0*
3	*1*
4	*0*

3. Two coins were tossed six times. The number of times 2 tails occurred was recorded. This was repeated 300 times. The results are shown below. Find the mean number of times that 2 tails appeared.

2 tails	frequency
0	5
1	30
2	64
3	93
4	75
5	27
6	6

$$mean = \tfrac{1}{300}(0+30+128+279$$
$$+ 300 +135+36)$$
$$= \tfrac{1}{300}(908)$$
$$= 3.02\overline{6}$$

4. Describe a model, a trial and the statistic of interest for the following.

A. What is the expected number of girls in a 5 child family?

Model *Coin H → girl*
T → boy

Trial *Toss coin 5 times (once for each child)*

St of int *Record the # of heads (girls)*

B. An excellent softball player has a .400 batting average. How many times in a row would you expect her to bat without getting a hit?

Model *Cards Hit A,2,3,4(ignore J,Q,K)*
No Hit 5,6,7,8,9,10

Trial *Draw a card until a A,2,3,4(hit)occurs*

St of int *Record the number of 5 to 10's (no hit)*

C. In a multiple choice test with 3 responses for each question, what is the expected number of correct answers obtained by guessing if there are 25 questions on the test?

Model *Die 1-2 correct*
3-6 wrong

Trial *Toss die 25 times (once for each question)*

St of int *Record the number of 1 and 2's*

D. A market research company claims that .75 of persons called agree to answer survey questions. Under this assumption, how many people in a row could be expected to respond to the researcher's questions?

Model *Cards Club, Diamond, Heat → answer*
Spade → no answer

Trial *Draw a card until a spade (no answer) occurs*

St of int *Record the number of non spades used.*

Note : different models could be used.

Test

Chapter 3 Sections 4-6   Name _____

1. A two dimensional walk of 10 steps was taken. This was repeated 5 times. Find the terminal point, the distance from the origin for each walk and the mean distance for the 5 walks.

HH → N
HT → S
TH → W
TT → E

Steps	Point	Distance
HT HH TT HT HH TH TH HT HH	*(0,0)*	*0*
HT TT TH HH HT TH TH TT TT TH	*(-1,-1)*	*1.41*
HH HH TH TH HT TT HT HT TT	*(-2,0)*	*2.00*
HH HH TH HT TT HT TH HH TH HH	*(-2,2)*	*2.83*
TH TH HH HT HT TT HH TH TT HH	*(-1,3)*	*3.16*

The mean distance is   *1.88*

2. To find the approximate temperature at the point (4,2) on the steel plate (see page 72) 250 random walks were taken. The results were:

temp	3°	15°	30°	40°
no. of walks	25	88	6	131

Find the approximate temperature.

$$T = 3\times25 + 1320 + 180 + 5240$$
$$= \frac{6815}{250}$$
$$= 27.26$$

3. Describe a model, a trial and the statistic of interest for the following:

In a multiple choice test with 3 responses for each question, what is the expected number of correct answers obtained by guessing if there are 50 questions?

Model: Die 1-2 correct 3-6 wrong

Trial: Toss die 50 times, once for each question

St. of Int.: Record the number of 1 or 2's (correct)

The teacher who keeps her classroom locked and the loose keys in her purse now has only four keys. She still pulls out a key and tries it. If the key does not fit, she returns it to her purse and tries again. On the average, how many tries will she have to make before she succeeds in opening the door?

Model: 2 Coins HH is correct key, HT, TH, TT wrong key

Trial: Toss coins until HH (correct key) occurs.

St. of Int.: Record # of tosses necessary to obtain correct key. (models may differ)

4. The following number of steps were taken before reaching a barrier at 5 or -5 in a one dimensional random walk. Make 5 statistical statements concerning these data.

25, 9, 19, 27, 49, 23, 33, 15, 15, 8,
14, 14, 6, 11, 7, 21, 37, 9, 11, 21
21, 5, 17, 15, 35, 10, 5, 21, 9, 5
15, 31, 13, 7, 9, 31, 13, 7, 62, 14

Answers will differ

mean is $\frac{719}{40}$ or 17.975

median is 14.5

no mode

range is 62-5 or 57

5. Perform 10 trials for the following problem.

What is the expected number of people necessary to obtain a 'shared' birth month?

Model 12 outcomes (a coin and a die as indicated below)

Trial Toss coin and die; record result. Continue to toss until one result (month) is repeated.

St. of int. Record the number of tosses necessary to obtain a repeated result (duplicate birth month)

Repeat 20 times

Mean value =

Trial \ month	1 (1h)	2 (2h)	3 (3h)	4 (4h)	5 (5h)	6 (6h)	7 (1t)	8 (2t)	9 (3t)	10 (4t)	11 (5t)	12 (6t)	TOTAL
1													
2													
3													
4													
5													
6													
7													
8													
9													
10													

Answers will differ

Test

Chapter 4   Name _____

1. Find the estimated probabilities for the following. (The capital P represents an estimated probability). Give answer in decimal form.

Airline records show that 6640 people actually showed up for flights when 7000 reservations had been made.

P(showing up for a flight) = .9486
P(not showing up for a flight) = .0514

A baseball player had 137 hits in 465 times at bat.

P(getting a hit) = .295

In picking from a deck of cards, I obtained a king 11 times and non-king 89 times.

P(picking a king) = .11

In rolling 2 dice 20 times, I obtained a sum of 8 three times.

P(sum of 8) = .15

2. Find the theoretical probabilities for the following. Give answer in fraction form. (The small p represents the theoretical probability).

Two dice are rolled

p(sum of 4) = 3/36 or 1/12
p(sum of 10 or more) = 6/36 or 1/6

A card is drawn from a well shuffled deck

p(club) = 13/52 or 1/4
p(four of diamonds) = 1/52
p(jack) = 4/52 or 1/13

Four coins are tossed. Use a tree diagram to illustrate the outcomes.

p(0 heads) = 1/16
p(1 head) = 4/16
p(2 heads) = 6/16
p(3 heads) = 4/16
p(4 heads) = 1/16

Write the 5 step procedure for the following. Do not perform the trials.

3. The probability of being left-handed is .10 (10%). In a class of 23 students, what is the probability of having 4 or more left-handed students?

Model: 1 digit RN   0 is lefty
                     1-9 not left

Trial: Read 23 1 digit RN (one for each student)

Successful trial: Occurs if 4 or more 0's (lefties) appear.

Repeat
P(4 or more lefties) =

4. A restaurant has found that 15 percent of those making reservations do not show up. If that restaurant has 25 tables and has taken 28 reservations, find the probability that everyone who shows up will be accommodated.

Model: 2 digit RN   01-15 No show
                    16-99 + 00 show

Trial: Read 28 RN (one for each reservation)

Successful trial: occurs if 3 or more RN appear in 1-15 interval.

Repeat
Problem (3 or more "no shows") =

5. Perform 15 trials for the following. Use your random number sheet.

The probability of rain in Chicago is .7 and the probability of rain in San Juan is .4; find the probability of rain in both cities.

Model   1 digit R N

   1 to 7 rain in Chi; 8,9,0 no rain in Chi
   1 to 4 rain in San Juan; 5 to 9 and 0 no rain in San Juan

Trial   Read two one-digit random numbers (one for each city)

Succ. Trial occurs if first digit is in 1 to 7 interval and second digit is in 1 to 4 interval.

Repeat 15 times

(e) To determine the "life" of a set of 10,000 batteries, the researcher used 5 until they burned out.

Sample	Population
(a) 5000 people	all Tribune Readers
(b) 2100 families	all TV watchers
(c) small amount of fudge	Pot of fudge
(d) 60 NT Seniors	all NT Seniors
(e) 50 batteries	10,000 batteries

2. Why is sampling used? Give two reasons.

To find out something about the population. Too costly to use entire population, "use up" if test all bulbs.

Write the six steps for the following

3. CBS News carried a report on March 21, 1979 concerning research done in Japan on predicting earthquakes. It had been noticed that out of 20 occasions, the whiskers of catfish were observed to wriggle on 17 occasions just before earthquakes took place. Suppose that catfish whiskers wriggling has no relation to earthquakes' happening. What is the probability that the wriggles would take place 17 out of 20 times by chance? Do 100 trials.

model coin   H → Wriggle
             T → No Wriggle

Trial: toss coin 20 times, once for each earthquake

Outcome: Record the number of heads (Wriggles). Repeat.

Prob (17 or more wriggles) = Proportion of successful trials

Prob (rain in both cities) = $\overline{15}$

Trial	Rain in Chi 1 to 7	Rain in S J 1 to 4	Success
1			
2			
3			
4			
5			
6			
7			
8			
9			
10			
11			
12			
13			
14			
15			

What is P(rain in Chi)?
What is P(rain in S J)?

What is P(rain in Chi) · P(rain in S J)? =
What is p(rain in Chi) · p(rain in S J)? =

Answers will differ

Name _____

Test
Chapter 5

1. For each of the following, identify the sample and the population.

(a) 5000 people responded to a Tribune survey concerning the effect of the economy on Chicago area residents.

(b) A national survey of 2100 families rated Dallas as the top TV show.

(c) When cooking fudge, I dropped a small amount into cold water to see if it had cooked long enough.

(d) A poll of 60 New Trier seniors was taken to find out how many graduation ceremonies would be preferred. (1200 seniors attend New Trier.)

4. A producer of television sets believes that the transistors they are getting from a supplier are not as reliable as they used to be. In the batch of 100 that they just received, they find 9 defectives. Is this conclusive evidence that the manufacturer's claim is not correct? The claim is 5% defective.

The claim is 5% defective.

Model: 2 digit RN 01 to 05 defective 06-99 + 00 not

Trial: Read 100 RN one box each transistor

Outcome: Record the number of 01 to 05 (defectives) =

Repeat

Plot (9 or more defective) = proportion of successful trials.

5. A girl's batting average is .260 before attending a training camp. Following her attendance, she obtained 11 hits in her next 30 times at bat. Can you conclude that her hitting has improved?

model RN 01-26 hit
27-99 and 00 no hit

Trial: Read 30 RN (One for each time at bat)

Outcome: Record number in 01-26 interval (# of hits) = proportion of successful trials.

Repeat

Plot (7 or more hits) =

6. I am interested in how many girls are in a class of 30. Use your printout for sample size 30 and p = .50 to find

P(exactly 15 girls) = .15

P(20 or more girls) = .04

P(less than 12 girls) = .11

P(13 to 18 girls inclusive) = .69

If a class of 30 included 25 girls, would you believe that the population from which the class was drawn was evenly divided between boys and girls? Explain.

No; P(25 or more girls) = 0
very unlikely

7. In general, 80% of certain seeds germinate when planted correctly. You have carefully planted 20 seeds. Use your printout for sample size 20 and p = .80 to find

P(exactly 16 germinate) = .27

P(19 or more germinate) = .05

P(10 or less germinate) = 0

P(13 to 19 inclusive germinate) = .98

If only 12 of your seeds germinated, would you be justified in claiming that your seeds were inferior? Explain.

yes P(12 or less) = .02
a rare event

SIZE OF EACH SAMPLE = 30
50% MARKED
NUMBER OF SAMPLES = 100

FREQUENCY

```
0
1
2
3
4
5
6
7
8   ^1
9   ^1
10  ^^^^4
11  ^^^^^5
12  ^^^^^^^^^11
13  ^^^^^^^7
14  ^^^^^^^^8
15  ^^^^^^^^^^^^^^^15
16  ^^^^^^^^^^^^^^^^^^^19
17  ^^^^^^^^^^^^12
18  ^^^^^^^^8
19  ^^^^^5
20  ^^^3
21  ^1
22
23
24
25
26
27
28
29
30
```

SIZE OF EACH SAMPLE = 20
80% MARKED
NUMBER OF SAMPLES = 100

FREQUENCY

```
0
1
2
3
4
5
6
7
8
9
10
11
12  ^2
13  ^1
14  ^^^^^^^^^^^^^^^16
15  ^^^^^^^^^^^^^17
16  ^^^^^^^^^^^^^^^^^^27
17  ^^^^^^^^^^^^^17
18  ^^^^^^^^^^^15
19  ^^^^^5
20
```

Test

Chapter 6   Name _____

1. Toss your die 30 times and record the outcomes. Then find $\underline{D}$ and χ^2

OUTCOME	EXPECTED	OBTAINED
1	5	
2	5	
3	5	
4	5	
5	5	
6	5	

{ answers will differ

2. Draw a relative frequency polygon for the chi squares shown below. These values were obtained from 50 trials of 120 rolls of a six sided die.

Interval	Freq	Prop
0 - .9	1	.02
1 - 1.9	3	.06
2 - 2.9	4	.08
3 - 3.9	8	.16
4 - 4.9	9	.18
5 - 5.9	10	.20
6 - 6.9	7	.14
7 - 7.9	3	.06
8 - 8.9	2	.04
9 - 9.9	1	.02
10 -10.9	1	.02
11 -11.9	1	.02

Shade the area of the graph which represents the probability of obtaining your χ^2 from problem 1.   answers will differ

3. Use Appendix A on page 426 to complete the following.

(a) $p(\chi^2_3 \geq 6)$ = .10

(b) $p(\chi^2_{20} > 20)$ = .50

(c) $p(\chi^2_9 > 17)$ = .05

(d) $p(\chi^2_5 > 15)$ = .01

(e) The mean value of χ^2 with n degrees of freedom is __n__.

4. Five boxes of different brands of canned salmon were examined for high quality specifications. The number of cans which failed to meet specifications are indicated below. Is there a significant difference among these brands? Explain using chi square.

Brand	Expected	Obtained		
A	7	5	2	$\chi^2 = 70/7$
B	7	14	-7	$\chi^2 = 10$
C	7	6	-1	$P(\chi^2_6 \geq 10) \approx .05$
D	7	3	4	yes a significant
E	7	7	0	difference

5. According to Mendelian Inheritance theory, offspring of a certain crossing should be colored red, black or white. The chart below gives the theoretical proportions and the number actually obtained. Do these data substantiate the theory? Use chi-square to answer.

	Expected		Obtained	
Red	9/16	81	69	12
Black	3/16	27	37	-10
White	4/16	36	38	-2

$$\chi^2 = \frac{144}{81} + \frac{100}{27} + \frac{4}{36}$$

$$= 5.587$$

$P(\chi^2_2 \geq 5.587) \approx .05$

Data do not support theory

(Ans problem optional - depends on Sect. 13.1.)

Form an interval table for the chi-squares listed below. These data are the result of 60 trials of 90 rolls of a 6-sided die.

Chi-square	freq.
.4	2
1.46	1
1.6	1
1.86	5
2.13	1
2.26	1
2.4	1
2.53	1
2.66	1
2.8	1
2.93	2
3.33	1
3.46	3
3.6	1
3.73	1
3.86	2
4	2
4.4	1
4.53	1
4.8	1
5.2	1
5.33	2
5.46	1
5.6	2
5.73	1
6.13	1
6.26	1
6.53	1
6.66	1
7.46	2
8	1
8.53	1
8.66	1
11.46	2
12.93	1
14	1

Mean chi-square = 4.76

interval	frequency
0 - .99	2
1 - 1.99	7
2 - 2.99	8
3 - 3.99	8
4 - 4.99	5
5 - 5.99	7
6 - 6.99	4
7 - 7.99	2
8 - 8.99	3
9 - 9.99	0
10 - 10.99	0
11 - 11.99	2
12 - 12.99	1
13 - 13.99	0
14 - 14.99	1

Test

Chapter 7   Name _____

1. What two variables are of interest in the following questions?

Is the age of a car related to its trade-in value?

age of car   *trade in value*

Is crime related to the rate of inflation?

amount of crime   *rate of inflation*

Does the amount of snow in the North affect tourism in the South?

amount of snow   *amount of tourism*

Is the amount of alcohol drunk by a pregnant woman related to the size of the baby at birth?

amount of alcohol drunk   *size of baby*

Does life insurance cost more as one gets older?

Cost of life insurance   *age*

2. Find the following

The equation of a line with slope .85 and Y intercept -5.2

$$y = .85 x - 5.2$$

The slope of the line containing the points (5,8) and (2,10)

$$m = (8-10)/(5-2) \text{ or } -2/3 \text{ or } -.\overline{6}$$

The point (18, 43) is on the line Y = 2X + C.   Find C

$$c = 7 \quad (\text{see below})$$

$$43 = 2(18) + C$$
$$43 - 36 = C$$
$$7 = C$$

The equation of the line shown at the right

$$y = -5/3 x + 5$$

3. Graph the following on the same axis

$Y = \frac{1}{3}X - 6$

$Y = -2X + 1$

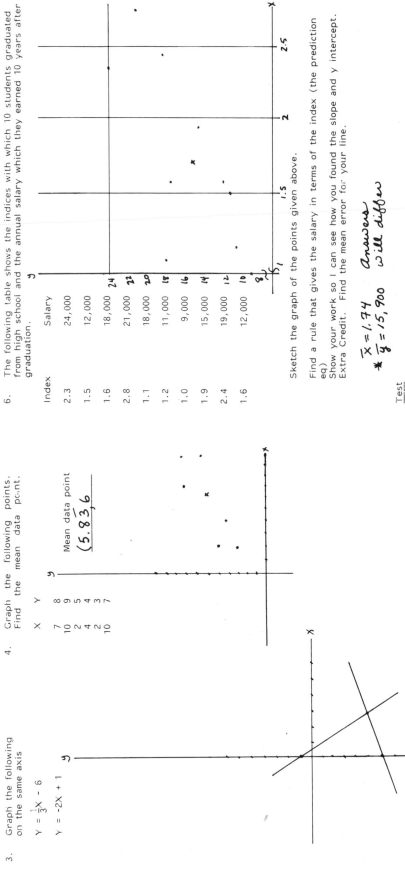

4. Graph the following points. Find the mean data point.

X	Y
7	8
10	9
2	5
4	4
2	3
10	7

Mean data point

$\underline{(5.8\ \overline{36}\ )}$

5. Complete the following equation and find the mean error for the given equation.

$Y' = .1x + 1.10$

X	Y	Y'	Y - Y'
2	1.2	1.30	-.10
3	1.3	1.40	-.10
4.5	1.45	1.55	-.10
7	1.80	1.80	0
10	2.00	2.10	-.10
15	3.00	2.60	-.40
20	4.75	3.10	1.65

6. The following table shows the indices with which 10 students graduated from high school and the annual salary which they earned 10 years after graduation.

Index	Salary
2.3	24,000
1.5	12,000
1.6	18,000
2.8	21,000
1.1	18,000
1.2	11,000
1.0	9,000
1.9	15,000
2.4	19,000
1.6	12,000

Sketch the graph of the points given above.

Find a rule that gives the salary in terms of the index (the prediction eq)
Show your work so I can see how you found the slope and y intercept.
Extra Credit. Find the mean error for your line.

$\bar{x} = 1.74$

* $\bar{y} = 15,900$

Answers will differ

Test

Chapter 8

Name _____

1. The following questions refer to the article at the right.

What variables are reported to be related?

driver accidents

and { being over weight
{ smoking
{ irregular hours

A recent study of driver accident rates was conducted in 5 major American cities. It was found that severely overweight drivers have double the accident rate of slightly or non-overweight drivers. Also, the accident rate was found to increase roughly proportionately to the number of packs of cigarettes smoked per week. Finally, it was found that individuals maintaining irregular hours had 40% more accidents on the average. (Imaginary data)

The following data are the height and weight for 7 college men. Complete the table and find the information requested.

ht X	wt Y	X − X̄	Y − Ȳ	(X − X̄)(Y − Ȳ)	(X − X̄)²	(Y − Ȳ)²
72	185	3	26	78	9	676
68	163	-1	4	-4	1	16
66	142	-3	-17	51	9	289
70	162	1	3	3	1	9
69	152	0	-7	0	0	49
64	127	-5	-32	160	25	1024
74	182	5	23	115	25	529
				407·4 / 403	70	2592

$\bar{X} = $ __69__

$\bar{Y} = $ __159__

var(X) = __10__

var(Y) = __370.3__

covar (X,Y) = __57.6__

$$m = \frac{403/7}{70/7} \text{ or } 5.76$$

$$y' - 159 = 5.76 (x - 69)$$

What causal relationship is implied?

accidents are caused by excessive weight, smoking and irregular hours

Chicago Tribune, April 3, 1983

What do you think about this information?

Answers will vary

2. The following statistics were computed for a set of data.

$\bar{X} = 68.6$ $\bar{Y} = 156.8$

var(X) = 12.1   var(Y) = 570.8   covar(X,Y) = 75.9

Find the equation of the least squares best fitting line.
(Hint: find the slope of the line using the formula; then find the Y intercept using the mean data point.)

$$m = \frac{75.9}{12.1} \text{ or } 6.27$$

$156.8 = 6.3 \ (68.6) + C$

$-275.4 = C$

$y' = 6.3x - 275.4$

Find the correlation between X and Y.

$$R = \frac{75.9}{\sqrt{12.1} \ \sqrt{570.8}}$$

$$= \frac{75.9}{3.48 \ (23.89)}$$

$$= .91$$

3. Would you expect strong or weak positive, strong or weak negative, or no correlation between the following pairs of data?

(a) The weights and lengths of newborn babies. positive strong

(b) Weight of a car and miles per gallon of gas. negative weak

(c) Hat size of adults and their I.Q. scores. none

(d) Ages of husbands and their wives. positive weak

(e) Speed of travel and travel time. negative strong

4. Describe the correlation presented in the following graphs.

See graphs sent for problem

a   strong positive   b   weak negative

c   strong negative   d   weak positive

e   none

Test

Chapter 9 Sections 1-5   Name

1. Transform the following scores as indicated. Then find the new mean and the new standard deviation. Use original scores for each transformation.

SCORE	Slide -14	Shrink ÷ 5
52	38	10.4
58	44	11.6
63	49	12.6
74	60	14.8
82	68	16.4
MEAN 65.8	51.8	13.16
SD 10.9	10.9	2.18

2. Suppose you receive a score of 107 on both Test I and Test II. Find your z-score for each.

	mean	SD	z-score
Test I	98	7.2	1.25
Test II	125	21.4	-.84

3. Find the transformed score for each of the following z-scores.

z	new mean	new SD	Transformed score
-.57	400	80	354.4
1.18	100	15	117.7

4. Transform the following quiz scores so that they have a mean of 50 and a standard deviation of 10.

Score	Dev	z	Transformed score
5	-5	-1.28	37.2
6	-4	-1.00	39.7
11	1	.26	52.6
13	3	.77	57.7
15	5	1.28	62.8

$$\bar{X} = 50/10 \sim 10$$
$$Var = (25+16+1+9+25)/5$$
$$= 76/5$$
$$= 15.2 \quad so \quad SD = 3.90$$

6. The following data give mass transit fares and the mean number of annual riders.

Fare in cents Rider (thousands)

X	Y	Y'	Y - Y'	(Y - Y')²
45	200	180.7	19.3	392.49
50	180	174.2	5.8	33.64
60	150	161.2	-11.2	125.44
75	120	141.7	-21.7	470.89
90	115	122.2	-7.2	51.84
100	110	109.2	.8	.64
125	90	76.7	13.3	176.89

$\bar{X} = 77.9$ $\bar{Y} = 137.9$

(a) Graph the data

(b) For the equations Y' = -1.3X + C, find C.

(c) Complete the chart above and find the mean square error.

$$137.9 = -1.3(77.9)+C \qquad MSE =1231.83/7$$
$$239.2 = C \qquad\qquad MSE =175.98$$

(graph axes labeled 80, 100, 120, 140, 160, 180, 200 vertical; 40, 50, 60, 70, 80, 90, 100, 110, 120 horizontal)

Test
Chapter 10   Name _____

1. In an experiment measuring the percent shrinkage in drying, 40 clay test specimens produced the following results:

19.3	20.5	17.9	17.3
15.8	16.9	17.1	19.5
20.7	18.5	17.1	19.1
18.4	18.7	19.4	16.8
14.9	12.3	18.8	17.5
17.3	19.5	17.4	16.3
21.3	23.4	18.5	19.0
16.1	18.8	17.5	18.2
18.6	18.3	16.5	17.4
20.5	16.9	17.5	18.2

(a) Organize these data using a stem and leaf table.

(b) Draw a histogram of these data.

Stem	Leaf
12	3
13	
14	9
15	99583
16	391455354
17	465383522
18	354510
19	755
20	3
21	
22	
23	4

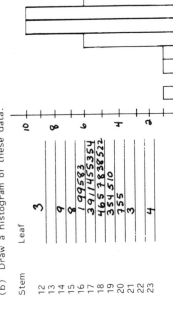

2. Three groups of students measured a chalkboard known to be 6 meters long. They obtained these results:

Group I	Group II	Group III
6.03	6.05	6.09
6.05	5.97	6.07
5.89	6.04	6.05
5.93	6.08	6.10
6.10	5.92	6.08

Group I: $\bar{X} = -6$ $SD = .078$ $SD_{n-1} = .087$

Group II: $\bar{X} = 6.012$ $SD_n = .058$ $SD_{n-1} = .065$

Group III: $\bar{X} = 6.078$ $SD_n = .017$ $SD_{n-1} = .019$

(a) What are the mean and standard deviation of each group?
see previous page

(b) Which group seems to have the smallest error?   III

(c) Which group seems the most biased?   III

(d) What recommendations would you make for improving the results?
answers will differ

3. Find the least squares regression equation for estimating the 1980 median price for a house in the New Trier district. (New Trier West serves students from the suburbs listed below.) The median price for 1970 is given in thousands and is represented by X. The median price for 1980, also given in thousands, is represented by Y.

	X	Y
Glenview	41.9	111.9
Kenilworth	50.0	200.0
Northfield	48.4	117.9
Wilmette	46.5	121.8
Winnetka	50.0	172.0

$\bar{X} = 47.4$ $CofAR = 77.79$
$\bar{y} = 144.7$ $Var\, x = 9.116$
$Var\, y = 8.5$
$y - 144.7 = 8.5 (X - 47.4)$

$x - \bar{x}$ $(x-\bar{x})(y-\bar{y})$
-5.5 -32.8 180.4
-2.0 -55.3 143.8
-1.0 -26.8 -26.80
-1.9 -22.9 20.61
2.6 27.3 70.98
                388.97

Sum of $(x - \bar{x})^2 = 45.58$

Test
Chapter 11   Name _____

1. Identify the sample, the population, the statistic and the parameter in each of the following.

   The owner of a small store wishes to estimate the proportion of those who enter her store who actually buy something. She carefully observes 20 randomly selected people who enter the store and finds that 13 of them make a purchase.

Sample: 20 randomly selected people
Population: all who enter store
Statistic: 13/20 or 65% of sample buy
Parameter: 65% of all who enter will buy.

A group of 100 Central High students was asked "Approximately how many hours per week do you study?" The responses ranged from 0 to 23 and the mean was 8.4

Sample: 100 New Trier students
Population: all New Trier students
statistic: mean amount of time studied = 8.4 hours
Parameter: mean study time in 8.4 for all

2. Use the stem-and-leaf plots from Tables 11.12 a,b,c; page 321 & 322 the numbers represent the unbiased variances from 100 samples. Find the following.

For $n = 4$, $P(90 \leq var \leq 110) = $ .15 $P(80 \leq var \leq 120) = $ .23

For $n = 16$, $P(90 \leq var \leq 110) = $ .43 $P(80 \leq var \leq 120) = $ .68

For $n = 36$, $P(90 \leq var \leq 110) = $ .62 $P(80 \leq var \leq 120) = $ .88

What conclusions can you draw from your answers?

Answers will differ.
Example: Longer sample gives larger proportion in given interval.

3. Give the meaning of the following:

Statistical bias - systematic over or under estimating the population parameter.

The sample mean is unbiased - mean of sample is a good estimate of the population mean.

The sample variance is biased - variance of sample is not a good estimate of the population variance.

The Central Limit Theorem - if more and more samples of size N are taken from a population with mean μ and SD σ, the distribution of sample means becomes more like a normal distribution with mean μ and SD $\frac{\sigma}{\sqrt{N}}$

4. A random sample of 49 adults is tested for pulse rates. The resulting mean is 75.8 beats per minute. Assume standard deviation of the population is 10 and find the 95% Confidence interval for the means of all such samples.

Sketch a graph of this information.

95% CI $Z = \pm 1.96$
$\bar{x} = 75.8 \pm 1.96 \left(\frac{10}{7} \right)$
$= 75.8 \pm 2.8$
73 to 78.6

73   75.8   78.6

5. Find the mean, the biased and unbiased standard deviation of the data below. Show your work neatly. You may check using the calculator BUT I MUST see your work.

72.89   62.37   76.32   52.49   75.33

$\bar{x} = 67.88$
$S.D._n = 9.16$
$SD_{n-1} = 10.24$

5. A coin was tossed 1,000 times; 457 heads and 543 tails resulted. Use a chi-square test to decide if the coin is fair.

	E	Ob	Diff	
H	500	457	43	.849
T	500	543	-43	.849

$x^2 = (3698)/500$ or 7.396

$P(x^2 > 7.396)$ is small, so conclude coin is not fair.

6. Three hundred cards were drawn at random from a bridge deck. Draw a relative frequency polygon. Sketch in an appropriate smooth curve.

Clubs	84	.28
Diamonds	72	.24
Hearts	75	.25
Spades	69	.23

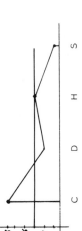

7. The following table gives the weights of 50 Girl Scouts at a summer camp. Draw a frequency polygon and sketch in a smooth curve which seems appropriate for the data.

Interval	Frequency
70 - 79	4
80 - 89	7
90 - 99	9
100 - 109	13
110 - 119	8
120 - 129	6
130 - 139	3

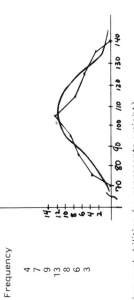

(w represents weight)

Find the following probabilities (w represents weight)

$P(w < 90) = \dfrac{11}{50}$ or .22

$P(w \geq 120) = \dfrac{9}{50}$ or .18

$P(90 \leq w < 120) = \dfrac{30}{50}$ or .60

8. The following numbers represent final scores on a statistics test. Classify the data using the stem and leaf method.

88	54	91	70	93	62	89	61	81	67
72	87	80	76	83	58	75	86	78	92
80	56	75	60	73	69	97	77	65	81
92	71	63	71	64	79	88	62	51	73
85	67	95	50	75	71	72	90	78	69

Stem	Leaf
5	46081
6	730429 2579
7	21506135915 57883
8	80570398611
9	2153702

Interval	Freq.
52 - 59	5
60 - 69	11
70 - 79	16
80 - 89	11
90 - 99	7

The mean of these data is 78.8 and the standard deviation is 11.9. Assume the data are normally distributed and find an interval around the mean in which about 68% of the scores are found.

78.8 ± 11.9

66.9 to 90.7

How <u>many</u> grades are actually in this interval?

$1 + 11 + 16 + 4 = 32$

What percent of the grades are actually in this interval?

$\dfrac{32}{50}$ or 64 %

Test

Chapter 9 Sections 6-8

Name _____

Complete the following and illustrate information on the graph.

1. p(z < 1.28) = **.8997**

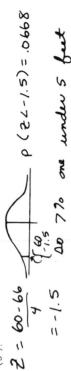

2. p(z < -2.13) = **.0166**

3. p(z > 1.75) = **.0401**

4. p(z > -1.05) = **.8531**

5. p(z < **-.52**) = .30

6. p(z < **1.04**) = .85

7. p(z > **1.28**) = .10

8. p(z > **-.67**) = .75

9. Assume that the heights of women are normally distributed with a mean of 66" (5'6") and a standard deviation of 4".

(a) What percentage of women would you expect to be under 60" (5')?

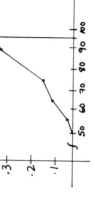

$$z = \frac{60-66}{4}$$

$$= -1.5$$

$$p(z < -1.5) = .0668$$

So 7% are under 5 feet

(b) What is the lowest height that would place a woman in the tallest 10% of the group?

$$z = 1.28$$

$$T = 4(1.28)+66$$

$$= 71.12$$

So about 5'11" would place woman in top 10%

10. The following stem and leaf diagram gives the final statistics grades for a class of 19 students. Draw a relative frequency polygon and answer the questions.

Stem	Leaf	
9	8 5 5 4 2 1 0	.37
8	8 8 5 4 3 0	.32
7	9 5 2	.16
6	8 0	.11
5	3	.05

P(71 < G < 87) = **.37**

P(G ≥ 88) = **.47**

P(G ≤ 65) = **.11**

The median is **85**

Is the distribution normal? **no**

What observations can you make about this class? **Answers will differ**

Test

Chapter 12

Name _____

1. A school district is interested in whether student achievement in mathematics is significantly higher than the nationwide mean of 75. A random sample of 50 students takes the test and gets a mean of 77 and a standard deviation of 7.3.

To answer the question experimentally 100 random samples of size 50 were taken from a population with mean 75 and s.d. 7.3. What answer do these data suggest?

72	2
73	7
74	28
75	36
76	21
77	4
78	1
79	1

$P(\bar{x} \geq 77) = \dfrac{6}{100}$

Achievement is higher

To answer the question by theoretical means, find the z score and use the normal curve chart. What conclusion do you draw based on this information?

$$z = \frac{77-75}{7.3/\sqrt{50}} = 1.93$$

$P(z \geq 1.93) = .0262$

$\sim 3\%$

achievement is higher

Sketch a graph illustrating your theoretical results.

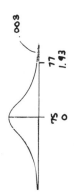

.003

75   77
0   1.93

2. Write the six steps and perform 10 trials for the following problem.

In a large set of applicants for similar jobs, there are 60 men and 40 women applying. If 20 jobs are to be filled and 16 are given to men, would you say that there is evidence of discrimination in the selection process?

Model   1 digit RN   1-6 man   7-9&0 woman

Trial   Read 20 RN   (one for each applicant)

Outcome   Record # of 1-6's

Repeat   10 times

Probability   P(16 or more men) = _____

Decision   answers will differ

3. (a) Define:

Type I Error   Rejecting a claim that is true

Type II Error   Accepting a claim that is not true.

(b) Complete. Use t table

df = 15 $p(t < -1.34) = .10$

df = 24 $p(t > 2.49) = .01$

df = 4 $p(t < -2.78) = .025$

df = 8 $p(t > 1.86) = .05$

4. A survey of 9 automobile drivers indicated that the mean number of miles driven per day was 32.7 with a standard deviation of 6.8 miles. Find a 99% Confidence Interval for the mean distance travelled in a day. Also find a 90% Confidence Interval.

90 CI t≈1.83
99 CI t=3.25

$99\% \ CI = 32.7 \pm 3.25 \frac{(6.8)}{\sqrt{9}}$
$= 32.7 \pm 7.4$
25.3 to 40.1

$90\% \ CI = 32.7 \pm 1.83 \frac{(6.8)}{\sqrt{9}}$
$\approx 32.7 \pm 4.1$
28.6 to 36.8

5. A random sample of 16 college freshmen indicated that they studied the following number of hours per week:

40	5	27	21
28	20	35	30
33	19	38	58
61	32	37	0

Do a statistical test to determine if these freshmen differ significantly from the national mean of 32 hours per week.

$\bar{x} = 30.25$ $t = \frac{30.25 - 32}{15.99/\sqrt{16}} = \frac{-1.75}{4} \approx -.4375$
$\sigma = 15.48$
$\sigma_{n-1} = 15.99$

$P(t < -.4375) a P(t > .4375)$ on big — so data do not significantly.

Test
Chapter 13

Name _____

1. A survey of 32 four-children families was conducted. The expected and observed number of sons is given in the following chart. Use chi square to determine if the observed is consistent with the expected.

Number of sons	expected		observed	
0	1/16	2	4	-2
1	4/16	8	8	0
2	6/16	12	9	3
3	4/16	8	9	-1
4	1/16	2	2	0

$x^2 = \frac{4}{4} + \frac{0}{8} + \frac{9}{12} + \frac{1}{8} + \frac{0}{2}$
$x^2 = 1.875$
$P(x^2 \geq 1.875) \approx .76$
yes consistent

---

2. A certain drug is claimed to be more effective in curing headaches. In an experiment with 150 people, half were given the drug, and half were given sugar pills. The patients' reactions to the treatment are recorded in the following table. Test the hypothesis that the drug and the sugar pills yield similar reactions.

	Helped	Harmed	No reaction	
Drug	50 45.5	8 9	17 20.5	75
Sugar Pill	41 45.5	10 9	24 20.5	75
	91	18	41	150

$x^2 = 2\left(\frac{20.25}{45.5}\right) + 2 \cdot \left(\frac{1}{9}\right) + 2\left(\frac{12.45}{20.5}\right)$
$= .89 + .22 + 1.20$
$P(x_3^2 \geq 2.31) \approx .35$

It appears drug and sugar pills do yield similar reaction.

3. Use Pascal's Triangle, for six tosses of a fair coin, to find the following:

p(0 Heads) = 1/64
p(2 Heads) = 15/64
p(5 Heads) = 6/64

4. A random sample of 100 college students indicated that the average number of classes missed per week was 4.2 with a standard deviation of .85. Is this significantly different from the University's statement that students missed 3.5 classes per week?

$z = \frac{4.2 - 3.5}{.85/\sqrt{100}} = 8.23$

$P(z > 8.23)$ is ~0 so conclude sign difference.

5. Take-home question. Use a local phone book as a source of random digits. Select 400 digits.

(a) Describe how you selected the digits.

(b) Perform two tests of your choice to determine if the digits are in fact random.

Answers will differ.

APPENDIX
E
References

American Statistical Association. (1984). Proceedings of the Statistical Education Conference. American Statistical Assoc. 103 p. (See Ch II: Statistics in the High School).

American Statistical Association. Quantitative Literacy in the Schools. Program literature and instructional units.

Anderson, Clive and Barnett, Vic. IN STEP with the Microcomputer. Teaching Statistics, Vol. 5 No. 1 Jan. 1983:2-7.

ASA-NCTM Curriculum Committee. Annotated Bibliography.

ASA-NCTM Newsletter. Order free from Ann Watkins, Dept. of Mathematics, Los Angeles Pierce College, Woodland Hills, CA 91371.

Barnett, V. (ed) (1982). Teaching Statistics in Schools throughout the World. Voorburg, Netherlands: International Statistics Institute.

Barnett, V. (1979). Statistical Education and Training for 16-19 yr. olds. Sheffield: Centre for Statistical Education.

Beyer, William H. (1985). Handbook of Tables for Probability and Statistics. Chemical Rubber Co. 642 p.

Boardman, Thomas J. (1982). The Future of Statistical Computing on Desktop Computers. The American Statistician, Vol. 36 no 1 Feb 1982:49-58.

Boling, John C. and Kirk, Herbert J. (1983). Teaching experimental design: Proper and improper use of Statistical Software. Proceedings of the Statistical Education Section. ASA Annual Meeting 1983:10-13.

Breiman, Leo. (1973). Statistics: With a View Towards Applications. Houghton Mifflin.

Brockett, Patrick and Arnold Levine. (1984). Statistics and Probability and Their Applications. Holt, Rinehart and Winston. 571 p.

British Columbia Ministry of Education (1984). A discussion paper on Secondary Graduation Requirements. Victoria.

Careers in Statistics. (1984). American Statistical Association Pamphlet.

Chambers, John; Cleveland, Kleiner Wm.; Tukey, Paul. (1983). Graphical Methods For Data Analysis. Wadsworth.

College Board. (1985). Academic Preparation for College: What Students Need to Know and Be Able to Do.

Conference Board of the Mathematical Sciences (1982). The Mathematical Sciences Curriculum K-12: What is still fundamental and what is not. Washington D.C.: The Board: 1982.

Cordano, Gerolamo. (1953). The Book on Games of Chance. Princeton University Press.

Del Grande, J., Bissett, W. P. and Swift, J. H. (1976). Mathematics - Insights and Applications. Toronto: Gage.

Durran, J. H. (1970). The School Mathematics Project. Statistics and Probability. Cambridge University Press. 487 p.

Erickson, B. H., T.A. Nosanchuk. (1977). Understanding Data. McGraw-Hill Ryerson Limited. 388p.

Fabricand, Burton. (1979). The Science of Winning. Von Nostrand.

Ferbes, Robert; Sheslsley, Paul; Turner, Anthony; and Wlaesberg, Joseph. What Is A Survey? American Statistical Association Pamphlet.

Freedman, David, and David Lane. (1981). Mathematical Methods in Statistics. A workbook. W. W. Norton and Co. 204 p.

Freedman, David, Robert Pisani, and Roger Purves. (1978). Statistics. W.W. Norton and Co. 506p.

Freedman, David, Robert Pisani, and Roger Purves. (1978). Instructor's Manual for Statistics. George J. McLeod, Limited. 135p.

Griffin, Diane L. and Mosteller, Frederick. (1983). Beginning Statistics with Data Analysis. Solutions Manual to Accompany Mosteller, Fienberg, and Rourke. Addison-Wesley, Publ. Co. 292p.

Groenewald, Rickland A. (1979). An Introduction to Probability and Statistics Using BASIC. Marcel Dakken.

Hansen, Viggo P., Marilyn J. Zweng. (1984). Computers in Mathematics Education. The National Council of Teachers of Mathematics, Inc. 244p.

Hecht, James E. (1980). Using the Monte Carlo method to teach probabilistic problem solving to ninth grade general mathematics students. Ph.D. Thesis: Urbana: University of Illinois.

Hoffer, Alan R. (1982). Development of Teaching Materials at the School level. Proceedings of the First International Conference on the Teaching of Statistics, Sheffield (UK): 1982: p.263.

Hoffer, Alan R. (1978). Statistics and Information. Organization Math Resource Project. Oregon State System of Higher Education. 888p.

Hogg, Robert V. and Elliot A. Tanis. (1983). Probability and Statistical Inference. Macmillan Publ. Col., Inc. Copy #1 533p.

Holmes, P. (1982). Assessment Methods and their Effect on Teaching Statistics. Unpublished discussion paper for a workshop at the First International Conference on Teaching Statistics.

Holmes, P., Kapadia, R. and Rubra, G. N. (1981). Statistics in Schools 11-16: A Review: Schools Council working Paper 69. London (UK): Methuen Educational.

Hooke, Robert. (1983). How to Tell the Liars from the Statisticians. Marcel Dekker, Inc. 173p.

Ingram, John A. (1977). Elementary Statistics. Menlo Park: Cummings Publishing Company.

Kotz, Samuel and Donna F. Stroup. (1983). Educated Guessing. How to Cope in an Uncertain World. Marcel Dekker, Inc. 187p.

Ladany, Shaul and Machol, Robert. (1977). Optimal Strategies in Sports. North Holland.

Miller, Irwin and John E. Freund. (1977). Probability and Statistics for Engineers. Prentice-Hall, Inc. 2nd Ed. 529p.

Moore, David S. (1979). Statistics, Concepts and Controversies. W. H. Freeman and Co. 313p.

Moore, David S. (1979). Statistics, Concepts and Controversies. Instructor's Guide. W. H. Freeman & Co. 101p.

Morrison, Donald F. (1976). Multivariate Statistical Methods. McGraw-Hill. 415p.

Mosteller, Frederick, Stephen E. Fienberg, and Robert E. K. Rourke. (1983). Beginning Statistics with Data Systems. Addison-Wesley. 585p.

Mosteller, Frederick, William H. Kruskal, Richard F. Link, Richard S. Pieters, Gerald R. Rising. (1973). Statistics by Example. Detecting Patterns. Addison-Wesley, 166p.

Mosteller, Frederick, William H. Kruskal, Richard F. Link, Richard S. Pieters , and Gerald R. Rising. (1973). Statistics by Example. Finding Models. Addison-Wesley, 145p.

Mosteller, Frederick, William H. Kruskal, Richard F. Link, Richard S. Pieters, Gerald R. Rising. (1973). Statistics by Example. Exploring Data. Addison-Wesley, 125p.

Mosteller, Frederick, Robert E. K. Rourke, George B. Thomas Jr. (1961). Probability with Statistical Applications. Addison-Wesley. 125p.

Mosteller, Frederick, John W. Tukey. (1977). Data Analysis and Regression. A second course in statistics. Addison-Wesley. 588p.

National Council of Supervisors of Mathematics (1973). A position paper on Basic Skills. The Council, Washington DC.

National Council of Teachers of Mathematics (1980). An Agenda for Action: Recommendations for School Mathematics of the 1980's. Reston, Va: The Council.

Neter, John and Wassesman, Wilham. (1974). Applied Linear Statistical Models. Irwin.

Niven, Ivan. (1965). Mathematics of Choice or How to Count without Counting. Mathematical Association of America. 202p.

Noether, G. E. (1983). Statistics in the School Curriculum – A Statistician's Viewpoint. Proceedings of the Statistical Education Section. ASA Annual Meeting 1983:46-49.

Nemetz, T. (1982). Teaching Statistics to 16-18 yr olds: Dreams and Reality. Proceedings of the First International Conference on the Teaching of Statistics, Sheffield (UK): 203-4.

O'Dell, Jerry W. (1984). Basic Statistics: An Introduction to Problem Solving with your Personal Computer. Tab Books, Inc. 452p.

Packel, Edward. (1981). The Mathematics of Games and Gambling. Mathematical Association of America. 141p.

Pisani, Robert. (1985). Statistics: A Tutorial Handbook. W.W. Norton.

Rowntree, Derek. (1984). Probability without Tears. Charles Scribner's and Sons. 196p.

Rowntree, Derek. (1981). Statistics without Tears. A Primer for Non-mathematicians. Charles Scribner's and Sons. 199p.

Sedgewick, Robert. (1983). Algorithms. Addison-Wesley, 549p.

Shulte, Albert P. and James R. Smart. (1981). Teaching Statistics and Probability. National Council of Teachers of Mathematics, 146p.

Smith, Gary. (1985). Statistical Reasoning. Allyn & Bacon, 705p.

Statistics as a Career: Women at Work. American Statistical Association Pamphlet.

Swift, Jim (1984). Exploring Data with a Microcomputer. In Computers in Mathematics Education, 1984 Yearbook of the National Council of Teachers of Mathematics, ed. Viggo P. Hansen, Reston, Va: The Council, 1984: pp. 107-114.

Tanur, Judith M., Frederick Mosteller, William H. Kruskal, Richard F. Link, Richard S. Pieters, and Gerald R. Rising. (1972). Statistics. A Guide to the Unknown. Holdan-Day, Inc. 430p.

Thisted, Ronald A. (1979). Teaching Statistical Computing using Computer Packages. The American Statistician, Vol. 33 no 1 Feb 1979: 27-35.

Tufte, Edward. (1983). The Visual Display of Quantitative Information. Graphic Press.

Tufte, Edward R. (1974). Data Analysis for Politics and Policy. Prentice-Hall, Inc. 179p.

Velleman, Paul F. and David C. Hoaglin. (1981). Applications, Basics, and Computing of Exploratory Data Analysis. Duxbury Press. 354p.

Williams, Bill. (1978). A Sampler on Sampling. John Wiley and Sons, N.Y. 254p.

Willoughby, Stephen S. (1977). Probability and Statistics. Agincourt, Ontario, GLC Publishers.

Zelinka, Martha and Michael Sutherland. (1973). Statistics by Example: Exploring Data. Teacher's Commentary and Solutions Manual. Addison-Wesley, Publ. Co. 79p.

Zelinka, Martha and Michael Sutherland. (1973). Statistics by Example: Finding Models. Teacher's Commentary and Solutions Manual. Addison-Wesley, Publ. Co. 47p.

Zelinka, Martha and Sanford Weisberg. (1973). Statistics by Example: Weighing Chances. Teacher's Commentary and Solutions Manual. Addison-Wesley, Publ. Co. 71p.

Zelinka, Martha and Sanford Weisberg. (1973). Statistics by Example: Detecting Patterns. Teacher's Commentary and Solutions Manual. Addison-Wesley, Publ. Co. 56p.